KU-548-663

To the love of my life, whose eyes glaze over when I talk about designing video games but who always listens regardless. I couldn't have done this without you!

Acknowledgments

For the creation of this book, there have been many supporters, especially from the Unity game development community. Several individuals helped tailor this book into a suitable fit for the readers, including Emi Smith, Kezia Endsley, Clayton Crooks, Melba Hopper, and the rest of the fine folks at Cengage Learning. I also want to thank Andrius Kuznecovas, whose multiplayer tutorial for Unity I couldn't have done without, and Jeremy Alessi, who came up with the initial inspiration for this book.

About the Author

Michael Duggan is a Southern-based author and illustrator of nine textbooks on the subjects of video game design and digital media. He is also an applications developer and computer art instructor at North Arkansas College. A member of the International Game Developers Association (IGDA), he currently resides in the Ozark Mountains with his wife and step-children. His love for making games comes from long days spent thinking up role-playing games as a kid.

IPAD®
MULTIPLAYER
MAGIC

Michael Duggan

Course Technology PTR
A part of Cengage Learning

COURSE TECHNOLOGY
CENGAGE Learning

038927

Australia, Brazil, Japan, Korea, United Kingdom, United States

COURSE TECHNOLOGY
CENGAGE Learning®

iPad® Multiplayer Magic
Michael Duggan

Publisher and General Manager, Course Technology PTR: Stacy L. Hiquet

Associate Director of Marketing: Sarah Panella

Manager of Editorial Services: Heather Talbot

Senior Acquisitions Editor: Emi Smith

Marketing Manager: Mark Hughes

Project/Copy Editor: Kezia Endsley

Technical Editor: Clayton Crooks

Interior Layout: Jill Flores

Cover Designer: Mike Tanamachi

Indexer: Sharon Shock

Proofreader: Melba Hopper

© 2012 Course Technology, a part of Cengage Learning.

ALL RIGHTS RESERVED. No part of this work covered by the copyright herein may be reproduced, transmitted, stored, or used in any form or by any means graphic, electronic, or mechanical, including but not limited to photocopying, recording, scanning, digitizing, taping, Web distribution, information networks, or information storage and retrieval systems, except as permitted under Section 107 or 108 of the 1976 United States Copyright Act, without the prior written permission of the publisher.

For product information and technology assistance, contact us at
Cengage Learning Customer & Sales Support Center, 1-800-354-9706

For permission to use material from this text or product, submit all requests online at **cengage.com/permissions**
Further permissions questions can be emailed to
permissionrequest@cengage.com

iPad, iPhone, iTunes, and iPod are registered trademarks of Apple Inc. Unity is a trademark of Unity Technologies.

All other trademarks are the property of their respective owners.

All images © Cengage Learning unless otherwise noted.

Library of Congress Control Number: 2011936053

ISBN-13: 978-1-4354-5964-9

ISBN-10: 1-4354-5964-4

Course Technology, a part of Cengage Learning
20 Channel Center Street
Boston, MA 02210
USA

Cengage Learning is a leading provider of customized learning solutions with office locations around the globe, including Singapore, the United Kingdom, Australia, Mexico, Brazil, and Japan. Locate your local office at: **international.cengage.com/region**

Cengage Learning products are represented in Canada by Nelson Education, Ltd.

For your lifelong learning solutions, visit **courseptr.com**

Visit our corporate website at **cengage.com**

BOLTON COLLEGE LIBRARY

Acc. No.	038927
Class No.	794.8151 DUG
Sup.	Dawson
Date	10/12 £18-99
Site	DR SFL

Printed in the United States of America
1 2 3 4 5 6 7 13 12 11

Contents

Chapter 2
Game Design Principles 49

Chapter 3
Your Grimoire to the iPad 77

Chapter 7
Mixing the Brew Together   201

Chapter 8
What's Next   239

Appendix
Online Resources   258

Glossary   264

Index   282

Introduction

You probably already know about or possibly even own Apple's latest darling in its line of mobile devices: the iPad. The iPad is a thin touchscreen tablet that has a mission to revolutionize mobile computing and portable media consumption. It does this through unprecedented access to apps—including games.

In 2008, Apple launched the iTunes App Store, with only 500 native apps from third-party developers. In 2010, the iTunes App Store grew to include more than 200,000 apps, and it grows daily as software developers target Apple mobile devices. As of late 2010, over 120 million iOS devices are connected as active users. That's a huge potential target market!

The iPad is not just all about playing games. However, iPod Touch and iPad games have made Apple a dominant force in the portable gaming field. Steve Jobs, founder of Apple, went onstage in September 2010 to announce to an audience in San Francisco the latest version of the iPod, and during his speech, he wowed listeners by boasting an astonishing statistic: Apple had cornered 50 percent of the mobile gaming market! This number has only increased since that time, as the iPod Touch, iPad, and iPhone mobile devices have repeatedly outsold similar mobile products from other vendors.

This alone should tell you that if you want to start making mobile games, you should go to the source and develop for the Apple iOS. Not only that, but the Apple App Store provides a direct sales and distribution conduit unlike any other. You can literally make an iOS game and turn around and start making profits off it.

What sets the tablet apart? This is a relatively new category of mobile technology, somewhere between a laptop and a smartphone. Netbooks have tried bridging the gap but failed, because they are only small form-factor laptops and nothing more. A tablet device, on the other hand, imitates a notepad and thus can be effortlessly ported around and held at just about any angle for comfort. Users can carry a tablet device easily to work, the coffee shop, the dentist's office, the couch, the bed—and even the bathroom! This makes the iPad ideal for playing casual games online.

Who Should Read This Book

iPad Multiplayer Magic is a beginner's guide to developing multiplayer games for the iOS devices—specifically the iPad. You don't need previous iOS or Macintosh application development experience, either. In fact, you're expected to be a beginner, and I hope you're eager to learn a new method for doing things.

What This Book Will Teach You

By the time you have finished reading *iPad Multiplayer Magic*, you will have traveled the path from being a novice or someone who doesn't know anything about mobile game development to being someone who can crank out a respectable, playable game for the iPad all on your own. You can look at this book as a cookbook, providing you with a recipe for creating a delicious gaming experience that can be played on an iPad, and then—with what you learn from this particular "cooking" exercise—you can go on to master other dishes!

This book distills hundreds of Apple documentations down to the nitty-gritty, glossing over concepts you don't have to know to get started. This book also acts as a guide to using Unity iOS, a complex and versatile game authoring tool that makes developing multiplayer games for iOS devices faster and less of a hassle. Along the way, you will also be introduced to several other game editors that can be used to make games for the iPad, but after much deliberation, I chose the Unity iOS for its ease-of-use, the fact that it can actually make 3D mobile games (most other game development tools can only handle 2D graphics), and because it can be used to fashion multiplayer games.

How to Read This Book

Code examples used in this book appear in mono font so they stand out a bit better. This means that the code you see will look like this:

```
var sensitivity : float = 3.0;
```

Also, anything you are asked to type will appear in **bold**.

If you are ever uncertain about anything in the code, you can always look at the source code on the Internet at www.courseptr.com/downloads. You can search by title, ISBN, or author's name to find this book. From time to time, we might provide updates for the code there and other things you might find useful.

What You Need

The following are items you will need to complete the lessons in this book.

A Macintosh Computer

To begin creating a multiplayer game for the iPad, you will need an Intel-based Macintosh computer with the latest version of the MacOS on it. You cannot program iPad applications on an iPad! Some of the game-authoring software you will use *will* work on a Windows PC, but for final production and distribution, you will still need a Macintosh computer, so why not just start with one?

I used MacOS X Snow Leopard for the writing of this book and creating the illustrations herein.

An iPad

You will also need an actual iPad. You don't run your game on the iPad right away. In the initial phases of mobile game development, you test your product in an emulator, but eventually you will need to test your application on a real, live iOS device. Having an iPad at your disposal will be beneficial.

An Apple iOS Developer Account

Next, you need to become a registered iOS developer on Apple's website. This is so you can download the iOS SDK (software development kit), which is free, and utilize the other great iOS developer tools. Don't worry; I show you how in Chapter 3.

Unity iOS Software

Last—but certainly not least—you need a copy of Unity iOS, the game engine you'll use to make the multiplayer iOS game featured in this book. Using Unity iOS is ideal, because it will save you a lot of time scratching together the framework of a game engine by yourself—especially if you're new to programming. Unity iOS, as opposed to the other game toolkits I discuss, allows you to make iPad games set up for multiplayer online play.

You can easily purchase Unity iOS or Unity iOS Pro by visiting the Unity web store at https://store.unity3d.com/shop/. I show you how to download and install Unity iOS in Chapter 3.

1

Brief History of Gaming and What You Need to Know

When I say "games," I mean "video games." Games by themselves—including card, dice, and board games—have been around almost as long as mankind has. A game is a variety of entertainment that people created as a means of amusing themselves when they weren't busy hunting, gathering, preparing, cooking, or taking care of business. And this is still true today, in this digital age, with video games.

A video game, by definition, is an electronic game wherein graphic images can be manipulated by the player, thus the word "video" added in front of "game."

In 1961, Digital Equipment Corporation donated their latest computer to the Massachusetts Institute of Technology (MIT). It was called the Programmed Data Processor-1, or PDP-1. Compared to most computers at the time, the PDP-1 (featured in Figure 1.1) was comparatively modest in size, only as big as a large automobile.

Figure 1.1
The PDP-1
computer.

Like most universities, MIT had several campus organizations, one of which was the Tech Model Railroad Club, or TMRC. TMRC appealed to students who liked to build things and see how they worked. They programmed on the PDP-1 for fun.

Steve Russell, nicknamed "Slug," was a typical science-fiction-loving nerd who joined TMRC. He put nearly six months and two hundred hours into completing an interactive game where two players controlled rocket ships. Using toggle switches built into the PDP-1, players controlled the speed and direction of their ships and fired torpedoes at each other. Russell called his game *Spacewar!* Thanks to "Slug" (seen in Figure 1.2), one of the very first arcade video games came into being.

Figure 1.2
Steve Russell at the Computer History Museum's PDP-1 computer in 2007.

Icons in Game Development

Now, take a look at some of the landmark game companies and the evolution of the media.

Atari

Although many electronic devices had near-game-like qualities, *Computer Space*, developed by Nolan Bushnell and Ted Dabney in 1971 and based on Steve Russell's *Spacewar!* game, was arguably the first true example of a video game. It used a black-and-white television for its video display and had a computer system made up of 74 series TTL chips. The coin-operated video game (shown in Figure 1.3) was actually featured in the 1973 science-fiction film *Soylent Green*, a show famous for the phrase, "It's people. Soylent Green is made out of people!"

Figure 1.3
The *Computer Space* arcade game.

Nolan Bushnell and Ted Dabney went on and in 1972 started a company called Atari, which revolutionized gaming. The word "Atari" comes from the Japanese strategy game Go and means about the same as "checkmate!" The Atari company (whose iconic logo can be seen in Figure 1.4) was primarily responsible for the formation of the video arcade and modern video game industry.

You don't see as many video arcades as you used to, but back in the day, these were places where upright coin-operated game machines stood in rows and, with their bright lights and loud noises, drew the attention of the young and interested everywhere.

Note

Nolan Bushnell later left Atari to start a chain of video arcade pizza parlors in 1977. He called his theme restaurant Chuck E. Cheese's Pizza Time Theatre, and it was the first family restaurant to combine food, animated entertainment, and an indoor video arcade.

Figure 1.4
The Atari
rainbow logo.

By November 1972, Atari finished its keynote game *Pong*, which featured a black-and-white television from Walgreens and a coin mechanism from a laundromat with a milk carton inside to catch coins as they were deposited. *Pong* was placed in a Sunnyvale, California, tavern called Andy Capp's to test its viability. When Atari workers showed up the next morning to fix the machine, which had died around 10 o'clock the night before, they met a line of people waiting to play the game. On examination, they discovered what had caused the *Pong* game to quit working was that the coin collector was overflowing with quarters, and when gamers kept shoving quarters in anyway, the machine shorted out. The Atari folks realized they had a hit on their hands, and after that, video games really took off!

Another leap came when Bushnell had the idea in 1975 to make a home console machine. By early 1976, the Atari 2600 home console system (shown in Figure 1.5) became one of the hottest commercial items in history, followed by several successors and competitors. The home console machine was the first way gamers had of bringing the video game arcade into their domiciles. It was a huge marketing success.

Figure 1.5
The Atari 2600
home console
system.

However, Atari's success turned out to be ephemeral. As with all things that go up, they invariably must fall, and so, too, did Atari.

The North American video game crash of 1983, also known as the Atari Debacle, brought an end to what is considered the second generation of video game consoles in North America. There were several viable reasons for the crash, but mainly too many game consoles, too many companies, and a constant price war to catch as many gamers as possible flooded the market with hundreds of cheap low-quality games that resulted in consumer confidence loss.

One of these high-profile titles that did incredibly poor in the market was the 1982 game *E.T. the Extra-Terrestrial*, a movie tie-in with the Spielberg franchise. *E.T. the Extra-Terrestrial* is often quoted as being "one of the worst video games ever." Thousands of the *E.T. the Extra-Terrestrial* game cartridges were returned unsold to the manufacturers and eventually dumped in landfills in the desert.

Atari was dissolved in 1985.

Nintendo

Nintendo is a multinational corporation located in Kyoto, Japan. According to Nintendo's *Touch! Generations* website, the name "Nintendo" translated from Japanese to English means "leave luck to heaven." Nintendo was founded in 1889 by Fusajiro Yamauchi to make handmade trading cards for the game Hanafuda.

In 1956, Hiroshi Yamauchi, grandson of Fusajiro Yamauchi, visited the U.S. to talk with the United States Playing Card Company, the dominant playing card manufacturer in America, and found that the world's biggest company in his business was headquartered in a rinky-dink office. This was a turning point, because Yamauchi realized the limitations of the playing card business and knew Nintendo needed to do "something different" to survive.

By 1963, Yamauchi renamed Nintendo Playing Card Company Limited to Nintendo Company, Limited, and the company had been occupied in, or tried out, several other entrepreneurial ventures, including a taxi cab company, an instant rice manufacturer, a television network, and a love hotel. None of these panned out. Then in 1974, Nintendo secured the rights to distribute the Magnavox Odyssey home video game console in Japan. By 1977, Nintendo began producing its own Color TV Game home video game consoles.

Nintendo hired a student product developer named Shigeru Miyamoto (seen in Figure 1.6) about this time. Among his first tasks was to design the casing for several of the Color TV Game consoles. However, Miyamoto had some pretty spectacular ideas of his own, and in 1981, Nintendo released Miyamoto's creation *Donkey Kong*, which changed the history of Nintendo forever.

Figure 1.6
Shigeru Miyamoto, creator of *Donkey Kong*.

Eventually, Nintendo became the software development company it is today, with a U.S. market value of over $85 billion, and is listed as the fifth largest software company in the world.

The Nintendo Seal of Quality (currently Official Nintendo Seal in NTSC regions) is a golden starburst seal first used by Nintendo of America and later Nintendo of Europe. You can see an example of it in Figure 1.7. The seal is displayed on any game licensed for use on one of Nintendo's video game consoles. The seal tells buyers the game has been properly licensed by Nintendo (and, in theory, checked for quality). Part of the reason for the Nintendo Seal was that gamers were understandably wary of game makers when the Nintendo Entertainment System (NES) came out in 1985, especially after the decline of the console market. Currently, the seal makes no guarantee of quality software, instead referring to the truth that the game has been published or licensed by Nintendo.

Figure 1.7
The Nintendo
Seal of Quality.

Nintendo has long been viewed as a "family company" because of its strict policy toward releasing only family-friendly titles. In 1994, when the ESRB video game ratings system came out, Nintendo chose to abolish those policies in favor of consumers making their own choices about the substance of the games they played.

In 1980, Nintendo launched Game & Watch, a handheld video game series developed by Yokoi. In 1989, Yokoi came out with an even greater follow-up: the GameBoy. This spawned a new age in video games, where a handheld console device could be taken with you anywhere, in a bag or pocket. When the GameBoy Advance came out a decade later, it continued the handheld gaming fever, and the GameBoy Advance SP, a flip-screen version, introduced something remarkably new at the time: a rechargeable, built-in battery supply, ending the need for AA batteries in handheld units.

The Nintendo outdid its GameBoy system in 2010 with its release of the 3DS. The Nintendo 3DS was a complete revamping of its previous DS handheld system. The 3DS was the first auto-stereoscopic handheld Nintendo engineered, and it included 2GB NAND flash memory for storage and 3D-capable 24-bit color. The 3DS currently competes against all other handhelds on the market, even with the cloud of controversy about its possible health-risks amongst children concerning vision problems due to persistent play.

Nintendo conceived the Wii console in 2001 just as the GameCube console was being launched. According to an interview with Nintendo's game designer Shigeru Miyamoto, the concept for the Wii involved focusing on a new form of human interaction: "The consensus was that power isn't everything for a console. Too many powerful consoles can't coexist. It's like having only ferocious dinosaurs. They might fight and hasten their own extinction."

The Wii console (presented in Figure 1.8) is best known for its unique interface device, often referred to as a "magic wand." A game controller is an input device used to control a video game that is typically connected to a console or personal computer. A game controller can be a keyboard, mouse, gamepad, joystick, paddle, or any other device designed for gaming that can receive input. Special purpose devices, such as steering wheels for driving games, light guns for shooting games, and fishing rods for fishing games, have also existed. Rhythm games like *Guitar Hero* and *Rock Band* have utilized controllers that are shaped and/or act like musical instruments, dance games like *Dance Dance Revolution* and *Pump It Up* use dance mats with sensors in them to detect foot motion, and some games have used microphones and voice-recognition software.

Figure 1.8
The Wii console system.

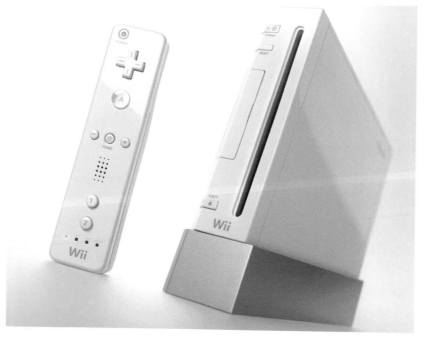

The Wii continues to dominate the console wars in North America, maintaining Nintendo's legacy.

Sega

A small Hawaiian company called Standard Games began its operations in 1940. In 1951, Raymond Lemaire and Richard Stewart moved the company from Hawaii to Tokyo, Japan, in order to develop and distribute coin-operated amusement games like jukeboxes and slot machines. At that time, they renamed the company Service Games and dispersed their machines to American military bases throughout Japan.

An American Air Force officer named David Rosen came up with a two-minute photo booth business in Tokyo in 1954. He started making coin-operated games in 1957 and began competition with Service Games. Finally, round 1965, David Rosen merged with Service Games and changed the name of the company. Using the first two letters of Service Games, the company became known as Sega. Rosen helmed Sega until 1984.

Sega, whose logo is presented in Figure 1.9, prospered heavily from the video game arcade boom of the late 1970s, with revenues climbing over $100 million by 1979. In 1982, Sega's revenues eclipsed over $214 million, but in the following year, following the North American video game crash, Sega's revenues dropped to $136 million. Sega then pioneered the use of laser disks and built their first video game console machine (the SG-1000) around the concept.

Figure 1.9
The Sega logo.

Sonic the Hedgehog became a virtual mascot for Sega in 1991 in an effort to compete with Nintendo's Mario character. With his hip attitude and style, Sonic was marketed to seem "cooler" than the plumber. This effort worked in Sega's favor, pushing the Sega Genesis machine over the top in the console wars for a short time.

Sega enjoyed some market hits, including the Dreamcast machine, but after early denials, they officially announced they were quitting the console market race in early 2001. Although dropping out of hardware manufacturing, Sega continues in software development and video arcade distribution. In fact, Sega has even released an interactive urinal called Toylet (shown in Figure 1.10), whereby players control a series of onscreen action games using their urine stream.

Figure 1.10
A conference display of Sega's interactive urinal Toylet.

Sony

Sony Computer Entertainment (SCE) is a video game company subsidiary of Sony Consumer Products & Services Group. The company was established in late 1993 prior to its launching of the original PlayStation video game console.

Sony's first PlayStation (codenamed PSX during development; now known as PS1) was initially developed to be a CD-ROM drive add-on for Nintendo's Super Nintendo Entertainment System (SNES) as a response to the Sega CD. Negotiations between Sony and Nintendo fell through, so Sony decided to release its add-on as a standalone game system. Nothing prepared them for how well received it would be.

The PlayStation 2 (PS2), released in 2000, was the first video game console to have DVD playback functionality included straight out-of-the-box, making it a dual-purpose entertainment device. You can see the PS2 console in Figure 1.11. Even though the proprietary hardware and multifaceted development technologies received a lot of criticism at first, the system still received widespread support from third-party developers and went on to sell over 150 million units internationally. The successor, PlayStation 3, was released in 2006.

Figure 1.11
The Sony
PlayStation 2.

The PlayStation Portable (PSP) was SCE's first foray into the handheld gaming market, which had been dominated by Nintendo ever since its invention of the GameBoy. First released in 2004, the PSP has since seen significant redesigns, including smaller size, more internal memory, better quality LCD screen, and slimmer fit. The latest design, the PSP Go, came out in late 2009 and supports Bluetooth. It is 45 percent lighter and 56 percent smaller than the first PSP.

Sony Ericsson has also taken the smartphone market with its Xperia phone (see Figure 1.12), which combines the popular Android and HD screen technologies and puts them together in one mobile device. "Xperia" is derived from the word "experience" and is used in the Xperia branding.

Figure 1.12
The Sony Ericsson Xperia smartphone.

Besides hardware, Sony had a strong and persistent software angle as well from the very start. Sony Computer Entertainment Worldwide Studios (SCE WWS) is a subsidiary of SCE and is a group of video game developers fully owned and operated by Sony. This includes Naughty Dog, which has such title recognition as *Crash Bandicoot*, *Jak and Daxter*, and the *Uncharted* series.

Microsoft

In 1998, engineers from Microsoft's DirectX team—including Seamus Blackley, Ted Hase, and Otto Berkes—disassembled some old Dell laptops to construct a prototype Windows-based video game console. The team hoped their console would compete with the Sony PlayStation 2, which had been luring players away from Windows games. Early on, their prototype was named the "DirectX box"—but this was later shortened to "Xbox" because of the name's popularity with the test demographic.

In 2000, Bill Gates unveiled the Xbox (viewed in Figure 1.13) at the Game Developers Conference to rave reviews. Games like *Halo: Combat Evolved* helped secure Xbox's place in households worldwide.

Figure 1.13
The Microsoft Xbox.

The Xbox was the first video game console to feature a built-in hard disk drive, used primarily for storing game saves. This eliminated the need for separate memory cards. Xbox users could also rip music from audio CDs to the hard drive, and these songs were often used as the custom soundtracks in some of the Xbox games.

In November 2002, Microsoft launched its Xbox Live online gaming service, allowing subscribers to play online Xbox games with other subscribers around the world and download new, improved game content directly to the system's hard drive. Approximately 250,000 subscribers signed up within the first two months, and by May 2009, that number had swelled to 20 million subscribers.

By August 2005, NVIDIA ceased making Xbox's GPU, and Xbox became a dinosaur. At the same time, Microsoft launched the new and improved Xbox 360 (shown in Figure 1.14), which featured superior storage, audio, and video capabilities.

Figure 1.14
The Microsoft
Xbox 360.

Microsoft announced as part of its Live Anywhere initiative that it would bring the Live online gaming and entertainment network to a wide host of platforms and devices, including the Xbox, Xbox 360, Windows PC, Windows Phone 7, Zune, and more. As part of the Live experience, Microsoft is encouraging new developers to make games for these media to be integrated into the Live network. This has drawn an audience of amateur game developers to learn Microsoft XNA Studio and related technologies.

Macintosh

Before the very first Macintosh was released by Apple, marketing execs voiced their concerns that including a game in the completed operating system would only exacerbate the notion that the Mac was toy-like and what with the narrow amount of RAM, fitting a game into the operating system would be nigh impossible.

Eventually, however, developer Andy Hertzfeld created a desk accessory called *Puzzle* that used only 600 bytes of memory and was shipped with the Mac in 1984. *Puzzle* remained a constant part of the Mac OS until 1994, when it was replaced by *Jigsaw*, a jigsaw puzzle game that came with Mac OS 7.5.

In the 1990s, Apple computers didn't attract the same amount of video game development as Windows computers did, largely in part due to the high popularity of Windows and, especially useful for 3D gaming, Microsoft's DirectX technology.

In recent years, however, the introduction of Mac OS X and support for Intel processors has eased the porting of many games, including 3D games that use OpenGL. Virtualization technology and Boot Camp (a product that allows Intel-based Macintosh machines to boot directly into Windows) have also permitted the use of Windows games on the Mac.

The Valve Corporation shocked a lot of users when, in 2010, they hinted at a Mac version of Steam, their online gaming distribution and multiplayer communications platform. Steam had become well known for Windows game usage. Rather than typical Mac emulations, Valve plans to have downloadable full native content for Macs. The first game to be released simultaneously for Mac and Windows by Valve was *Portal 2*.

An even more successful movement by Apple was mobile gaming. A mobile game is a video game played on a mobile phone, smartphone, PDA, handheld computer, or portable media player. This is not to be confused with handheld video games such as the GameBoy, Nintendo DS, or PlayStation Portable (PSP).

The Apple iPhone, a smartphone first unveiled in 2007 (see Figure 1.15), combines a video camera, a camera phone, a media player, and a web browser with phone technology that accepts both text messages and voice mail and uses WiFi and 3G for Internet connection. Development of the iPhone first began in 2005 when Steve Jobs, former Apple CEO, decided Apple engineers ought to investigate touchscreens. It proved to be a huge success, mostly due to its native integration with Apple iTunes, one of the top stores for MP3 media, and mobile gaming.

Figure 1.15
The Apple
iPhone.

The iPod Touch (shown in Figure 1.16) is an improvement on the original iPod design. Essentially, it is a portable media player, personal digital assistant (PDA), handheld game console, and WiFi mobile platform. The iPod Touch runs iOS, the Macintosh operating system custom-designed for mobile technology. The iPod Touch was the first to add the multi-touch graphical user interface to the iPod line and was also the first iPod to have wireless access to the iTunes store; similarly, it has direct access to the Apple App Store, enabling content to be purchased and downloaded directly to the device.

Figure 1.16
The Apple iPod
Touch.

The Apple iPad (covered in more detail in Chapter 3, "Your Grimoire to the iPad") is Apple's tablet computer design, primarily a platform for audio-visual media such as books, periodicals, movies, music, games, and web content. It was released in 2010 and sold 3 million units in the first 80 days. The iPad, which you can see in Figure 1.17, runs the same iOS as the iPod Touch and iPhone and can run its own iPad apps as well as most iPhone apps. This makes it the ideal target platform for game designers wanting to tap into the iOS market.

Figure 1.17
The Apple
iPad.

Several games are making use of the iPad's lightweight on-the-go size and touchscreen functionality to give players unique experiences. You can see examples of these in the following illustrations from various rising iPad games: *Gangstar* (see Figure 1.18), *Dragooo* (see Figure 1.19), *Pocket Legends* (see Figure 1.20), and *The Deep Pinball* (see Figure 1.21).

Besides new games just made for the iPad, you can find all kinds of games from other platforms being ported to the iPad because of its target audience, including popular games like *Dead Space* (see Figure 1.22) and *FarmVille* (see Figure 1.23).

Figure 1.18
Gangstar, a game obviously inspired by *Grand Theft Auto,* takes you on an open-world crime spree.

Figure 1.19
Dragooo proves virtual pet games aren't boring by letting you raise and nurture fire-breathing dragons.

Figure 1.20
In the free-to-play multiplayer online fantasy game *Pocket Legends*, from Spacetime Studios, all the heroes are cute animals.

Figure 1.21
The Deep Pinball, from Gameprom, features a detailed pinball table and play by tilting the iPad itself back and forth.

Figure 1.22
Dead Space brings the survival horror game to the iPad.

Figure 1.23
Instead of going from the big screen to the little, *FarmVille* goes from your Facebook to the marginally larger screen of the iPad.

The Game Center is an online multiplayer "social gaming network" released by Apple. It allows users to "invite friends to play a game, start a multiplayer game through match-making, track their achievements, and compare their high scores on a leader board." Game Center (shown in Figure 1.24) was announced during an iOS 4 preview event in the summer of 2010 and was released later in September 2010.

Figure 1.24
The Apple Game Center.

Being a Game Developer

Game development uses cutting-edge computer technology to create video games. Why do people do it? Besides the sheer pleasure of making games, they do it because video games make money!

ABI Research, an independent technology market research firm, estimates that video game sales from 2005, around $32.6 billion, are going to double to around $65.9 billion in 2011. Right now, sales of video games have topped sales of CDs, videos, and DVDs—making more money than the movie or music industry. This global economic expansion has ushered in a need for skilled programmers and talented game artists. Game design schools have sprung up across the globe in order to meet the rising demand for game developers.

A single game may require a team of 20 to 300 or more individual programmers, artists, animators, sound engineers, and directors—and may cost upwards of $500,000 (usually around $50 million for a big triple-A title) to make. A game dev team is often funded by a game publisher, such as Microsoft, Nintendo, Electronic Arts, or Activision, for exclusive publishing rights. Once the game is made, it must hit the store shelves running and make as much money in the first month as possible, or it might wind up in the bargain bins or returned to the manufacturer as unsold product.

> **Note**
>
> The *triple-A (AAA)* game title description refers that an individual title's success or anticipated success if it is still under development. Triple-A titles are defined by the cost and the return on investment. Most triple-A title games cost between $10 to $12 million to make and become a smash hit, selling well over a million copies.

Game developers are often hired based on personality. This is because of the team-based work structure, and because everyone on the team must get along and work well together. Game developers also get hired based on their skills. Developers fall into several classes based on skill sets and specializations. The broadest classes of individuals making up a game development team are

- **Programmers**—These people make the most money because they have to program the code that tells the computer what to do and how to react to the players playing the game. Programmers in the industry today are expected to know a lot of different programming languages (no single language standard exists in software development). According to the Fall 2009 issue of *Game Developer* magazine's *Game Career Guide*, the average entry-level salary of game programmers is around $64,500 per year. If you're really good at math and excel in linear algebra, programming is probably for you.

- **Artists and designers**—These people create the game's assets, including its environments, characters, props, weapons, vehicles, monsters, and more. The look of a game, readily noticeable in its graphics, can make or break its commercial viability. Game art and design reduces to 2D and 3D art, both of which are important in video game design. 3D artists should learn to use two or more major 3D modeling and animation packages, including 3ds Max, Maya, Softimage XSI, and Lightwave. Designers are often differentiated from artists in the industry, because designers are often in charge of UI layout and level design and use different toolsets to accomplish both. According to the Fall 2009 issue of *Game Developer* magazine's *Game Career Guide*, the average entry-level salary of game artists is around $47,692 per year. If you're good at drawing, or can visualize imaginary objects and people really well, you might have what it takes to be a game artist or designer.

- **Writers**—Not only are writers responsible for constructing the storyline behind the game, they also script the dialogue and events that take place in the game and write the game manual, too. It takes proper use of grammar and written expression to be a game writer. Writers are typically outsourced on a game project, so most of their income is from freelance jobs. If you find yourself making up stories and coming up with unique characters and events, you could probably be a game writer.

- **Sound engineers**—The engineers set up the sound effects, compose the music mixes, and make the games sound sweet. Ever play a video game on mute? It's not the same experience, is it? Sound is vital to the total gaming experience. According to the Fall 2009 issue of *Game Developer* magazine's *Game Career Guide*, the average entry-level salary of audio developers is around $53,269 per year. If you enjoy music and sound and have a distinct ear for the way things sound, you could make a decent sound engineer.

- **Testers**—There's a persistent myth that game testers get paid big money to play games all day, but that's not true. Testers are outsourced by game developers to bring a pair of fresh eyes to their games. Testers sit in offices, testing just one level or one part of the overall game, day in and day out, and they have to fill out lots of paperwork on a regular basis. Testers let the team know what works and what doesn't, and then they test the same area where there was an issue to see if that issue has been fixed. The majority of programmers, artists, and other game developers get their start as game testers, so one reason to get a job as a game tester is to get your foot in the door. An informal apprenticeship exists between testers and designers, producers, or associate producers, with the more experienced group shepherding talented quality assurance (Q/A) personnel who are determined to find a lasting career in the business. According to the Fall 2009 issue of *Game Developer* magazine's *Game Career Guide*, the average entry-level salary of Q/A testers is around $27,894 per year.

- **Leaders**—The leaders communicate between the rest of the team, making sure that everyone is doing what they should and that the game development deadlines are reached. Leaders include directors, team leads, producers, and managers. Leaders often have to communicate with everyone, from artists to engineers, so understanding the culture and vocabulary of these groups can add to their effectiveness. According to the Fall 2009 issue of *Game Developer* magazine's *Game Career Guide*, the average entry-level salary of game designers is around $45,259 per year and producers is around $45,259 per year. If you often find yourself coming up with ideas and talking your friends into making those ideas a reality, you would probably make a great leader on a game design team.

Pay is commensurate with location, as well. Most game companies are headquartered in large metropolitan areas like Austin, Texas, and San Diego, California. Companies pay better in those areas. A game artist working in New York may make close to $68,000 a year, whereas a freelance game artist living in the sticks in Wisconsin may only make $27,000. However, the guy living in New York will have higher living expenses, as the cost of living is higher there than for the guy living in Wisconsin. So a lot of salary earning must be balanced with your comfort level and where you want to live.

Skillsets are vitally important within a game design team. In fact, if you graduate from a game school, the majority of employers will judge you not on the classes you took in school but by your skills in computers or the portfolio of work done previously. So if you want to get a job in the industry as a 3D animator, you have to show an employer what 3D software you know really well—and you will have to show them a portfolio of original 3D artwork you've personally created. An employer may also want to see a demo reel of any animations you have made yourself.

Note

For more information on game design jobs and projected salaries, visit www.gamecareer guide.com today. The makers of *Game Developer* magazine can help you get prepared for a future career in game design.

Tip

"My primary responsibility at Rockstar San Diego is to build buildings that will populate the environment of the game I'm working on. To do my job, I've got to keep up with various levels of technology, all the way from simply making cool stuff in Maya (based on a detailed photo reference) to applying various shaders to these objects so that they look good within the context of the finished game."

—Tom Carroll, environment artist at Rockstar San Diego

How to Get Into the Game Biz

There are two ways to get started as a game developer: the "insider" way, which means going to school for it and getting a job at an existing company, where you work your way up; and the "outsider" way, which means making games "on the cheap" for yourself or for profit.

Get Educated

Electronic games are spanning the earth and this global expansion has ushered in a need for skilled programmers and talented game artists. Most tech schools have started offering degree programs in game design to help fill this need, creating a brand new foundation in game education.

If you decide game design will be your career goal, look for a technical college that teaches game software development or game art. Perhaps there is one near you. Here are a few:

- **3D Training Institute**—www.3dtraining.com
- **Academy of Art University**—www.academyart.edu/game-design-school/
- **Collins College**—www.collinscollege.edu/game-production.asp
- **Daniel Webster College**—www.dwc.edu/admissions/programs/gamedesign.cfm
- **DeVry University**—www.devry.edu
- **DigiPen Institute of Technology**—www.digipen.edu
- **Digital Media Arts College**—www.dmac.edu
- **Emagination Game Design**—www.computercamps.com
- **Ex'pression College for Digital Arts**—www.expression.edu
- **Full Sail University**—www.fullsail.edu
- **iD Tech Camps**—www.internaldrive.com
- **International Academy of Design and Technology**—www.iadt.edu
- **ITT Technical Institute**—www.itt-tech.edu/teach/list/degd.cfm
- **Pacific Audio Visual Institute**—www.pacificav.com
- **Seneca College's Animation Arts Centre**—www.senecac.on.ca/school/animationartscentre.html
- **The Academy of Game Entertainment Technology**—http://academy.smc.edu
- **The Art Institutes**—www.artinstitutes.edu
- **The Florida Interactive Entertainment Academy**—www.fiea.ucf.edu
- **The Guildhall at SMU**—http://guildhall.smu.edu
- **University of Advancing Technology**—www.uat.edu
- **Vancouver Institute for Media Arts**—www.vanarts.com
- **Westwood College of Technology**—www.westwood.edu/programs/

To become more proficient at the technology used in game development and to build your resume for future job applications, you can go to a school that offers a game design program, but honestly you don't *have* to have a formal education to become a computer-age rockstar. In fact, most employers, recruiters, and headhunters will be looking at your *portfolio*, or a list of what you've done successfully in the past, as an indication of whether you'd fit within their company. Thus, it is imperative you start right away making games.

If you have a few games of your own to show inside your portfolio, you have a much better chance attracting the attention of a game development company.

Get a Job

If you have your education and want to get a job at a game development company, like Bungie Software, chances are you will have to start with an entry-level position.

The most common entry-level position at game development companies is as a game tester. Game testers perform focus testing and beta testing and take part in quality assurance for games being developed. They write a lot of reports, as they have to document bugs or glitches they find.

It's not all about getting paid to play games; in fact, it can be downright tedious and nerve-wracking sometimes. Yet if you show a good head for design and stick with it, you can see promotion to another job title in the company in your future.

Occasionally, if you have a connection or a really good job placement counselor at your college, you can bypass servitude as a game tester and start out with a good game job title. It really helps, too, to have an amazing body of work or portfolio to show employers. Again, to get a job making games, you have to show employers you can make games. The best way to do this is to start right now, with what you learn in this book, by making as many cool games as you can to put into your portfolio.

Dance to Your Own Drumbeat

Of course, you might not want to even get a job at a game development company. In that case, it's not imperative for you to go to college and get a job (although you'll certainly need to do something to support yourself, when you're not living at home—and trust me, living in mom and dad's basement and piddling with making video games in your spare time when you're 30 years old just isn't cool!).

You might want to make video games for yourself, your friends, and/or your family—more as a hobby than anything else. That's okay, too.

Or you might decide you want to make indie games for money, and you start your own in-house company. That's even better. Just know that you will have to find the funding and the time to invest in an enterprise like that, that it's not easy but it's not impossible, either. You'll have to spend just as much time promoting yourself and your indie games as you'll spend making them.

Either route you go, the "insider" or "outsider" way, this book can help you get started making games of your very own!

Indie Game Development

The music industry has existed for a lot longer than the game industry, and as anyone who knows music can tell you, the Top 40 pop music lists are fine for most listeners, but if you want to really hear some edgy tunes that take tired formulas for a ride on the wild side, indie music is where it's at. Indie musicians are artists who aren't afraid to take risks. They settle for smaller gigs and less pay to play the music they want to and experiment with their sonic art. Indie musicians are often seen as rebels who thumb their noses at the big industry giants.

Games work precisely the same way. When a corporate giant such as Electronic Arts pours thousands of dollars into creating a big-market game, they expect huge payoffs to compensate for their costs. They are understandably against taking risks, even if the payoff might come in better innovation or storytelling. This undeniable fact is why you see so many game sequels and imitation knockoffs instead of original or ground-breaking games on store shelves. If you want to see real innovation in the game industry, you have to peer at the margins, at the indie game designers.

Indie games are often shorter, cheaper-made games developed by fewer than 20 people, and are free or sell for a low price over the Internet. Indie games usually rise out of amateur and hobbyist game designers. Just giving away your game doesn't sound very smart, and when you see prices at $10 a purchase, it makes you wonder if indie developers ever make their money back—but if they can sell a minimum of 4,000 copies in one year, at $10 a pop, that comes to $40,000 in gross profit! Not bad for a part-time hobby, eh?

The indie game movement grew out of the modification community, where players of popular games such as *Quake* and *Unreal* modified the components to build their own game experiences and swap them online. With ever more affordable game software licenses, more schools teaching game development, and regular indie game festivals, almost anyone can become an indie game developer!

Although much of the game industry's big-budget efforts come from large team efforts, toiling on the production line is not the only model for game development out there. Lovingly crafted creations from indie game developers have proven that creativity flourishes when the development process is put back into the hands of a solo designer.

As an indie developer, you can make any game you want. Because you're not taking anyone else's money to make your game, you can try radical things no one else has tried before. Working alone to build a game with art, music, and compelling play may seem daunting to a first-timer, but it's never been easier for developers to create original titles without committing themselves to programming from scratch or shelling out an exhaustive budget.

And best of all, there is no reason to wait for permission to start working on a game. You can start right now and do it all yourself. Working alone on a game not only gives you complete control, but also it infuses your work with a personality that big team development rarely has.

iPad Multiplayer Magic and the Unity iOS software will give you all the tools you need to make your own indie games for the iPad. In this book, you will learn how to make a multiplayer online game where the players are witches flying on brooms and shooting potion bubbles at one another (see Figure 1.25), but what you learn, you can apply to just about any iPad game you want.

Figure 1.25
The *SorcerRun* game you will build.

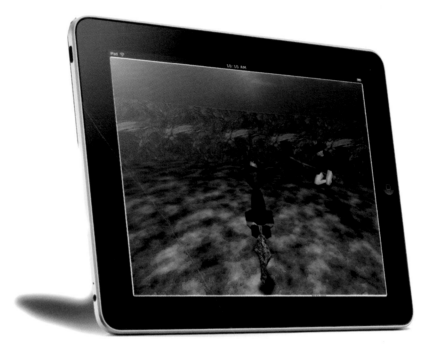

Casual Gaming

When video games entered homes during the console movement, the rules for video games became more complex and only the most hardcore gamers dominated the consumer market. However, this is not the only type of video game audience out there, and developers—especially mobile game developers—have recognized that.

A casual game is a video game targeted at or used by an audience of casual gamers. What are casual gamers? Casual gamers are those who do not have the time, patience, or obsessive passion to learn difficult, complex video games but still want to be entertained. Casual gamers include the young and old but are more often female, with over 74 percent of casual gamers having a pair of ovaries. Casual gamers tend to seek out games with comfortable gameplay and a pick-up-and-play entertainment that people from almost any age group or skill level can enjoy.

Casual games can be any type of genre, but they are distinguished by a simple set of rules and particular lack of time commitment required. Casual games often have one or more of these distinguishing features:

- Extremely modest gameplay, such as a jigsaw puzzle game that can be played entirely with a single-button mouse click or cell phone keypad
- Gameplay that can be accomplished in short episodes, such as during work breaks or—especially in the case of mobile games—on public transportation
- Either the capacity to quickly attain a finishing stage or continuous play with frequent or no need to save your spot in the game
- Usually free or try-before-you-buy downloads

Microsoft's *Solitaire*, which comes free with Microsoft Windows, is widely considered the very first casual game, with more than 400 million people having played it since its inception. When Nintendo released their GameBoy, the free built-in *Tetris* game, a casual game if there ever was one, was partially credited with the success of that handheld console. And with the invention of the Flash 2D interactive animation software, there came a sudden boom of web-based casual games, one of the most prominent titles being *Bejeweled*. Even former president Bill Clinton admitted to being addicted to playing *Bejeweled*. Flash game sites have cropped up left and right on the Internet, and Facebook third-party application developers also got into the action with casual games like *Farmville* and *Mobsters*.

The arrival of Apple's iPod in the casual gaming market made more powerful games widely available in a portable format. PopCap Games created *Peggle*, which was an instant success on Apple's music player, proving the need for more high-quality casual games on mobile devices. You can see *Peggle* in action in Figure 1.26.

Today, casual games—especially on the web and on mobile devices—have exploded, with a wider and much more approachable audience than any other known game type.

Casual games are also remarkably well placed for indie game developers to get their foot in the door.

Figure 1.26
Peggle, a casual
game from
PopCap
Games.

Figure 1.26 *Peggle*, a casual game from PopCap Games.

How Video Games Are Made

A video game is not created willy-nilly. Every game has a process behind its development.

There are many levels, or steps, to developing video games you probably aren't aware of. When you play a game, you don't see the years of sweat and hard work it took to polish that game into the final piece of electronic make-believe you play. Although there are many steps taken to getting that game into your hands, the procedure can be broken down into three categories: pre-production, production, and post-production.

Pre-Production

The pre-production stage is where the concept is created and finalized, funds are sought after, and a team is put together to produce the game. The game design document is written, a game proposal or short demo may be shopped around to publishers, and a general inventory takes place before the developers get started.

Concept Creation

The game concept has to come from somewhere. A board meeting might brainstorm ideas until one or two trickle together that show merits of profit-making potential. A bunch of people sitting around eating pizza may be joking about what games they would like to see and suddenly one of them says, "That's it!" Or one game developer may be taking a break from it all, enjoying a hot shower at home, and suddenly jumps out and grabs a notepad because a great idea has hit him. Whatever the concept is or looks like, it has sparked the development process.

Concept Finalization

The core team of the game's creators, often starting with the lead game designer, starts fleshing out the game.

The artists come up with concept artwork, including drawings and paintings of the characters, vehicles, environments, and weapons that may be used in the game. The writers write a game design document, which tells the team all the details of the game, including what levels there will be, who will be the characters in it, and how the player controls work. The asset artists and programmers begin hashing together a short playable demo—what is often referred to as a *prototype*. The lead game designer works with his team to prepare a game proposal that is sure to knock the socks off of prospective financial backers.

Preparation

The team takes inventory of what software and hardware they have to start with, whether they have the office space needed to produce in, and how many members of the team they need to add by either hiring or outsourcing. This inventory helps shape their list of needed funds. Once they have the needed funds, they can get the help or tools necessary to produce the game.

Production

The team is now ready to begin game development in earnest.

The asset artists design 3D models, 2D artwork, textures, and environments on their computers. The programmers code the player controls and character behaviors, as well as the physics engine. The writers set out dialogue and scripted events. The cinematic artists take storyboards and create short animatic cut-scenes that appear throughout the game (*cut-scenes* are those pauses in games where the player's controls are taken away, and she must watch and listen for story exposition purposes). The leaders make sure the office doesn't burn down and that the team members don't walk off the job.

The production process often starts off dreamy and becomes tenser the closer the deadlines get. Team members will often work obscene hours during the "crunch" time, even sleeping underneath their desks and avoiding their families.

Post-Production

After the game is finished, it is still not finished. Testing, quality assurance, and bug-fixing commences, followed up by a PR (public relations) scheme that will market the game to its target audience. Even after the game is released and sitting on store shelves, more bug fixes may be required in the form of patch software.

Testing and Q/A

Testing involves the team members who are finished with the earlier tasks of playing the game over and over carefully. They follow checklists to make sure every possible glitch is rooted out. After the team tests their game, they may pull in people not related to the team to test the game with fresh eyes. A beta version of the game may even be released online, requesting players to tell the team if a bug is discovered or offering prizes if players discover any glitch.

Team leaders are responsible, primarily guided by the project manager or head game designer, for making doubly sure that the game's overall look and playability remain consistent with the original concept. It can often happen that while 40 or so designers are working on a single project, some of them will start jumping off on tangents or try to change the look of the game part of the way through the build. So it's imperative that quality assurance, or Q/A, is maintained at every stage of production, especially during post-production.

Marketing

The game has to start selling well before it even hits store shelves, so the PR department of a game company makes sure people know about the game before its release and that the target audience wants to buy it. Game magazines will feature previews of early prototypes of the game or interviews with its developers. Web forums are also a great place to hit the target audience. Any way that the PR people can whet the appetite of the public and make folks curious about an upcoming game is a good way to advertise it long before its release.

Expansion

Although the designers never intend for bugs to happen, the game may need patches to fix bugs that still occur in the product after it's shipped. The game may also prove wildly successful, and the developer may want to start work on expansion packs or sequels. If not, the game design team might get a moment to take a few breaths before starting their next new game project.

Popular Game Genres

Now, take a look at some traditional video game genres and what they are made of.

Action Games

Action games are made up of all the kinds of games where the player's reflexes and hand-eye coordination make a difference in whether she wins or loses. The most popular action games include the following:

- **First-person shooters**—Seen through the eyes of the main character, these games focus on fast-paced movement through detailed game levels, shooting and blowing up everything in sight. Because of the intimacy of "being the character," these games have the deepest player immersion. However, because of the frantic pacing of these games, the player rarely has time to stand still and take in the scenery. *Doom*, shown in Figure 1.27, is an icon of the first-person shooter market.

Figure 1.27
Doom, made by id Software.

- **Third-person shooters**—The player sees the action through a camera, which is aimed from behind the main character or over its shoulder. These games still focus on shooting and blowing stuff up, but the character is always visible onscreen and may have additional controls for actions like jumping, climbing, and performing martial arts. A cartoon variety of this kind of game made the *Sly Cooper* series a success. Naughty Dog's *Uncharted* series (see Figure 1.28) has surpassed previous third-person shooters with its smart enemies and realistic motion captures.

Figure 1.28
Uncharted features clever bad guys and fast action. The player becomes treasure-hunting hero Nathan Drake.

- **Platform games**—The player's character is seen onscreen, sometimes from a side angle. The action no longer focuses on shooting and blowing up bad guys; instead, the main action focuses on the character running and jumping from one platform to the next in a fast-paced animated world. Although the first platform games were side-scrollers, where the two-dimensional characters started on the left of the screen and ran and hopped their way to the right of the screen, games like *Mario 64*, *Ratchet and Clank* (see Figure 1.29), and *Crash Bandicoot* revolutionized platform jumpers by bringing them into fully-realized 360-degree 3D game worlds.

- **Racing games**—Racing games feature fast vehicles along nasty tracks and difficult terrain in an all-out race to the finish line. The goal is usually to come in first and as far ahead of the rest as possible.

- **Sports games**—Featuring rules and scenarios just like the real-world counterpart games, sports games focus on (what did you expect?) sports. Popular sports found in video games include golf, soccer, basketball, football, volleyball, and baseball, but any pastime can be a prospective electronic game.

- **Fighting games**—Fighting games have the player competing against a single opponent in an arena, where they must duke it out using feet and fists in elaborate combination moves. Games such as *Street Fighter*, *Mortal Kombat*, and *DOA* revolutionized the genre.

Figure 1.29
Ratchet and Clank: Crack in Time.

- **Stealth games**—For those players who don't like to rush into battle, there are games that reward the players for sneaking into and out of places without being seen and striking silently. Sometimes the player is taking on the role of a master thief (*Thief: Deadly Shadows*), while at other times the player is a slick assassin (*Hitman: Absolution*—see Figure 1.30).

Figure 1.30
Hitman: Absolution.

Adventure Games

Adventure games traditionally combine puzzle-solving with storytelling. What pulls the game together is an extended, often twisting narrative, calling for the player to visit different locations and encounter many different characters. Often the player's path is blocked, and she must gather and manipulate certain items to solve some puzzle and unblock the path.

Zork (shown in Figure 1.31) was one of the first interactive fiction games ever played on a computer and one of the best games ever released for the Commodore 64, one of the first home computers. The name Zork is hacker jargon for an unfinished program, but by the time Infocom's Zork was released and going to be named *Dungeon* in 1979, the nickname *Zork* had already stuck. For many, the name *Zork* conjures up dim images of a computer game prehistory, before graphical adventures had become the norm. *Zork* set several precedents for the genre.

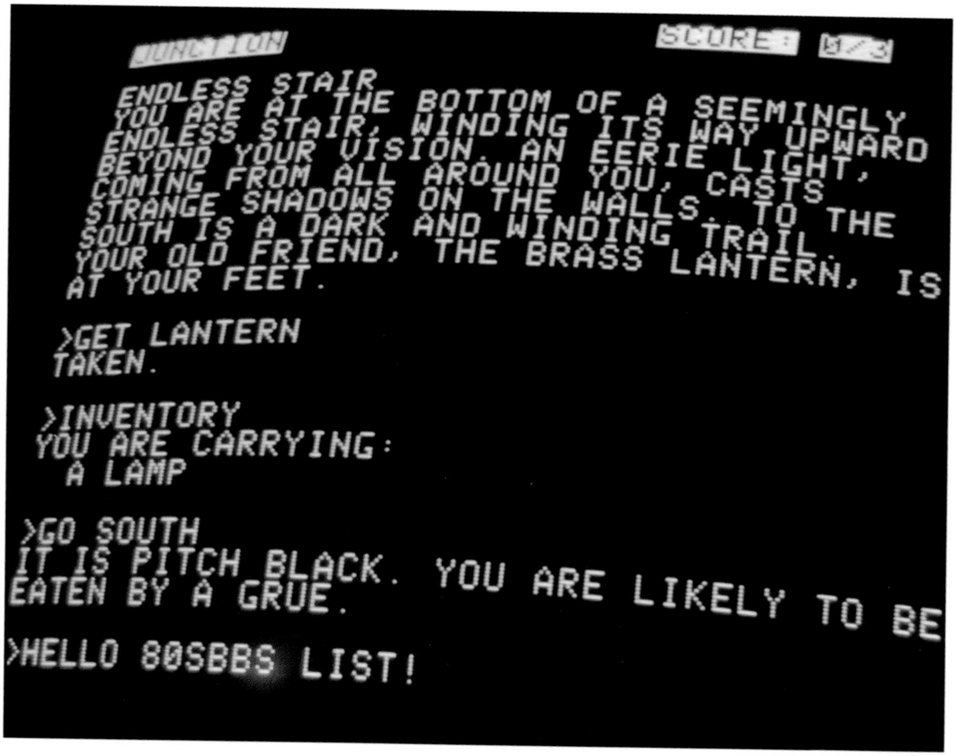

Figure 1.31
Zork was an interactive text-based fantasy game in 1979.

```
JUNCTION                          SCORE: 0/3
ENDLESS STAIR
YOU ARE AT THE BOTTOM OF A SEEMINGLY
ENDLESS STAIR, WINDING ITS WAY UPWARD
BEYOND YOUR VISION. AN EERIE LIGHT,
COMING FROM ALL AROUND YOU, CASTS
STRANGE SHADOWS ON THE WALLS. TO THE
SOUTH IS A DARK AND WINDING TRAIL.
YOUR OLD FRIEND, THE BRASS LANTERN, IS
AT YOUR FEET.

>GET LANTERN
TAKEN.

>INVENTORY
YOU ARE CARRYING:
  A LAMP

>GO SOUTH
IT IS PITCH BLACK. YOU ARE LIKELY TO BE
EATEN BY A GRUE.

>HELLO 80SBBS LIST!
```

Adventure games primarily center on story, exploration, and mental challenges. Most, if not all, adventure games don't even have violence in them. Many have players solve mysteries through gathering up specific clues, as in Toshimitsu Takagi's 2004 game *Crimson Room*.

There are at least four different types of adventure games. There are completely text-based adventure games, graphic adventure games, and visual novels (which are a popular Japanese variant featuring mostly static anime-style graphics and resembling mixed-media novels).

Another type of adventure game you might have seen—and even played before—is the hunt-the-pixel or "hidden image" adventure game. This manner of adventure games, a trendy genre for amateur game developers to undertake, is a series of graphic puzzles that takes the player on a virtual scavenger hunt.

Examples of adventure games include *Colossal Cave*, *Secret of Monkey Island*, *Myst*, *Siberia*, *Clue: Fatal Illusion*, *Still Life* (see Figure 1.32), *Legend of the Broken Sword*, *Gabriel Knight*, *Grim Fandango*, and *Maniac Mansion*.

Figure 1.32
Still Life.

There are several great game-authoring tools you can look into if you are interested in making an adventure game. Most require Windows, however. They are

- **WinterMute Engine (WME)**—http://dead-code.org/home/
- **Adventure Game Studio (AGS)**—www.adventuregamestudio.co.uk/
- **Lassie Adventure Studio**—http://lassiegames.com/lassie/about/

Role-Playing Games

Role-playing games, or RPGs, got their start in pencil and paper in the 1970s with Gary Gygax's *Dungeons and Dragons*. A variation of British war-gaming (which used miniature soldiers and world maps), RPGs required players to sit around a table and imagine they were wizards, warriors, and rogues exploring vast treacherous dungeons in a fantasy world.

Today's more complex computer role-playing games, like *Neverwinter Nights, Asheron's Call, World of Warcraft,* and *Elder Scrolls V: Skyrim* (see Figure 1.33), help players create their own characters from scratch, and the goal of each game is often making their characters stronger and finding better weapons while facing a rising level of adversity. And adversity comes in many startling guises, from trolls to giant spiders to fire-breathing dragons.

Figure 1.33
Elder Scrolls V: Skyrim.

One of the major resources you see in almost every RPG is experience. Players get experience for completing missions and beating monsters, and they spend experience to raise their character's skills or gain new powers. Another popular part of RPGs is communicating with non-player characters, or NPCs, through multiple-choice conversations called *dialogue trees*. Depending on what players decide to say to NPCs, they might make friends, or they might find the NPCs rushing them with swords drawn!

There is a really great application you can use to make fantasy RPGs. It's called RPG Maker, and if you want to learn more about it, look for my book *RPG Maker for Teens*, from Course Technology PTR, 2011. In my book, I show you how to make a fantasy game RPG using Enterbrain's RPG Maker software. It's fast and easy to learn.

Strategy Games

Strategy games envelop a great deal of mental challenge-based games, including real-time strategy (RTS) games, turn-based strategy (TBS) games, and construction-management simulations (CMS). In each, the core play has the player building an empire, fortress, realm, world, or other construct, managing the resources therein, and preparing against inevitable problems like decay, hardship, economic depravity, revolution, or foreign invaders. Strategy games emphasize skillful thinking and planning in order to achieve victory. In most strategy games, the player is given a godlike view of the game world and indirectly controls game units under her command. Thus, strategy games are a closer comparison to classic British war-games than RPGs, even though RPGs originated from war-games.

Keynote strategy games that have helped define the genre include *Age of Empires* (see Figure 1.34), *Civilization*, *StarCraft*, *Command & Conquer*, and *Shattered Galaxy*.

Figure 1.34
Age of Empires 3.

Other Game Genres

Besides the genres already mentioned, there are many more:

- **Traditional games**—Chess, Poker, Texas Hold 'em, Solitaire, Mahjong, trivia games, and others share a clustered category under traditional games. These are all games that have been played in a physical milieu and are given a virtual makeover in order to become video games. In some cases, the video game versions become more popular than the originals.

- **Online games**—Any game played through an Internet connection, including Xbox Live games, are considered online games. Ones with lots of players joining together in a co-op or versus mode in the same game realm are called *massive multiplayer online games* (*MMOs*). Although Blizzard's *World of Warcraft* is an RPG, it is also an MMO, which is why people in the industry classify it as an MMORPG.

- **Artificial life games**—The player of an A-life game cares for a creature or virtual pet. In *Nintendogs*, for instance, players feed, play, and care for virtual canines. A game that first started out as an A-life game and grew to encompass multiple games in an online community is *Neopets*.

- **Puzzle games**—These games never have much of a story. Instead, they focus on single-player mental challenges. Popular examples include *Bejeweled* and *Tetris*. One very addictive game that has truly redefined the puzzle game genre is *Plants vs. Zombies*, where the player controls cute but tough cartoon plants against an oncoming zombie horde. You can see a screenshot from *Plants vs. Zombies* in Figure 1.35.

- **Serious games**—Serious games are a serious business; many of them are educational games, which help schools teach subjects in the guise of having fun, or they can be training games, helping companies to instruct their employees in specific tasks. This is developing into a much larger genre as years go by, and some professionals have started referring to it as "edutainment."

Tip

"One of the more interesting trends today is the plethora of 'mixed-genre' games. It seems that one way to mitigate risk, while still trying to innovate, is to take several popular genres… and mix them to create a new style of game. Deus Ex is a great example of this hybrid."

—Tracy Fullerton, Assistant Professor, Electronic Arts Interactive
Entertainment Program at USC School of Cinema-Television

Figure 1.35

Plants vs. Zombies from PopCap Games.

Tip

"I tend to de-emphasize genre in my designing and thinking. I feel that genre is a bit of a double-edged sword for designers. On one hand, genres give designers and publishers a common language for describing styles of play. . . . On the other hand, genres tend to restrict the creative process and lead designers toward tried-and-true gameplay solutions. I encourage students to consider genre when thinking about their games from a business perspective, but not to allow it to stifle their imagination during the design process."

—Tracy Fullerton, Assistant Professor, Electronic Arts Interactive Entertainment Program at USC School of Cinema-Television

---

Playing Perspective

There is another principle to consider when designing a game besides genre. It's called playing perspective. This is also known as the point-of-view, or POV, just as in the development of fiction stories. In film, cinematographers have to arrange the composition of all their camera shots to tell the story, but games use fixed or active cameras, thought of as floating eyes, to witness the action in the games. The position of these cameras, whether fixed or not, defines the POV of the game. The following are the most popular playing perspectives seen in video games today.

First-Person View

Just as fiction has a first-person perspective, the "I," "me," and "our" voice, told from the perspective of the narrator, so too do games have a first-person perspective. The approved choice of 3D shooters because of the ease of aiming, first-person perspective enhances the sensory immersion of a game by putting the player in the shoes of the character she is playing; she sees through the eyes of her character, and usually the only part of the player's character that can be seen is the hand holding the gun out in front of her (see Figure 1.36).

Figure 1.36
Call of Duty 4: Modern Warfare is an example of a first-person view game.

It is important to remember when designing a first-person game that the player will start to think of herself as the avatar character, so cut-scenes that suddenly show her character or asides where a particularly grating voiceover supposed to belong to her character will take away the player's suspension of disbelief and (worst-case scenario) cause frustration.

Suspension of disbelief, a concept first postulated by poet Samuel Taylor Coleridge, is that magical realm where the audience goes along with fantastical fiction elements as long as they aren't brought back down to reality by some flaw in the writing. This concept is best demonstrated by watching a stage magician performing: You want to believe in his act, that he's really doing magic, but your suspension of disbelief gets worn out if he constantly goofs or shows you how he's doing his tricks.

Third-Person View

Just as in fiction writing, where the third-person (or omniscient) style is typified by the "he," "she," "they," and "it" voice, games, too, have a third-person perspective. The third-person perspective is much more cinematic and immediate. The gamer can see her character on the screen and watch every move she makes. This leads to a greater identification with the player character but less immersion overall.

Compare the two perspectives in Figure 1.37.

Figure 1.37
The game *Mirror's Edge* as seen in third- and first-person. When you're teetering on the edge of a sky-scraper in first-person, you feel the dizzying effects of height worse, but in third-person, you feel more like you're watching a movie.

The worst restriction to this viewpoint is that the character is *always* onscreen, and often seen from behind, so the character must look exceptional or gamers are going to complain about always looking at an ugly butt. Mario from *Mario 64* and Lara Croft from the *Tomb Raider* series were used in this perspective and rose to "movie star" fame because they literally became game icons and representatives of their gameplay.

Film cinematography features an over-the-shoulder, or OTS, camera view, which has recently seen its way into video games as a variation of the third-person perspective. Surprisingly well-done examples of this are Capcom's *Resident Evil 4* and *5* (see Figure 1.38).

Figure 1.38
Leon, in
Resident Evil 4,
is shown from
over-the-
shoulder
perspective,
which often
makes aiming
at infected
enemy heads
easier.

Top-Down (Aerial) View

The top-down or aerial view is a view looking straight down at the playing field. This perspective is most often seen in games like *Solitaire*, the early *Ultima*, or *Zelda: Link to the Past*. It limits the horizon for the player, so she has a harder time seeing what obstacles might be coming up, but it does add greater detail to what is on the surrounding map. *Grand Theft Auto*, before its 3D days, began as a vintage 8-bit top-down game.

Isometric View

Isometric is the favored tilted "three-quarter" view hovering off to one side of certain RPGs such as *Diablo, Baldur's Gate, Bard's Tale*, and *Planescape: Torment* (see Figure 1.39). This perspective is often used to give a fair impersonation of 3D even when the characters and environments are really 2D. Isometric games for this reason are popular in RTS and RPG but rarely seen in action shooters because of the limitations to aim and visibility. Isometric games offer player movement in eight directions: north, north-west, west, southwest, south, southeast, east, and northeast.

Figure 1.39
*Planescape:
Torment* has an
isometric view.

Side View

The side view perspective reflects the traditional view of Sega and Nintendo's side-scrolling platformers as popularized in *Sonic the Hedgehog, Super Mario Bros.,* and *Earthworm Jim.* Although largely unused in newer games, thought of as too "retro," this view can be mimicked quite well even when working in 3D if you set up satellite cameras from the side and provide a fenced-in path terrain.

Adventure Scenes

Adventure games are well known for having 3D characters exploring pre-rendered 2D backdrops using an invisible box model, with each scene thus becoming a diorama. Or sometimes there isn't a player character at all, just a diorama to explore.

The player navigates and clicks through each adventure scene, sometimes having to backtrack many times or click throughout a scene to find elements to interact with, and if the designer is not careful, this can quickly degenerate into "hunt-the-pixel" frustrations. This type of perspective is fixed and unmovable. Whenever the player moves to an exact location onscreen, say a door leading to a hallway, another scene is drawn, say the interior of that hallway.

Closed-Circuit Cameras

This perspective style was first pioneered by *Alone in the Dark* and became the basis for the *Resident Evil* cameras. The style was later copied by *Silent Hill* and countless other survival horror games in succession, because it made for better suspense.

In this closed-circuit camera view, fixed cameras pan to follow the 3D player models wandering through pre-rendered settings. When a player character gets too far away from one camera, another camera will "switch on" and pick up the action so that the player character is always on display. Unfortunately, this perspective style has gotten a lot of flak: Players have griped that this style, while able to maintain a suspenseful mood, can be downright frustrating when trying to shoot enemies around corners or for seeing if you are about to walk up on a potential hazard (see Figure 1.40). This complaint is one of the reasons that *Resident Evil*, starting with RE4, switched to using over-the-shoulder third-person perspective.

Figure 1.40
As you can see by this screen grab from *Resident Evil 3*, even if you were armed with a Gatling gun, you *still* couldn't see to shoot the approaching zombies because of the tricky fixed camera positions.

What's Next?

You've already learned some basic game principles, such as playing perspectives and popular game genres. In the next chapter, you will learn more about the ins and outs of game design, and you'll discover the ingredients used in the video games you love to play.

RESTART GAME

SETTINGS

HELP

GENERAL STATS

ENJOY YOUR OWN SUDOKU

auto-fill

TIME ELAPSED
3m 27s

Easy Normal Hard Insane

4	1	5	7			3		9
6				5	9	4	1	8
9			1	4	6	2		
		9	5	3	2		8	4
1	2	3				5	7	6
8	5	4	6	7				
			4	6	7	8		5
3		7	9	1	5			2
5			2		3		9	1

1   2   3   4   5

←   6   7   8   9   ✕   →

2

Game Design Principles

Now that you know how video games got started and how they are made, you're ready to make your own, right? Wait! Perhaps it would help if you had clearer guidelines for making a video game before you begin.

There are accepted practices in game design that will assist you if you happen to get stuck. I will outline these practices within the context of 4FOGGD: The Four Fs of Great Game Design. Refer back to this chapter whenever you find yourself at an impasse for what and how to design your game.

The Four Fs of Great Game Design

There are Four Fs of Great Game Design, or 4FOGGD, that are listed in order of priority and should be considered whenever you have to make any design decision. They help ensure the game you build will be fantastic.

The Four Fs of Great Game Design are Fun, Fairness, Feedback, and Feasibility.

Fun

> **Tip**
>
> "I still think that people who make their own games forget that it's supposed to be fun. I still play enough games where I'm really into it, and there's something just amazingly frustrating. Never give your player a reason to put your game down."
>
> —Todd Howard, Bethesda Softworks

Games are intended to be fun by their definition. Fun is a word often synonymous with play. Fun is a short and simple word, easy to spell, and it is innate. Even the smallest child will begin inventing his or her own personal game when bored, an innate instinct meant to stave off ennui.

You know what fun is intrinsically, but fun is actually very abstract and subjective. You can't dissect fun and have it laid out before you in its constituent parts. It loses its nature when you do so. Yet there are some tricks you can do to make sure your game will be fun.

A game, first of all, is any fun activity conducted in a pretend reality that has a core component of play. Because it is play—and not work—that is a huge distinction to keep in mind when making a game. However, every play has rules.

Rules of Play

Play is any grouping of recreational human activities centered on having fun. The pretend reality of most games is based on the mental capacity to create a conceptual state self-contained within its own set of rules, where the pretender can create, discard, or transform the components at will. The complexity and character of people's games evolve with their age and mental acuity. A game that outreaches a participant's age or understanding will swiftly tire the participant and leave her bored. A boring game is no fun at all, as boredom is the antithesis of fun.

Remember that boredom is the antithesis of fun!

The pretend reality created by a game's rule set is referred to by experts as Huizinga's Magic Circle, which was first established by Johan Huizinga (see Figure 2.1) in 1971. Huizinga's Magic Circle is a concept stating that artificial effects appear to have importance and are bound by a set of made-up rules while inside their circle of use.

Figure 2.1
Dutch historian Johan Huizinga.

For example, the American game of football is about guys tossing a pigskin ball back and forth to each other, but inside Huizinga's Magic Circle, the players abide clearly outlined rules to reach a victory for one team or the other. Consequently, the concepts of winning and losing are not essential to all games, but they do make a game more exciting, competitive, and positioned within a clear frame of reference.

Video games are special games where the Huizinga's Magic Circle is tied within an electronic device, whether that device is a computer screen and keyboard, TV screen and console, or handheld machine. Video games have graphics, audio, and interaction, but beyond those things, the elements of a video game differ widely based on game genre and platform.

Video games are different from traditional board or card games: In video games, most of the rules are hidden. The game still has its own rules, but those rules are rarely written down for the player to consult before jumping into play. Instead, video games allow players to learn the rules of the game as they play. Harder games, or ones with entirely new/unheard-of rules, will sometimes offer players training levels to learn the rules pretty early in the game. These are levels where players are taught the rules by moderated experimentation. Given this route for learning rules, players with more practice playing a specific game will be better informed and can optimize their choices.

Hiding the rules offers video games one huge advantage over traditional games: Because the computer sets the boundary of the Huizinga's Magic Circle, the player no longer has to think of the game as a game! This level of immersion is found lacking in most traditional games.

Tip

"Communication is hard because players are not here to learn; they're here to play. But if they don't learn, they will never know how to play."

—Tom Smith, Senior Producer, Disney Mobile

Teaching Players to Play

You should never forget to teach your player how to play your game. Every game is slightly different in the way it is played. Games of the same genre are generally more similar in their gameplay, and thus players can figure them out quicker than games of opposite genres. But never assume your players know what to do when they need to do it, or you'll only foster confusion and frustration.

Things to think about when teaching a player to play your game include

- Who is the player in your game?

- What can the player do in your game? What are the controls?

- Why should the player do anything in your game? What are the goals and rewards?

Probably the easiest way to tell the player how to play the game is through a short briefing before the game starts (see Figure 2.2). This briefing can be so short it takes up a single screen with a picture of the game controls, or so long as to be an entry level in the game itself, like a training level. Or you could weave the instruction into the beginning levels of the gameplay, where short pop-up messages give the player hints about how to play the game, like "Press A to jump over obstacles." See Figure 2.3 for an example.

(continued)

Teaching Players to Play (continued)

Figure 2.2

As in *Chocolatier: Decadence by Design* (iPad), each mission has a briefing before you start that clearly defines the goal.

Figure 2.3

Cut the Rope for the iPad is a physics-based game where you must bring the candy closer to the green critter called Om Nom. This screenshot shows in-game player hints.

(continued)

Teaching Players to Play (continued)

There are some games that use these pop-up messages as gates, blocking the player from moving on in the game until the player demonstrates that she understands the control system. As in *Conker's Bad Fur Day* for the Nintendo 64, the player is told how to use the squirrel tail as a propeller to jump farther and is immediately given a challenge that forces the player to do so or else she can't escape from the waterfall's edge. Forcing the player to show they "get it" is a neat way of reinforcing your message, but it can also make your players feel like they aren't in control, rob them of their enjoyment, and on rare occasions even reveal weaknesses in the game interface.

Show the players the ropes and then step back and let them make the big choices governing the game's direction.

Components of Fun Video Games

Danc, a game designer, pixel artist, and tool maker in the industry, says that a really fun video game can be best described as an onion, with many layers: "A game is built like an onion. Each layer of the game polishes an aspect of the previous structure and makes it slightly more appealing. Areas near the inner core give you the most bang for your buck. Areas near the outer edges of the game design are easier to change without unbalancing the system, but don't make as big of an impact."

Danc lists the layers a video game has (see Figure 2.4) as such, from innermost out:

1. **Core mechanics**—The fundamental gameplay, with its risks and rewards. Gameplay is a commonly used term meant to describe the interactive aspects of video game design. Gameplay involves the player interacting with the game.

2. **Meta mechanics**—The rules that tie together the core mechanics. For instance, an RPG can be seen as a string of multiple battle scenes, but the meta mechanics tell a story and create an exploratory mode that pulls these battles together.

3. **Base setting**—The backstory of the game, its character description, and its setting. This is seen as a hook from a marketing perspective, because it gets the player excited to play the game.

4. **Tokens**—This includes the graphics and sound effects in the game. These are just like board game tokens, in a way. For instance, a gnarly snarling alien in the game Prey is a token that can hurt the character if not dealt with or avoided.

5. **Scenarios**—This includes the game levels and scripted events. The core mechanics often involve the interactions between various game tokens. Things like game levels and scripted events put the tokens into proper perspective.

6. **Story**—The narrative element of the game can provide an overall wrapper of context around the mechanics and tokens and give the player an evocative base for gameplay.

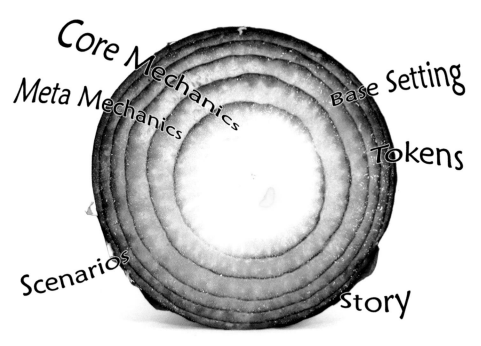

Figure 2.4
The onion layers of a video game.

A video game starts with at least two, sometimes three, layers. Some games have all six layers.

Take a look at the game of Chess, which is shown in Figure 2.5. Chess has well-defined core mechanics. The meta mechanics are limited to the game's start and end rules. The best you can say of the base setting for Chess is that it depicts an abstract conflict between two medieval armies. The tokens are the pawns, knights, queens, and so on, and the type of token they are defines how they can move on the game board. There are no scenarios and no game story going on in Chess.

Most of a game's core mechanics dwell on player interaction and gameplay. Now, look at these equally important elements separately.

Figure 2.5
The game of
Chess.

Player Interaction

When a player picks up the controller or takes over the keyboard and mouse, she wants to be able to explore make-believe worlds, encounter responsive creatures, and interact with her game environment. Games are not passive entertainment forms, such as watching football on television. Games are active: They put you into the football field and place a ball of pigskin right in your hands! They expect you to react.

Games are not like traditional stories. Stories are typically a series of facts that occur in a time-sequenced order suggestive of cause-and-effect relationships. In other words, a story plods from one step to another in a fairly linear fashion. A story is a great way to represent reality as cause equaling an effect. In a game, however, the audience cannot understand the story from a typical causal relationship but, rather, is free to make choices and come at the options from every angle.

This freedom of interactivity leads to immersion, which sells games. Indeed, a game that has a lot of immersion in it is a game that players will want to play over and over again to explore new opportunities and avenues for expression. A story is relatively static, while a game, on the other hand, is dynamic and constantly in motion!

Have you ever played a game that appeared to be one long cut-scene after another, with only short pauses in between where you got to run around as your character before hitting another cut-scene? These games are closer to film projects than really fun games. These games can be frustrating for many players, because games are meant to be interactive.

Players don't want to be told a story; they want to tell or discover the story themselves. Listening to long-winded expositions, being forced to watch long animated sequences, and even talking with characters should always be secondary to exploration, combat, manipulation, and puzzle-solving. In other words, story is supplementary to interactivity.

If you fail to empower the player with interactivity, you have failed as a game designer. Putting the controls in the player's hands can sound scary for any designer at first. You are abdicating some of your control to allow the player to interact with, and possibly lose, at the game you've provided. However, without elevating your player to the status of co-author of your game, you will never make a fun game because fun games are all about interactivity.

When your player picks up her game controller or sits at her computer to play your game, she wants to be able to explore make-believe worlds, encounter responsive creatures, and interact with her game environment in ways she can't get out of watching a show or reading printed words. If you fail to empower your player with interactive control, you fail as a game designer.

Giving Players Fun Choices to Make

Part of interactive control is giving the player fun choices to make. This involves two main things to be present in your game for it to work:

- Difficult, not easy, decisions that have to be made by the gamer

- Tangible consequences for making these decisions

There is a partnership between you, the game designer, and your future gamer. You essentially pass off partial control of your game and its contingent story to the person who plays your game. Doing this is exciting. It is even more exciting watching your testers for the first time playing through your game missions and seeing how they make different decisions than you would to come to the same resolution. See Figure 2.6.

(continued)

Giving Players Fun Choices to Make (continued)

Care for patients with real-world consequences...

Figure 2.6
As the catch-line for *Hospital Havoc 2* says, this iPad game puts players in the position of a doctor who must manage, manipulate, and medicate patients and health centers, earning muffins as rewards. One wrong choice and a patient might not make it out alive!

When creating decisions for the player to make, keep these simple rules in mind:

- **Make each choice reasonable**—Don't ask your player to go in a door marked "Great Stuff Inside," and then have a brick wall on the other side of it. Likewise, don't ask your player to choose between getting a magnificent sword and a pile of junk, because she'll pick the sword every time. The choices a player is given should be reasonable ones.

- **Make each choice real**—Don't invent arbitrary decisions, such as asking your player if she would rather go through Door A or Door B when both doors lead to the same place. To the player, this is as bad as cheating. The best choices of all to present your gamer with are difficult ones, especially when there is a perceptible tension surrounding the outcome of the decision.

- **Keep your player informed**—You must give the player enough knowledge to make a proper decision when faced with it. If you leave out the fact that if she keeps the Sword of Eons, she will have to slaughter her only surviving sibling, you are sure to see a player throw a tantrum.

Gameplay and Finding Balance

Gameplay is defined by developer Dino Dini as "interaction that entertains" and by developer Sid Meier as "a series of interesting choices." Gameplay comes first, because it's the primary source of entertainment in all video games. Art and story are seen almost as "window dressing" in many cases. When designing the core mechanics, gameplay must be the foremost element you consider.

Gameplay differs from game to game, based on the player actions, options, and challenges. The challenges are central to the game, often varying by the game genre, and the options are the interactive abilities open to the player in order to overcome challenges. The player actions are steps players take to achieve their goals throughout the game.

One of the thorniest facets of successful game creation is making sure that the game has balanced gameplay. If just one element in play gives the player (or for that matter, the enemy) too much power, the whole game is a wreck. For example, if the player learns that her crossbow beats all the monsters in the game, possibly by some programming fluke, then she'll never pick up another weapon during the course of play—not even when you attempt to give her a weapon she needs to complete a quest later on in the game!

Players try to find the laziest and most efficient way to beat any game, because they understand that games have an underlying competitive challenge, even when the only competition a player faces in a game is the computer brain itself. So be on the lookout for minor imbalances in the core mechanics and repair those imbalances so your player cannot cheat.

Tip

When you think you've found all the discrepancies, have a friend or two play it with fresh eyes and see what they discover. They might find a loophole or problem you missed. Don't feel bad if they find one, because even the large commercial game developers can be hit unexpectedly by a bug or problem within the game's programming.

Gameplay versus Graphics

So is gameplay (and thus core mechanics) more important in a video game than the graphics?

In truth, both are of fairly identical value, yet you should be aware: Look at the way graphics are not mentioned in the innermost layers of the game onion. Graphics come in, with audio, as a part of the context tokens and scenarios. Graphics, in other words, are essential to games insofar as putting the game mechanics in proper context for the player. Gameplay is crucial to having a working game, and graphics bind it all together.

Nevertheless, graphics have begun to dominate the video game industry.

In the early days of arcade games, the weakness of the display hardware seriously hampered the aesthetics, resulting in ugly and oversimplified graphics. With the growth of modern display technology, graphics have taken on a much greater role, one that some designers see as a handicap. In the 1990s, there was a major push by Hollywood film producers to take over the game industry, and to a certain extent because of this thrusting interest, game companies became focused more on outward appearances of the games they made.

Part of your job description as a game designer is to give players aesthetic entertainment. Any ugly or awkward game with poor artistic style, clumsy animation, and sloppy artwork won't cut it anymore. But a pretty game won't make up for a game lacking fun and innovative gameplay.

Speaking of which, you will also have to keep in mind the memory limitations on the iPad and factor that into your overall design plan. Many next-generation technology 3D games that do well on other platforms have to be simplified when they are ported to the iPad or else they suffer from runtime glitches and major lag. You may have to sacrifice pretty graphics for a smoother running game.

What about Narrative?

As you can see, game story comes in last at the sixth layer of the game onion.

Numerous games have narrative elements that give a context to the events that take place in a game, making the activity of playing the game less abstract and enhancing the game's entertainment value. But narrative elements are not always clear or present in a game. Some games, in fact, have no narrative at all. Sudoku (shown in Figure 2.7) is a classic example of a video game without story.

Besides providing a context for play, narrative elements of a game are primarily used in marketing the game, as the game story can help sell the game to players.

You might have heard catchy slogans like "Play as a Brutal Warrior in a Fantasy Land," or "Save the Mushroom Kingdom from the Evil Bowser," or "Discover the Magic of the Emerald City"—or similar slogans to that effect. These do not tell you the game's core mechanics or share with you how the game is played, but they do impart the storytelling aspect of the games to get you to try them out.

It is largely up to you whether your game will have story in it or not. A game can still be fun and addictive even without a story behind it.

Figure 2.7
Sudoku for
iPad.

Always Remember to Make Your Game Fun

Give your players a fun, fresh, and original experience, one that is sure to encourage replaying and word-of-mouth advertisement, and you've done your first duty as a game designer. If your game is the slightest bit offbeat, offers cathartic release, or is irreverent and funny, it will get played. For some inspiration, check out *Gangstar* (see Figure 2.8) or *Hector: Badge of Carnage* from Telltale Games (see Figure 2.9).

Games can seem like hard work and can sometimes be frustrating to play, but players are willing to put in as much work as required if they get back enough high-quality fun. Fun is what games are all about. If you find that your game is not providing the player with high-quality fun, you have to stop, rewind, and erase what you're doing right now and start building your game on the premise that every part of it has to be fun.

A typical rule of thumb when making games is, if you are not having fun making the game, your players probably won't have fun playing it. So enjoy what you do and do what you enjoy.

Figure 2.8
Gangstar, like its inspiration *Grand Theft Auto*, has you playing a street criminal bent on taking the hood and stealing rich people's money. The game's ethics have earned it criticism from some corners, but players have demonstrated their desire to play it.

Figure 2.9
Hector: Badge of Carnage is a cheeky game from Telltale Games. In it, you play a drunken, lewd, and violent detective. Filled with foul language, bathroom humor, and cartoon violence, *Hector* is not recommended for kids.

Fairness

Tip

"Play is supposed to be the opposite of work, but most video games are just jobs with a little bit of fun thrown in. These games can leave players feeling abused, frustrated, and overly aggressive. Your game can either irritate or alleviate. Which would you rather do?"

—Duane Alan Hahn, Game Aficionado

A player's time must be respected. A great game should offer the quickest, easiest ways to have fun and accomplish all the challenges—unless there is some really entertaining reason to prevent it. Frustration can be a healthy motivator in games, challenging core gamers to achieve greater heights for themselves, but frustration can also lead to the player giving up before beating the game. So tamp down frustration by playing fair with your player, and you'll receive better rewards in the end.

Do not force gamers to repeat complicated moves in the game or learn their lesson by seeing their character die over and over again. Endless repetition can be absolutely maddening, so don't let your player fall into a rut. Never set the player up so that she has to perform a knotty set of maneuvers to get her character avatar to the top of a 100-foot platform, only at the last minute having her fall all the way back down to the bottom and making her start all over again. Likewise, don't kill the player's character off suddenly or inexplicably without giving her a heads-up as to why.

Avoid meaningless repetition or wrist-slapping such as this. A player's experiences through the game should always feel new, yet the player should never know ahead of time what is coming. Keeping your game experience fresh and surprising is difficult but a major part of the fun factor.

Avoid frustration by making the game easier for the player. Don't remove challenges from the game completely, but relieve the build-up of tension that could potentially lose the player's attention. For instance, it is common practice now to have extremely brief death or game-over sequences and allow the player to jump right back into play without missing a beat. Although this reduces the realism of game scenarios, it is intrinsic in making the game seem fun and fair.

Now, take a look at proper methods for using game challenges and the types of game challenges you could use that are both fun and fair.

How to Make Your Game Challenging the Right Way

> ### Tip
>
> "You're always trying to find the right level of challenge. You can't be too simple or it's not fun. [Nolan] Bushnell's famous quote is something along the lines of, 'A game should be easy to pick up and impossible to master.' We want that sweet spot where there's always another threshold to cross. In *Halo 1*, as we improved targeting, we found it was too intelligent and too simple. It was pretty straightforward for the Bungie team to fix that."
>
> —Dennis Wixon, Microsoft Games Studios

A game wouldn't be a game if it didn't offer the player some goal to reach or challenge to overcome. Your game can be challenging while still being fair to the player. The types of challenges games offer vary widely, from the accumulation of resources to intellectual challenges to self-preservation. Many challenges are staples of the game genres they belong in; others fit with the gameplay and are thus included.

Types of Game Challenges

The most common game challenges include the following:

- **Gates**—Gates, also called lock mechanisms, fence the player in, preventing access to some area or reward in the game world until that moment when the player beats the challenge and unlocks the next area or recovers the reward. The simplest and most prosaic gate is a locked door. The player is so familiar with this kind of gate that she knows to immediately start looking for a key to unlock it. Some gamers are fed up with the overuse of locked doors, however, so use them sparingly. For example, did you know that *Silent Hill: Origins* (see Figure 2.10) features over 133 locked doors? That's ridiculous! *Blood locks* are another kind of gate. In a blood lock, the player is locked within a single area with lots of foes to defeat, and the exit from the area will not appear until the player destroys all oncoming enemies.

- **Mazes**—Below-average gamers can get lost in standard game levels, so making the level more difficult to get through by adding in lots of twists, turns, and dead-ends might quickly make for a player headache. On the other hand, if you use it wisely, a maze can become a wonderfully entertaining way to break the monotony of locked doors.

- **Monsters**—Battles with monsters typify the combat mechanic in many games, including fighting games, shooters, and role-playing games. As classic as the gateway guardians of mythic lore, monsters are another form of obstacle to be overcome, and always with a reward (see Figure 2.11). The toughest of all are the "boss monsters" that pose the largest threat in a level.

Figure 2.10
Screenshot from *Silent Hill: Origins.* I don't know about you, but I bet someplace listed on that map will have a locked door!

Figure 2.11
Minigore is a fast-paced arcade shooter for the iPad. It stars block-headed hero John Gore blasting monsters in the dark wilds of Hardland.

■ **Traps**—Traps are a hodgepodge of suspense, scenery, and intrigue. Good traps can have whole stories behind them. Give some thought to each and every trap you place. Traps, like monsters, have become a staple of popular games ever since the days of pen-and-paper games like *Dungeons and Dragons*. One of the earliest games to showcase traps was Atari's *Pitfall* in 1982. In it, the player character Pitfall Harry had to leap or swing over tar pits, quicksand, water holes, rolling logs, crocodiles, and more. There are some newer games, like *Plants vs. Zombies*, that put traps in the players' hands, letting them use traps to stop enemies like in Figure 2.12.

Figure 2.12
In the iPad version of PopCap Games' *Plants vs. Zombies*, players use an odd assortment of plants as living traps to stop the approaching zombie horde. Here you can see Buttered Popcorn blast zombies to blackened ash.

■ **Quests**—These are special sets of challenges that take place in both stories and games, thus linking narrative and play. Quest games, like the *King's Quest* series, have quests that make up activities in which the player must overcome specific challenges in order to reach her goal. When the player successfully surmounts the challenges of the quest and achieves the goal, it unlocks another part of the game story. As Jesper Juul explains in *Half-Real: Video Games Between Real Rules and Fictional Worlds*, "Quests in games can actually provide an interesting type of bridge between game rules and game fiction in that the games can contain predefined sequences of events that the player then has to actualize or effect." Many standard action or shoot-'em-up games, including 2K Games' *BioShock*, have implemented quests to reveal narrative and create further depth of player experience.

■ **Puzzles**—Aside from actual puzzle games like *Bejeweled* and *Tetris*, puzzles can be used to further the game story or as short games within a game. Some puzzles are cryptographic or clue-driven in nature, where the player must supply a crucial bit of info, such as a password, key code, whodunit, or similar, to pass by a guard or a locked door, open a wall safe, or close the case. To figure out what the code/password/other is, the player must search for clues. These clues are often left lying around in convenient journals, computer e-mails, tape recordings, or can be found by talking to people.

How Gamers Approach Challenges: The Game Loop

The most common way players handle difficult challenges is what Andrew Glassner calls the Game Loop, which is a cycle or repetitive steps the player takes to win a game challenge:

1. Player observes the situation.

2. Player sets goals to win the challenge.

3. Player researches or prepares.

4. Player commits to a plan and executes decisions.

5. Player stops and compares the results of his actions to his original intention.

6. Player evaluates the results.

7. Player returns to Step 1.

If you've ever taken a science class, the Game Loop may sound kind of familiar. This is because the Game Loop, which gamers have adopted over years of playing video games, is identical to the scientific method. Scientists use the scientific method to analyze hypotheses. Players use the Game Loop to win games.

> **Note**
>
> Another kind of "game loop" is one within software programming, whereby a cycle of logic continues until a condition is met, breaking the cycle. One such game loop might be a patrolling enemy: He will continue his patrol unless the player crosses his field of view (FOV) and then will break off to attack the player. This kind of game loop is unrelated to the one mentioned here.

The first step is the most crucial for fair challenges, because if a player observes the current situation and can see no way to overcome it, she'll become frustrated and quit playing your game. Help the player with these observations. In *Alice: Madness Returns* from American McGee's Spicy Horse, they added layers of hints. If a player is totally lost, she can shrink her character and simultaneously spy "with her little eye" hidden chalk messages that give her hints on where to go or what to do.

Seasoned players know they are not playing the game but playing against the game's underlying programming. Most of the cheats you find on the web have been discovered by sharp analytical gamers who figure out what developers miss.

How to Adjust Chance to Be Fair

Chance is that slim margin of luck that can make the gamer a winner or loser. However, chance is not a vague whimsy. As the game's developer, you usually have a lot of control over chance and can adjust the fairness of a video game by resolving issues of chance.

The following are types of chances you find in games:

- **Calculated risk**—The player knows there's a 50/50 chance and takes it.

- **Built-in chance**—The game's developer sets up parameters for the computer to calculate random odds of the player winning.

- **Player error**—The player or one of his allies makes a mistake and pays for it.

- **Opponent error**—The opponent makes a mistake and the player makes sure he pays for it.

- **System error**—The player discovers a brief flaw in the system and monopolizes on it, winning by cheating. Or the player is betrayed by a computer error, setting him back in the game. This is often the result of a system bug, but it can also be an unexpected faulty return.

No matter the type of chance, luck plays a role in the outcome of a game's challenges. At least for the most part, you can control chance in your video games in order to avoid undo player frustration. Test your game multiple times to remove system bugs and toggle game parameters to put the odds in your player's favor.

Feedback

Video games are all about pushing a player's buttons. A game world is little better than a Skinner Box (as shown in Figure 2.13), which is a special lab apparatus developed by psychoanalyst B.F. Skinner to show that you can train a rat to hit a button to get food. Speaking of which, if you know anything about psychoanalytic theory, you will do just fine in the game industry. Feedback is just one of the primary components of the human-computer interface. Providing the player with adequate feedback will help the player know what to expect out of the game and frames the choices she will make from then on.

In other words, if the player does something downright stupid, show her it was wrong to try that particular action by punishing her. On the other hand, if the player does something right, give her a reward. Give that player a Twinkie!

Figure 2.13
B.F. Skinner loved teaching rats how to hit the feeder bar for pellets.

Make Feedback Appropriate, Consistent, and Immediate

There are two critical rules of thumb to use with regard to punishments and rewards. First, you should have your punishments and rewards fit the actions and environment, and you should always be consistent with your use of them. Second, you should make your punishments and rewards happen immediately so the cause-and-effect relationship is reinforced.

Players are eager to know that they are doing something right or wrong so they can adjust their play style and master the game. They listen for the bells and whistles to instruct them in how to play better. You can use this knowledge to your advantage by creating a better game.

Don't hold back too long on the carrots, or your player will eventually give up. If you want the player to defeat all the Orcs in a single level of the game, you have to give that player some reason for doing so; and when she does beat the Orcs (especially depending on how long and hard it takes to do so), you have to give her some really significant reward, like loud fanfare, gold coins, or power-ups. Likewise, if you don't want your player to do something, like hack up innocent bystanders, you have to set up punishments.

Make Environments Reactive

The game world must react reasonably to the game's player. The environment, meaning the virtual world in a game, must be somewhat reactive. Having reactive environments means that the game world responds to the player in logical and meaningful ways that help immerse the player in that game world.

This can mean that if the player sees a guy standing around as if he's waiting for something, the player should be able to walk up to him (in the game) and talk to the guy to find out some information about the place the player's character has found herself in. Or if there appears to be a weak spot in a wall, a strong enough force should be able to knock a hole in it. Or if the player sees a neat-looking door and wants to open it, she should be able to do so, or you should let her know, "This door is locked. To open it, you must find the key." This empowers the player to explore the game's environment and to treat it as if it were its own self-contained world.

Nowadays, it's uncommon to find a 3D shooter where you aren't capable of putting holes through or blowing up just about anything you find in the game's environment. This is an important lesson about what players want and what you should provide. (On the other hand, you will still find flimsy locked doors in games that a well-placed shot-gun blast should open in reality that appear impervious to your character's weapons, but that's a small concession to have to make.) When in doubt about whether to make the game background more interactive, always opt for the affirmative answer, although it usually means more work for you.

Feasibility

> ## Tip
>
> "I would say simplicity is a key factor in any good game design—simplicity in interface, game systems, and so on. Simplicity does not have to mean few possibilities (just look at chess), but creating a really good, well-balanced, simple game system is a much harder task than creating a very complex one."
>
> —Thorolfur Beck, Founder, CCP

Encourage player immersion whenever and wherever you can in your game. To this end, avoid inconsistencies and a little terror called feature creep: Feature creep happens when a game designer gets too close to his project and begins adding "neat features" that really add nothing to the game or do not fit with the original game concept. Keep your games simple. Anything goes as long as it's fun, fair, provides adequate feedback, and makes sense.

You might say, "Most games don't make a whole lot of sense!" I understand that. Take *Super Mario Bros.*, for example. You play an overweight plumber who runs around killing strolling mushrooms and kamikaze turtles by squishing them with his own body weight. Meanwhile, you have to navigate giant pipes and flaming pits in a world full of titanic toadstools and platforms in the clouds, all to face off with a giant redheaded tur-tle to win a pink princess named Peach. The game doesn't make a lot of sense, but it is fun as well as feasible; the core mechanics, in other words, remain consistent, and the player understands the workings of the game world.

As president of Cerny Games and video game consultant, Mark Cerny puts it, "Keep the rules of the game simple. Ideally, first-time players should understand and enjoy the game without instructions." Keep your game rules simple and feasible.

How to Come Up with Game Ideas

An iPad game doesn't just happen on its own. It takes someone to invent the idea, hash it out as a game concept, and put it to paper. The paper is part of the game design documentation.

Game ideas can come from anywhere, including other games, TV shows, movies, and alternative media. But you can't outright steal another person's intellectual property. You can't make an iPad game based on *Pirates of the Caribbean* without stepping on toes at Disney, but you could make a fun game about pirates, like the one in Figure 2.14.

Figure 2.14
Bungie
Aerospace
Corporation's
iPad game
*Crimson: Steam
Pirates.*

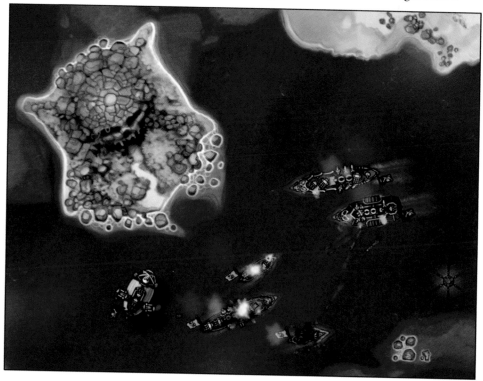

You can find game ideas almost anywhere but only if you're looking for them. Creativity is an active, not a passive, process. Be ready for it when you are struck by the video game muse.

I bet you have plenty of game ideas. A lot of times these ideas will come from playing other video games. You start by thinking, "I wonder if they did it this way…" or "I could make this totally better if only…" Write those ideas down. Get a notebook and start jotting down an idea the second you have it, because otherwise you might forget and lose the killer idea that could make a name for yourself as a game designer.

If my bet was wrong, and you don't have plenty of game ideas of your own, all hope is not lost. There are several ways to think of game ideas or find fresh angles to old ones.

Brainstorming Ideas

Chat with your friends. In this cheap and efficient idea-scouring way, you can hash out ideas for an iPad game over pizza while talking about games that interest you. Say your friend is complaining about a motion picture he saw recently, and you tell him you think it would make a much better game for the iPad. Light bulb goes "Ding!" Pretty soon you are both brainstorming ideas to complete an iPad game based on the premise.

Tracy Fullerton is the assistant professor at USC's School of Cinematic Arts, Interactive Media department, and co-director of the Electronic Arts Game Innovations Lab. She says, "Some of the best brainstormers are Imagineers [the kind of folks who work at Disney Imagineering]. They often have very large brainstorming sessions, with people from very different backgrounds, and they have physical toys to keep people loose. And somehow, tossing toys around gets the creative ideas flowing, and I find that very successful."

This process sounds wild and crazy, but it's actually encouraged in lots of companies that focus on creative entertainment. The more invigorating executives can make the work environment, the more productive their staff will be. This is one reason why you see so many toys surrounding game designers' work stations.

Researching Ideas

Next, you can search the library or Internet for ideas. Completely dry on fresh ideas? Google keywords and phrases like "iPad game idea" or "video game idea," and you will be surprised at how many sites you hit on the web where people are posting their own random concepts.

Don't just steal someone else's ideas, however. That's plagiarism. Ideas for games should come from within you. It is perfectly legit to have an inspiration when looking at the sorts of games other people would like to see made; it's just that your inspiration should be yours and yours alone. Plus, some of the top game producers browse sites like these to see what their target market wants, and they might recognize an idea you say you've had that you've actually stolen.

Playing Games to Get Inspiration

Another trick for coming up with game ideas I can never repeat enough: Play games! This advice sounds perfectly obvious, but that doesn't make it any less true. Great games beget other great games.

You can make a list of the details you like about iPad games you play most and what you could've done better. If you have ever played an iPad game, I bet you dimes-to-donuts you at some time have thought, "This bites! Why did the designers make the game like this?" or "Why did they put this in the game? It sucks." When you do start making critical remarks like this, write them down and consider, what would you do differently if you had to make the game over?

Every game that exists out there could be made better. You just have to figure out how and when you do you have the kernel of a killer game idea.

The Frankenstein Method

You could also try out the Frankenstein method of Hollywood. The Frankenstein method involves taking the best bits from disparate sources and merging them together into a single concept.

For example, take *GT Racing: Motor Academy*, a car racing game on the iPad, and *Final Fantasy III* for the iPad, a fantasy role-playing game, and create a new-fangled game idea out of the two. How many racing games on the present market do you see that incorporate magic fantasy elements? Why couldn't they?

Take several video games you like and pick out details about them to thrust together and see what comes out of the mix-up.

Write Your Game Idea Down

When that little light bulb comes on, you finally have a killer game idea. Write it down right away. Then flesh your idea out with more supporting details before attempting to write a game design document.

There is no greater test for a killer game idea than trying to put it into articulate words on paper. Usually ideas in and of themselves are sublingual, full of images, emotions, and vague details. Trying to put your idea onto paper and then reading it aloud to hear how it sounds helps you to focus and reveals weak spots that might have made it past your original mental process as you wrote the idea down. You might find there are words you used that don't work as efficiently as some others would.

After you have written your killer game idea down on paper, share it with your friends or family. Ask them to describe your idea back to you after they hear it, based on their own comprehension, and listen to them carefully. Pay particular attention to constructive criticism but avoid inappropriate or biased opinions.

The more you practice coming up with game ideas, the easier they will come for you.

Expressly you should write a game concept that encapsulates your killer game idea. A game concept is a short description of a game detailed enough to start discussing it as a potential project. The concept forms a general idea of how you intend to entertain someone through gameplay, and, more importantly, why you believe it will be a rich, compelling experience.

First, take stock of who your target audience will be. In a play-centric design, you put the players first and design the game around their expectations. You could design a game for yourself and hope that there is more than one person out there like yourself who will find your game as appealing as you do, but it has been proven that you will make more return on your initial investment of both time and money if you make a game for a specific group of gamers instead. So look around at types of gamers you see and who you think would like your game.

Try for inclusiveness and not universality. What I mean is, don't make a game that will appeal to everyone; just make a game that will appeal to the largest segment of gamers in your target market.

Next, write the game concept out on paper. As a minimum, your game concept should include

- A high concept statement that is a two-to-three sentence description of your game. Remember those blurbs of upcoming movies seen in the *TV Guide*? Keep your statement short and sweet.

- Who the players will be in the game, if they have a character they can see onscreen, and what role they're fulfilling.

- What the game world is like, if there is one.

- The game genre or a clarification of why its gameplay doesn't fit any known genre.

- The projected gameplay mode, including camera perspective, interaction, and gamer challenges.

- Who the target audience of the game will be, including their demographic (age, gender, how much money they bring in, and more).

- Property licenses the game will exploit, if any.

- A short summary of how the game will progress from level to level, including a synopsis of the storyline.

Look at the popular iPad game in the App Store, *Pocket RPG* (as shown in Figure 2.15), for example, and break it down using this list.

- **High concept**—Explore outdoor areas and dungeons in this fun *chibi*-influenced hack-and-slash game.

- **Characters**—Pick from three *chibi*-like character classes that have different playing styles and skill upgrades. Players receive automatic skill and stat additions based on items their characters have equipped. Each character has devastating combo moves as well.

- **Game world**—Amazing stylized 3D dungeons and wilderness maps. Random level generation, so no two maps will be the same on play-through (a bonus to replayability). Swarms of monsters to fight against, including boss encounters between levels.

- **Genre**—A fantasy role-playing game (RPG).

■ **Gameplay**—Full iPad support. Dual stick for moving and attacking. Besides attacking and moving, players can also loot areas to find better equipment for their characters. Top-down playing perspective. Players have two choices: Arcade play (includes multiple save points) and Rogue play (permanent death on failure). The game also includes leader boards (to see who's doing the best), Achievements (to share what you've mastered), and Unlockables (to gain extras).

■ **Target audience**—Boys and girls ages 8 and up who like anime and fantasy games.

Figure 2.15
Two screens from the iPad game *Pocket RPG*.

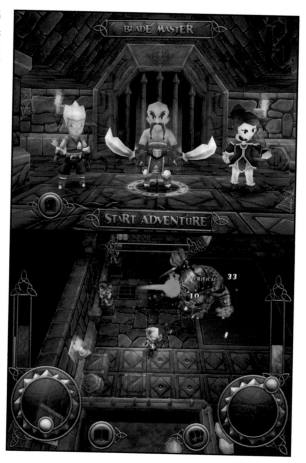

To read more about Pocket RPG, go to http://crescentmoongames.com/wordpress/pocket-rpg/.

What's Next?

You have learned the gist of what it takes to make an iPad game. Now it is time to examine the iPad itself. How did Apple come up with the iPad, and what are its major components? The next chapter will cover those questions in detail.

The Mac App Store. Thousands of Mac Apps. One simple new way to get them.

With the Mac App Store, getting the apps you want on your Mac has never been easier. No more boxes, no more disks, no more time-consuming installation. Click once to download and install any app on your Mac. The Mac App Store is now available as a software update for any Mac running Mac OS X Snow Leopard.

Get the Mac App Store. See how ▶

Overview   Great Mac apps

3

Your Grimoire to the iPad

This is your grimoire to the iPad. A *grimoire*, in fantasy RPG terms, is a book of magic spells. This chapter reflects the magic of the iPad and what you can do with it. The iPad is not the only computer tablet on the market and probably won't be the last, but it is the most popular and paradigm-setting one.

The iPad is one of a line of tablet computers designed, developed, and marketed by Apple. Speculative names for the device before its final release included "iTablet" and "iSlate." Apparently, the final name "iPad" was a nod to the science fiction show *Star Trek*, which featured a fictional device called a PADD that had an analogous look to the iPad. See Figure 3.1.

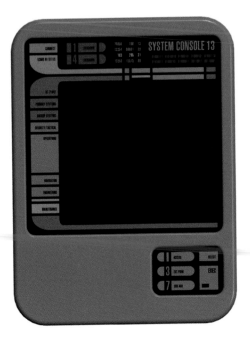

Figure 3.1
The PADD prop from the set of *Star Trek* looks and operates very similar to the iPad.

The iPad is primarily a platform for audio-visual media, which includes electronic-format books (ebooks), periodicals, movies, music, games, and web content. Its size and weight put the iPad in a category between Mac laptops and contemporary smartphones.

A Look at the iPad

This chapter starts off by taking a look at the history and development of the iPad, its applications, its hardware, and what those details mean to you as a game developer.

History of the iPad

In 1993, Apple created the Newton MessagePad, Apple's first stab at a tablet, which you can see in Figure 3.2. Critics considered it just an oversized personal digital assistant (PDA) instead of perceiving it as a true mobile computing device. Since the product never reached the acceptance the company hoped for, Apple discontinued the Newton in 1998.

When rumors first circulated back in 2009 that Apple was considering making another tablet, most people wanted to know what operating system (OS) it would run, because the OS would be a keynote in whether or not the tablet would have true sustaining power. Apple played it smart. Rather than stick their current Macintosh OS X on their new tablet, the company built an OS capably fixated on touchscreen navigation to create all-in-one mobile operations. The iPad is powered by a tablet-enhanced version of iOS. With millions of satisfied iPhone and iPod Touch users already familiar with the iOS interface, the iPad has an immediate and intuitive feel. It looks easy to use because it is, and people have raved about the cross-demographic simplicity.

Figure 3.2
The Newton
MessagePad
from Apple.

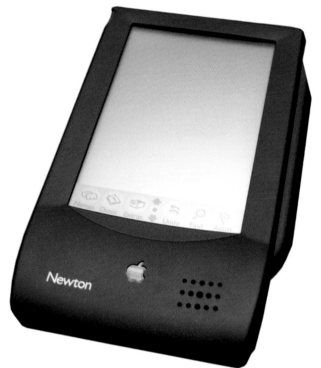

iPad Applications and Development

The iPad can run its own applications as well as applications built for the iPhone, which makes it easier to upgrade to for some consumers.

Although most of the 200,000 iPhone apps will run "as is" on the iPad, the small 480×20 pixel dimensions of the iPhone apps are less than half the dimensions of the iPad's 1024×768 pixel display (see Figure 3.3). Although the iPad includes backward-compatibility support for iPhone apps, the result is less than desirable. Apple provides just two options for running iPhone apps on an iPad. One is to display the iPhone app at normal size, centered in a black screen. The other is to view the app magnified double so as to fill the screen. The iPad's magnification works pretty well, but the apps still appear pixelated.

iPhone apps belong on the iPhone, and developers need to focus on native iPad apps instead, treating the larger display like a whole other platform, with its own design requirements.

The iPad only runs programs sanctioned by Apple and distributed via the Mac App Store (shown in Figure 3.4), with the exception of programs that run inside the Safari web browser. Applications the iPad ships with include Safari, Mail, Photos, Video, YouTube, iPod, iTunes, App Store, iBooks, maps, Notes, Calendar, Contacts, and Spotlight Search.

Figure 3.3
A visual comparison of the iPad and the iPhone.

Several of these apps are improved since their use on iPhone or Mac. Apple ported its iWork suite, Mac's answer to the Microsoft Office Suite, from the Mac to the iPad and sells pared down versions of Pages, Numbers, and Keynote apps in the Apple App Store. As of June 2011, there were about 90,000 iPad-specific apps in the App Store.

Critics have voiced concerns that Apple's centralized app approval process and control of the platform could throttle software innovation. In fact, Apple retains the facility to remotely disable or delete apps, media, or data from any iPad at any time. Apple employs Digital Rights Management with the intent to control certain software and prevent its transfer or use outside of the iPad. The iPad's development model also requires anyone who wants to create an app for an iPad to sign a non-disclosure agreement and pay for a registered developer subscription, which isn't cheap. Currently, it costs around $100 US to become an Apple developer, even if all you want to do is fiddle around with making apps. This has discouraged many software developers from entering the Apple market.

Many digital rights advocates have criticized the iPad for its digital rights restrictions. Apple has full control of what can go on and what can stay on an iPad, regardless of the iPad owner's wishes. Some critics consider this a breach of the freedom of speech provided for by the Bill of Rights.

Figure 3.4
The Mac App
Store.

GigaOM analyst Paul Sweeting was quoted as saying on National Public Radio, "Apple is offering you a gated community where there's a guard at the gate, and there's probably maid service, too." This concept of the iPad as a safe haven from viruses and malware is the one good thing about the digital rights restriction, but it makes becoming a developer for the platform much harder. As Paul went on to say, "With the iPad, you have the anti-Internet in your hands. It offers [major media companies] the opportunity to essentially re-create the old business model, wherein they are pushing content to you on *their* terms rather than you going out and finding content, or a search engine discovering content for you."

Like similar iOS devices, the iPad can be "jailbroken," a hack that allows applications and programs not authorized by Apple to run on the device. Once the iPad is jailbroken, whether through a "userland" jailbreak or other method, the user is able to download apps not presented in the Apple App Store as well as illegally pirated apps. The jailbreak app stores, of which there are several (Cydia, Icy, and RockYourPhone, among others), have apps that do pretty much anything you want on the iPad. Apple claims that jailbreaking voids factory warranty on the device in the United States, even though, officially, jailbreaking is legal. I am not condoning jailbreaking, but if you're not afraid to void your warranty, you can Google a how-to on jailbreaking (see Figure 3.5).

Figure 3.5
You can find apps that make jailbreaking a cinch, like JailbreakMe, shown here.

Answers to Questions about Jailbreaking

The following covers the most general questions you might have about jailbreaking.

Q: Does jailbreaking affect my App Store apps?

A: No, it doesn't. You can use your current apps from the App Store, buy new apps, and sync them to your computer just as you would normally.

Q: If I jailbreak my iPad, can I download App Store apps for free?

A: Yes, you can. Jailbreaking lets you circumvent the App Store and install apps for free. But this is really not a nice thing to do. It is treated similar to pirating software, and therefore is not suggested.

(continued)

Answers to Questions about Jailbreaking (continued)

Q: Will jailbreaking break my iPad?

A: Probably not, but downloading and installing apps can seriously mess up your iPad if you're not careful. You might even find yourself where a factory restore is required, and though there haven't been any reports so far, there's the outside chance you might break your iPad altogether. Also, you should keep future upgrades in mind, because Apple will patch the holes that make jailbreaking possible, and then you might be stuck.

Q: Does jailbreaking void the warranty on my iPad?

A: Yes, it does! When you jailbreak your iPad, you are essentially taking it off the grid. Apple Store Geniuses will regard your jailbroken device with complete and utter indifference. Of course, if you reset your iPad to its original factory settings, things should go back to normal, and it's possible no one will ever be wise to your shameful jailbreaking.

Q: Can I ever get my old iPad back?

A: Yes. Restoring your iPad to factory settings in iTunes will remove all traces of jailbreaking activity and lets you resume your previous iPad experience.

Q: Why should I jailbreak my iPad?

A: One of the most obvious reasons is to access content Apple wouldn't normally let you, especially apps that don't pass Apple scrutiny enough to appear in the App Store. Another reason is multitasking; currently, the iPad does not let you switch tasks, but Backgrounder, an iPhone jailbreak favorite, works great on the iPad and bestows upon you the capacity to browse the web while listening to your favorite music. You can also customize your icons and deck your iPad out with custom themes.

Q: How easy is jailbreaking?

A: It's very easy, in most cases. The Spirit jailbreak, for instance, is practically a one-click process. Any jailbreak system you use will have its own set of instructions. What's really important is to remember to not play around with your iPad or iTunes while jailbreaking and definitely do not unplug the device while the jailbreaking is taking place.

Q: How beneficial is jailbreaking in the long run?

A: Jailbreaking, believe it or not, has often been a trendsetter for official Apple revisions to its iOS. When a jailbreak app becomes exceedingly popular, you will likely see Apple release an official app very similar to it not too long after. Before you could do WiFi tethering on iOS devices, MyWi provided a jailbreak way to add WiFi tethering without having to go through a carrier. Apple later made WiFi tethering official with iOS 4.3. So jailbreak apps, in many ways, are like a testing ground for future iOS updates.

Besides digital content, another material issue in connection with the iPad is pornography. Steve Jobs actually told Valleywag's Ryan Tate in an e-mail that the iPad offers people "freedom from porn," because Apple's App Store, which provides iPad apps, imposes very strict censorship of all its content, which has led to many book and magazine writers and publishers being denied access to the platform. This marketing decision has many users, including user interface media artist Johannes P. Osterhoff (the middle initial "P" stands for "pixel"), up in arms over "freedom of speech."

Osterhoff created a giant, artificial iPad ad that was pornographic to grab the attention of passerbys in Berlin's Rosenthaler Platz station. Osterhoff said it was the original iPad ad, with the iPad placed on a man's lap, that inspired him to create the ad. He thought the iOS device would be the optimal porn delivery tool. He commented, "As one can see in the relaxed posture Apple imagines for its future users, the iPad is about to offer an entirely new porn experience. The user experience of the device and its dimensions will make it a perfect hand for porn viewers. If not it will be due to the platform only."

Steve Jobs made a formal statement about their censorship policies that, "We do believe we have a moral responsibility to keep porn off the iPhone. Folks who want porn can buy an Android phone." This policy apparently carries over to the iPad, as well, and will continue into Apple's future decision-making.

Technical Specs of the iPad

The following technical features will give you a better understanding of your iPad (see Figure 3.6).

Figure 3.6
The iPad front, back, and side.

The iPad's touchscreen display is a 1024×768 pixel liquid crystal display with finger-print-and-scratch-resistance glass. Like the iPhone, the iPad is engineered to be navigated by bare fingers. Normal, non-conductive gloves and styli won't work on it, although there are special gloves and capacitive styli designed for its use.

The display responds to other sensors, as well. An ambient light sensor adjusts screen brightness based on light source, and a three-axis accelerometer senses the iPad's orientation and switches back and forth between portrait and landscape view modes. The iPad supports screen rotation in every direction, even upside-down. The only item that stays consistent in comparison to orientation is the small, unobtrusive power button. This trait is capitalized on by several iPad apps, including iBeerKeg, which is shown in Figure 3.7.

Figure 3.7
The iBeerKeg app reacts almost realistically to the positioning of the iPad.

The iPad has two internal mono speakers located on the bottom-right of the unit. A volume switch is on the right side of the unit, and there is support for headphones (with or without microphones). The iPad contains a microphone for voice recording purposes.

The original iPad had no camera built-in, but the iPad 2 (released March 2011) has a front VGA camera and rear-facing 720p camera, both capable of taking still shots and 30fps video. The rear-facing camera also has a 5x digital zoom control for still images.

The iPad uses Wi-Fi network trilateration from Skyhook Wireless to provide location information to apps such as Google Maps. The 3G model supports A-GPS to allow its position to be calculated with GPS.

The iPad offers three capacity options for storage, including 16, 32, or 64GB of internal flash memory. All data is stored on the internal flash memory, with no expanded storage options. There is a camera connection kit with an SD card reader you can purchase separately for the iPad, but it can only be used to transfer photos and videos.

The iPad uses an internal rechargeable lithium-ion polymer (LiPo) battery. You can see the battery in the breakdown in Figure 3.8. The iPad is designed to be charged with a high current of 2 amperes using the included 10 W USB power adapter. Although it can be charged by a standard USB port from a computer, these are limited to 500 milliamperes, which equal about half an amp. As a result, if the iPad is running while powered by normal USB computer port, it may charge very slowly, if at all. The battery is supposed to provide up to 10 hours of video, 140 hours of audio playback, or one month on standby. Like any rechargeable battery, the iPad's battery loses its capacity over time. The battery is not meant to be replaced by the user but by Apple, who will do so at a specified cost. The battery can be swapped by an independent company, but you risk voiding the warranty if you do so. On the other hand, the warranty is usually gone before the battery goes bad anyway.

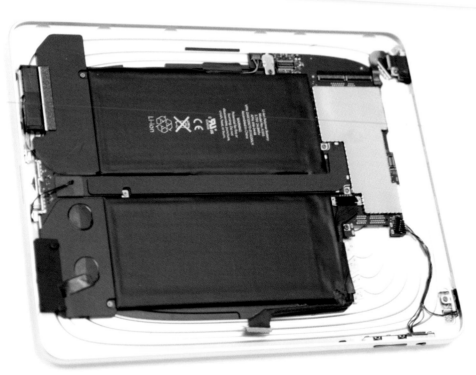

Figure 3.8
The iPad, broken down and showing its battery.

You can purchase a separate Bluetooth keyboard accessory or an upright docking station for the iPad, but it's not necessary.

Overview of iOS

The iOS comprises the operating system and unique technologies used to run applications on Apple devices like the iPad, iPhone, and iPod Touch. The iPad is shown in use in Figure 3.9. Although iOS shares a common background and some of the same infrastructure as Mac OS X, iOS was developed to meet the particular needs of Apple mobile devices.

Figure 3.9
The iPad uses iOS, which is typically finger-driven.

If you have ever developed applications for Mac OS X, you will probably find comfort in the similar technologies you will be using for iOS, but certain features like the multi-touch interface and accelerometer support may appear new to you.

The iOS runtime environment was designed to support mobile device users. This environment requires you to design applications differently than you would a desktop or even a laptop environment. By design, iOS restricts application to more effectively manage system resources and overall system security. These restrictions encompass everything from the way you manage memory and file sizes to how your application interacts with the hardware setup.

Uses for the iPad

Although the iPad is mostly used by general consumers, there are several growing user groups that have begun making the iPad a common sight in their prospective fields.

■ **Business**—Several companies are adopting iPads in their offices by distributing or making iPads available to their staff. A Frost & Sullivan survey shows that iPad usage in the workplace is linked to the increase of employee productivity, a greener and more paperless work environment, and increased revenues. The iPad is compact, making it easy to use to jot office notes down on, and its presentation apps can make in-office presentations—especially when connected to screen projectors—eye-catching and quicker to start.

- **Education**—The iPad has been adopted in the classroom and even praised in many circles as a much-needed tool for homeschoolers. Shortly after its release, reports came out that noted 81 percent of the top book apps were for school-age children. Many secondary educational institutions have also started using the iPad, even going so far as to make them available in student bookstores as a requisite learning utility.

- **Music**—In 2010, the rock band Gorillaz released an album called *The Fall* (shown in Figure 3.10) that singer/songwriter Damon Albarn created almost exclusively using just his iPad while he was on tour with the band. With its iTunes playback software and samplers, music creation is a snap on the iPad.

- **Flight**—In 2011, Alaska Airlines become the first airline to replace pilots' printed flight manuals with iPads in the hope of having fewer back and muscle complaints. The movement has spread with the U.S. Federal Aviation Administration approving the iPad for pilot use to cut down paper consumption.

Figure 3.10
The Fall album, by Gorillaz, was made almost entirely on the iPad.

The iPad is truly a "go anywhere" computer tablet, which makes it great for on-the-go casual gaming. Users can play games on the iPad wherever—as long as they don't disrupt the people around them, of course.

Developing iPad Apps

Syncode's Matthew Lesh said, "Apple has provided developers with some powerful and unique tools to create stylish applications for the iPad. The challenge now is to create them."

This is truly a mad-dash right now as developers seek ways to break into the iPad market. Take a gander at the available iPad apps out there if you need any more inspiration to get started. *iPad Multiplayer Magic* will show you how to make multiplayer online game apps for the iPad that are truly unsurpassed. And all it will take is a short skill curve and boundless imagination.

Of course, it will also take the right software tools.

Game Authoring Software for the iPad

When it comes to game development, most developers use a pipeline of technologies. They use paint editing programs to make 2D art, modeling and animation programs to make 3D graphics, sound editing programs for audio, and then put it together with a game engine. Big-name companies build their game engines from the ground up, but some game engines (especially Unreal) are becoming popular turn-to solutions even for corporate giants.

About Unreal

In less than two decades, Epic Games (see www.udk.com) has revolutionized PC game development with its next-generation engine technology. In 1991, four talented individuals (Tim Sweeney, James Schmalz, Mark Rein, and Cliff Bleszinski) got together to push ASCII-based games to their limits. In 1998, they published *Unreal* for the first time, and it changed everyone's minds about what was possible with 3D gaming. *Unreal* set whole new standards for multimedia graphics, AI, physics, level editing, and network gaming; in fact, *Unreal* lived up to its name!

Besides the game itself, Epic brought something else to the industry: the game engine that powered *Unreal*. *Unreal* shipped with a beta version of UnrealEd, an easy-to-use level editor that allowed gamers to make their own game levels and modify existing ones. Plus, it used UnrealScript, which hobbyists soon learned was an easy-to-learn scripting language whereby you could modify how the game operated and even make your own custom games.

With each new release of an *Unreal* game in the series, a new version of their Unreal engine also shipped. Game developers everywhere started purchasing licensing rights to use the Unreal engine to power their own game creations. The third and latest version, Unreal Engine 3, had everyone drooling at the 2004 Game Developer Conference, but what really made an impact was the 2009 launch of the Unreal Development Kit (UDK), a free version of the Unreal Engine 3. UDK awards free access to the same world-class tools and technology used by many video game developers and publishers. There is no charge for noncommercial or educational use of UDK. Over 100 academic campuses currently use Unreal as part of their game-development-related courses, and UDK has been a boon to educational institutions.

(continued)

> **About Unreal (continued)**
>
> Epic Games has recently released the September 2011 UDK Beta, the first version of the UDK with Mac OS support. For the first time, Mac game developers can access Unreal for development purposes, improving their pipelines. There is even an iPad app for UDK remote control for testing purposes.

GameSalad

Info on GameSalad:

- **URL**—http://gamesalad.com/products/creator

- **Price**—Free; $499 for pro version

- **Platforms**—Macintosh, iPad, iPhone, or HTML5 (Web)

- **Target audience**—Single player

- **Learning curve**—Easy or beginner

GameSalad Creator, which features a dynamic drag-and-drop game editor, comes with a variety of templates that you can use to start making any two-dimensional (2D) Macintosh, iPhone, or iPad game you want. GameSalad's biggest selling point is that the game creation tool doesn't require any programming knowledge to use, although a basic understanding of computer game logic and digital media is preferable. As they say on their website, "GameSalad aims to open the doors of game design to anyone who wants to create." With the editor's visual interface and versatile programming, their mission statement shows.

The best detail about GameSalad? It's free! There is a professional version, which costs $499 per year, that gives you promotional links to your games, a white-labeled loading screen, and priority tech support, but you can't beat "free!"

GameSalad (see Figure 3.11), as of June 2011, can also publish titles directly to HTML5, so that developers can embed those titles for play on any compatible web browser. "I'm not here to say that Flash is done, but we do envision that the web game industry will move towards the open standard of HTML5," GameSalad Chief Product Officer, Michael Agustin, reported to Gamasutra. "We're placing a bet: GameSalad wants to be ahead of the curve with HTML5.... It's widely expected to become the next standard language for the web, and is poised to quickly disrupt Flash." Since most major web browsers now support HTML5, GameSalad offers a much larger potential audience than Flash or Unity does currently. The company is also promoting emerging web-based games through the GameSalad Arcade section of their website.

Figure 3.11
GameSalad.

Unfortunately, GameSalad does not support 3D or multiplayer games yet. The latter is the main reason that GameSalad will not be featured prominently in this book. However, if you are looking to make a 2D game for an audience of one, give GameSalad a try. It's very easy to download and get started, with very little experience necessary. You can see it in action in Figure 3.12.

Figure 3.12
The
GameSalad
Creator's Scene
Editor.

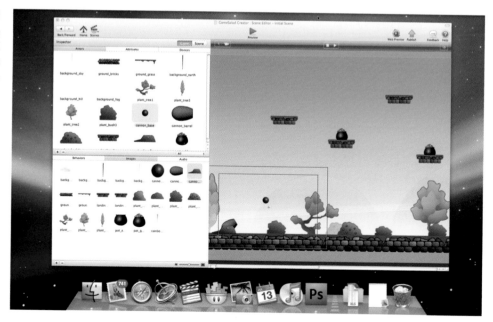

Optimizing Your GameSalad Experience

Here are a few ways you can optimize your game's performance.

- Keep all your assets small.

- Reduce audio file size using 22kHz/mono or less.

- Keep images close to the size they will be in the game.

- Keep image quality within standards.

- Set each dimension of the image sizes as close to a power of 2 as possible, like 32×32 or 32×64.

- Hide (turn off visibility attributes) or destroy actors if they are not supposed to be in the scene anymore.

- If an actor doesn't have to move around, turn off its movability attribute, which will switch off the physics callouts for that actor.

- This might seem very specific, but restrain from using the Constrain Attribute behavior too much, as its constant background calculating can be processor-intense. Use Change Attribute or Interpolate instead.

cocos2d for the iPhone

Info on cocos2d for the iPhone:

- **URL**—www.cocos2d-iphone.org

- **Price**—Free (open source)

- **Platforms**—Macintosh, iPhone, iPad, and iPod Touch

- **Target audience**—Single or multiplayer

- **Learning curve**—Intermediate

More than 2,500 App Store games reportedly use cocos2d for the iPhone.

cocos2d for the iPhone is a free, fast, and lightweight framework for building 2D games and other applications. The name itself is misleading, as cocos2d for the iPhone can be used to build iPhone, iPad, and iPod Touch games. It is entirely open source, so it is heavily community fed and driven. The language cocos2d for the iPhone uses is Objective-C and is a sight better than using direct OpenGL. Its core is very flexible, allowing integration with third-party code libraries, and it uses the OpenGL ES best practices and optimized data structures.

There are only two downsides to using cocos2d for the iPhone. One is that, at the time of this writing, cocos2d is for 2D game development only (hence the name). There is a 3D extension being released soon, but the developers who will release it (http://brenwill. com/cocos3d/) are waiting for cocos2d for the iPhone to update to the latest Xcode version first. (Xcode is Apple's suite of development tools for Mac OS X and iOS. You'll read more about Xcode later.)

The second issue is that cocos2d for the iPhone requires programming knowledge and experience, at least in Objective-C. This raises the bar ever so slightly for newbies trying to get started in game development or even those programmers who know unrelated languages. Often, you will find that is the price you pay for free game engines.

Here are some of the features of cocos2d for the iPhone:

- Scene management and transitions
- Basic menus and buttons
- Integrated behavior scripting
- Supports PVRTC format textures (8-, 16-, and 32-bit)
- Tile map and parallax scrolling support
- Particle system
- Special effects such as lens, ripple, waves, liquid, and twirl
- Two integrated physics engines
- Touch and accelerometer support for iOS
- Portrait and landscape modes for iOS

Parallax scrolling is a special scrolling technique in computer graphics where side-scrolling background images move by slower than foreground images, creating an artificial illusion of depth in a 2D game. This technique evolved from the multiplane camera technique used in traditional animation since the 1940s.

iTorque

Info on iTorque:

- **URL**—www.garagegames.com
- **Price**—Free to try; $99 to buy (price subject to change)
- **Platforms**—Macintosh, iPad, iPhone, or iPod Touch
- **Learning curve**—Easy or beginner

GarageGames, the makers of Torque, knew that their popular 2D and 3D game engines needed a wider audience of game platforms to be sustainable. So they began targeting platforms besides the PC and Mac computers. Following the release of Microsoft's XNA Studio, and the potential to develop Windows and Xbox 360 games, GarageGames launched their hugely successful TorqueX, a 2D game maker for Windows and Xbox 360 platforms. Most recently, they've set their sights on Apple's iOS mobile devices and have released the iTorque game engine.

iTorque can craft simple or complex games for the iPod Touch, iPhone, or iPad devices (see Figure 3.13). iTorque is simple to use and is just one level above drag-and-drop creation. iTorque provides the following features:

- A visual 2D editor at iPhone, iPad, or iPod touchscreen resolutions

- Supported technology for iOS 4.3 and Xcode 4

- Powerful and simple scripting language (TorqueScript) for rapid prototyping

- Multi-touch and accelerometer input support

- Tutorials and documentation to guide users of all experience levels

- Full source code included to integrate any other commercial middleware and customized expansions

- QuickTime movie playback and music playback support

Figure 3.13
iTorque.

You build your iOS game on a PC or Mac and then port it to the iPhone, iPad, or iPod Touch. A Mac is required to perform optimization, device deployment, and Objective-C coding, but if you're a diehard Windows user, you can still program your game on a PC with C++ before moving to the Mac.

There are two reasons this book doesn't focus on using iTorque, unfortunately—iTorque is based on the Torque 2D game engine and is limited to making 2D games, and iTorque, unlike the Torque 2D and 3D game engines, does not currently offer support for multiplayer functionality. This is currently in development but not available at the time of this writing.

Multimedia Fusion 2

Info on Multimedia Fusion 2:

- **URL**—www.clickteam.com
- **Price**—Free to try; $99 to buy (price subject to change)
- **Platforms**—Windows, iOS, and Android
- **Target audience**—Single player
- **Learning curve**—Easy or beginner

Clickteam, a software company founded in 1993 and headquartered in Paris, France, is best known for their easy-to-use game-making toolkits, including The Games Factory and Multimedia Fusion.

Multimedia Fusion is a flexible, powerful, and full-featured authoring tool with no programming skills or knowledge required, and it's used by many multimedia professionals, game creators, and more. You can create a frame containing any 2D graphics you desire and then insert objects called extensions into that frame by drag-and-drop. Set behaviors for those objects in an intuitive, grid-style Event Editor, and you're practically done!

Clickteam offers an iOS runtime option for Multimedia Fusion 2 and Multimedia Fusion 2 Developer, so that you can export games to be played on the iPhone or iPad.

Multimedia Fusion games can simulate Flash or point-and-click adventure games, but as they are not suited to online 3D content, this chapter does not focus on that software alternative.

Unity iOS

Info on Unity iOS:

- **URL**—http://unity3d.com
- **Price**—Unity is free (including full 30-day trails of Unity Pro and Unity iOS Pro); $400 for iOS add-on
- **Platforms**—Web, PC or Mac, iPad, iPhone, or iPod Touch (others available)
- **Target audience**—Single or multiplayer
- **Learning curve**—Beginner or intermediate

The engine behind the upcoming multiplayer fantasy game *World of Midgard* (shown in Figure 3.14), Unity is a popular high-end 3D graphics game engine that caters to most platforms. Through separate licenses, a single developer can publish to a PC or Mac, the Web to be played over a web browser (Unity Web Player plug-in required), Android, Nintendo Wii, Xbox 360, Sony PlayStation 3, and iOS devices. With a single tool and workspace, you can target multiple platforms at once. Plus, you have complete control over the way your project delivers to these platforms. The built-in Unity Editor emulates your selected platforms so you can see what your game will look like before you publish it.

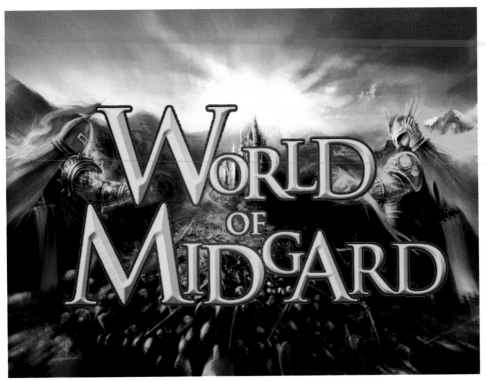

Figure 3.14
World of Midgard, a 3D fantasy MMORPG *World of Warcraft* clone, is being developed with Unity.

Popular Unity Features

Unity makes it a piece of cake to keep your program code working across multiple devices by abstracting away the preponderance of platform differences for greater convergence. When you need precise control based on platform, simply use code tag `#ifdef` to specialize code for each platform. Besides coding, Unity lets you specify graphic resolution and texture compression for the platforms you port to, so that you can use one Photoshop file and have it blend seamlessly on every device.

On top of cross-platform distribution possibilities, Unity has a next-generation look that has the feel of your most popular state-of-the-art triple-A game titles. Look at Figure 3.15 to see what I mean. Unity is optimized for speed and quality when rendering complex 3D environments and controlling ambient lighting and effects. It extensively uses fallbacks so you can make sure that everyone gets the best possible gaming experience. It also has preprogrammed physics that make those environments as close to reality as you can get. In fact, Unity contains the powerful NVIDIA PhysX Physics Engine, which is top-line in the gaming industry. On top of that, Unity also features the FMOD audio tools to give you extensive audio power, so your games will sound as good as they look.

Figure 3.15
The Unity
editor.

Add to that the options for multiplayer online support, and this is the game authoring kit for us. With Unity iOS, you can make unparalleled 3D multiplayer games for the iPad!

Unity Features Not Supported with iOS

There are some features of the fully capable Unity application not carried over with iOS, because of the particular needs and restrictions of Apple mobile devices. These are vital to keep in mind when developing games using Unity iOS.

- Ogg audio compression is not supported. Use MP3/AAC audio compression instead, as it is natively supported on iOS devices.

- Unity built-in multiplayer is not supported yet. Use .NET sockets instead.

- DXT texture compression is not supported. Use PVRTC texture compression instead, as it is natively supported on iOS devices and compresses textures both in memory and distribution size.

- Non-square textures are not supported by PVRTC formats.

- Pixel shaders are not supported.

- Render-to-texture is not supported.

- Movie textures are not supported. Instead, use full-screen streaming video playback.

- `GL` class is not supported.

- Unity's terrain engine is not supported. Unity's terrain engine is built to work with modern PC GPUs and so does not sensibly scale to iOS devices. Use low-poly meshes and occlusion culling to create your terrains instead.

- `OnMouseDown`, `OnMouseEnter`, `OnMouseOver`, `OnMouseExit`, `OnMouseUp`, and `OnMouseDrag` scripted events are not supported.

- Dynamic JavaScript features like duck typing, the `eval` function, and so on, are not supported.

- .NET 2.0 features are not supported. Generics will only give you compiler errors, so don't use them. Stick to .NET 1.1 instead.

- Video streaming via the `WWW` class is not supported.

- HTTPS is currently not supported by the `WWW` class.

- FTP is currently not supported by the `WWW` class.

Getting an Apple Developer Account and Downloading the iOS SDK

You cannot use Unity iPhone without first having a registered Apple developer account. To do so, follow these steps.

Note

This entire setup is performed through and dependent on Apple's developer website. As this is a complex process, and one that is subject to change if Apple reorganizes their development process, the best thing to do is to follow the instructions step-by-step from Apple's iOS dev center.

1. Apply for and become a registered iOS developer. Go to the Apple developer's website (shown in Figure 3.16) at http://developer.apple.com/iphone/program/.

Figure 3.16
The Apple
iOS developer
center.

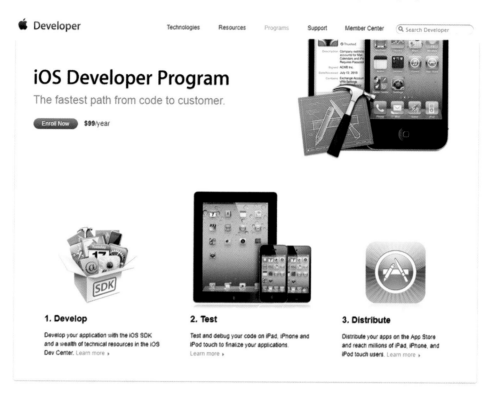

2. Standard registration at the time of this writing costs $99 for a year's membership. Registration gains you access to the iOS SDK (software development kit), which is used to build applications for iPad, iPhone, and iPod touch, as well as videos, sample code, documentation, and various forums.

3. If you need to, upgrade your operating system and iTunes installation. You must use the latest version of Mac OS X and iTunes. These are Apple-induced requirements as part of using their iPhone SDK and are not restrictions of Unity.

4. Download the iOS SDK. The iOS SDK contains the code, information, and tools you need to develop, test, run, debug, and tune applications for iOS. Go to the iOS development center and log in. After logging in, download and install the latest iPhone SDK. Do not download the beta version of the SDK. Note that downloading and installing the iPhone SDK will also install Xcode, which has a complete development environment of its own, including a source editor and graphical debugger. Xcode also provides the launch point for testing your applications on an iOS device and in iOS Simulator, which is a platform that mimics the basic iOS environment on a Macintosh computer.

5. Upgrade your device (iPhone/iPod Touch only). This could require you to purchase a $9.99 upgrade if you are using iPod Touch.

6. Get your device identifier. Using the USB cable, plug in your iOS device and launch Xcode. Xcode will detect your device as new. When it does, press the button labeled Use For Development. If that doesn't open the Organizer window, go to Window > Organizer. You should see your iOS device in the Devices list at left (see Figure 3.17). Select it and write down your device's unique identifier code. This code should be about 40 digits long.

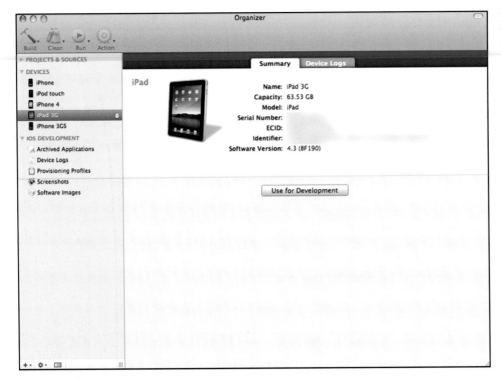

Figure 3.17
The Organizer window.

7. Add your device. Log in to the iOS dev center and enter the program portal. Go to the Devices page. Once there, click the Add Device button. Enter a name for your device (an alphanumeric name only) and your device's identifier code, which you wrote down in the last step. Click Submit when done.

8. Create a certificate. Within the iOS Developer Center, click the Certificates link and follow the instructions to generate a certificate (see Figure 3.18).

Figure 3.18
Create a
certificate.

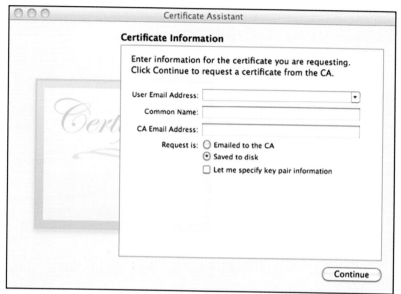

Figure 3.18
Create a
certificate.

9. Create a provisioning profile. The easiest way is within the iOS Developer Center; go to Certificates > Development and click the Request Certificate button. You can then upload the certificate you just created. Provisioning profiles are a little more advanced than that. They ought to be set up differently depending on how you've organized your team. Since there is no case that fits all circumstances, you can read up on how provisioning works on Apple's dev center at developer.apple.com/iphone/manage/provisioningprofiles/howto.action.

Downloading and Installing Unity iOS

Now that you have the necessary backend tools ready, it's time to install Unity iOS. If you're very lucky, you can get a free full version for OS X with Unity Pro, Android, and iOS trials added. If this limited-time opportunity is still available, you can download it by going to http://unity3d.com/unity/download/.

See Figure 3.19. If this opportunity is no longer available, you can purchase iOS from the Unity store.

Figure 3.19
You may be able to get a free trial version of Unity iOS.

1. Go to the following URL and select the appropriate currency rate.

   `https://store.unity3d.com/shop/`

2. Select Unity as your base product. You can view comparisons of the Unity and Unity Pro licenses online at

   `http://unity3d.com/unity/licenses`

3. Select iOS ($400 USD) as an add-on (see Figure 3.20).

4. Click Proceed and follow the online instructions to complete your purchase.

5. Once you have Unity iOS installer, run the executable file (which ends with .dmg on the Mac and .exe on a Windows PC) to begin installation. See Figure 3.21.

6. The Unity application requires activation before it can be used. Upon launching Unity, you will be taken to the online activation.

7. If you bought Unity, you will receive a serial number by e-mail. This code is unique to every customer. It should not be lost or shared with others. When activating Unity, you need to enter this serial number. The licensing system will take a fingerprint of your hardware and system software and send this fingerprint to the company's servers to lock the serial to your computer. The end-user license agreement permits you to install Unity on up to two computers. If you attempt to activate Unity on another computer besides two, you will be informed that your activation limit has been exceeded.

8. Once installed, double-check Unity iOS to make sure it was installed correctly. It should open into the editor with a project sample if you installed it successfully. If so, you're done!

Figure 3.20
Select Unity
and the iOS
add-on.

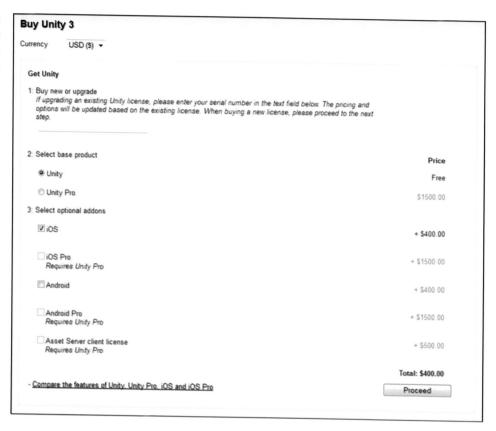

Figure 3.21
Installing
Unity.

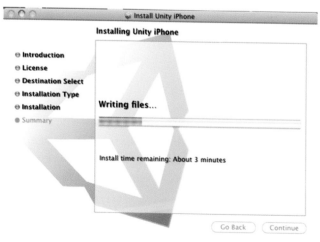

What's Next?

Now that you have become an Apple developer and set up the Unity game authoring software, the next chapter will help you explore its interface to find out how Unity works so you can make iPad games with it.

4

Unity Quick-Start Spellbook

This chapter contains information about the Unity user interface and how to navigate around the game environments you'll be creating. It also gives you starter instructions in how Unity works, how it's focused on game objects, and what you do with those game objects.

Unity, of course, is a game engine you can use to create iOS games. Game engines are not just software development kits (SDKs) but also run under the hood, driving your games. Everything from physics and collisions to graphic mapping and entity interactions are handled by the game engine, which in your case will be Unity.

Learning the Unity Interface

Take a look at the user interface of Unity, now that you have installed it on your Macintosh computer (assuming you are using a Macintosh, which is not required for the initial development cycle but is a definite must for distribution later on).

You can open Applications > Unity on Mac or Unity from Start > All Programs > Unity on Windows.

> **Note**
>
> If you are working on Windows, you may discover that Unity does not offer iOS support. For full iOS development, especially when it comes to testing, you should use a Mac.

When you first start Unity, the application gives you a welcome screen with links to video tutorials, documentation, and forums (see Figure 4.1). You can browse these on your own, but you don't need these to get your feet wet at this point, so go ahead and close the dialog box.

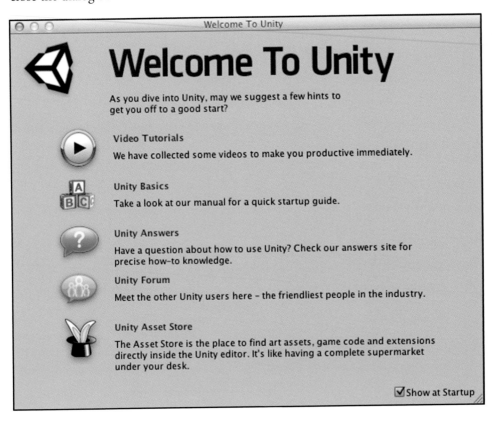

Figure 4.1
The welcome screen.

Typically, when you first start Unity, a demo project is already open. The current demo project is AngryBots, which is a third-person shooter game where the player is a starship trooper fighting an onslaught of angry robots. With AngryBots, you can see the possibilities and what you can do with Unity.

One aspect to keep in mind about Unity is that it was developed in Denmark and thus has a European minimalistic feel to its interface. The minimalistic layout is perfect for Apple developers, who are used to a minimal approach to interfaces. Another great thing about this type of interface is that you are not bombarded with hundreds of buttons or confusing menu commands that just clutter the interface. However, the drawback to all this is that the main features may be hidden or you need further instruction on how to find them. Someone new to the minimalist approach might find themselves lost, in fact, with no idea where to go.

For this reason alone, you'll need to review the Unity user interface first before you attempt to make a video game with it. As any game author will tell you, the first step in game creation is to become familiar with your software. There's nothing worse than not knowing what you're doing or not being aware of the best way to do something. Know your tools and your software, and you will see that it is much easier to build game environments when you actually know the toolsets you're using.

Unity's Tabs

Unity's main editor window is made up of separate tabbed windows, which are also called views. Each tab has a specific purpose. You can navigate between tabs, even while the game is running, to review different game functionality.

Scene Tab

The Scene tab (see Figure 4.2) is your basic editor and shows you everything going on in your game world. Scene does not reflect exactly what will be seen in-game but is instead a way for you to preview your game world as it is being built. You can select and move objects or even paint your terrains in the Scene pane.

If you are familiar with 3D editors like Blender, Maya, or 3ds Max, the Scene view and its functionality will appear very familiar to you, as it approaches 3D scene creation in Cartesian space (x, y, and z dimensions) in an identical fashion to those other editors. You will also find yourself accustomed to the red, green, and blue axes handles that come up. However, if you are totally new to 3D perspective views like this one, you need a firmer orientation.

Figure 4.2
The Scene tab.

What Does 3D Really Mean?

A Cartesian coordinate system specifies each point in a plane by a pair of numbers, which are distances from the point to two (or, as in the case of three-dimensional geometry, three) fixed perpendicular lines. Each reference line is called an axis, and the point where they meet is its origin. The system was invented by Rene Descartes in the 17th century and combines Euclidean geometry and Algebra. If it weren't for Descartes, there would be no 3D video games today.

Each point in Cartesian space is given a set of paired numbers. When considering 3D space, however, it is given a set of three numbers representing, in order, x, y, and z. So if you see a triumvirate such as 2, 3, 0, you know to go over 2 x, up 3 y, and stay at 0 z. This triangulation can tell you as well as the computer you're working on where a point exists in 3D space, whether it's in the real world or in a virtual landscape. This method is not only used for global positioning (GPS) but also for creating artificial realities.

Say you know where two points exist in virtual space. Now you can trace a direct line between them, which is often referred to in 3D editors as a line, segment, or edge. Once you have hundreds of points in space, you can map a connected framework of these lines to form a wireframe or mesh.

(continued)

What Does 3D Really Mean? (continued)

Where lines connect to form polygons a plane can be stretched across the void. Planes can be given a visible surface, and this surface, in turn, can have a 2D bitmap image covering it, making the once transparent wireframe object appear solid. This process is often referred to as mapping or adding materials. Materials can include bump-maps, which take the 2D bitmap image and a separate 2D grayscale image and extrapolate an imaginary "bumpy" surface out of them, giving flat plane surfaces a less rigid appearance. Materials can also include specular maps, which give surfaces the appearance of highlights, and many more maps.

So now you've come from having several points in 3D space to having lines bridging those points to having a wireframe to having visible planes and a surface that can be covered with material to appear like a real-live object. This object doesn't actually have any form or substance beyond what you can see, however. It takes programming and physics emulation to make 3D objects move and rub against one another and relate like real-live objects would. This is often handled by a game engine's scripts.

Now back to Unity!

Unity's Tools

There are several buttons in the top-left corner of the Unity interface, and these are tools that work within the Scene tab.

Move Tool

The cross-shaped icon button toggles the Move tool. The Move tool (see Figure 4.3) is used to select and move objects around in Scene. Try it by clicking on an object somewhere in the Scene tab.

Figure 4.3
The Move tool is the darker highlighted tool button shown here.

Note that a gizmo appears within the center of the object selected. This gizmo has a gray square in its center and red, green, and blue directional arrow-shaped axes handles, as shown in Figure 4.4. Red stands for direction x, green for direction y, and blue for direction z. You can move the object in any one of these directions by clicking and dragging the colored arrow handle corresponding to that direction. Whenever you click on a directional handle, it will change color to yellow to show it is selected. If you click the gray square in between the directional handles, you will move the object in more than one direction at once. It is preferred to move an object in a single direction at a time so that you have more control over an object's placement.

Figure 4.4
Arrow axis
handles.

Once you are done playing with the object, undo your actions by pressing Cmd+Z (Windows users use Ctrl+Z) until the model is back where it started.

Rotate Tool

Instead of the Move tool, you might decide to use the Rotate tool. The Rotate tool button looks like two arrows chasing one another around, as you can see in Figure 4.5. After you select it, circular colored lines will appear in orbit around the object's center.

Figure 4.5
The Rotate
tool.

By the way, an object's center is often referred to as its origin. Every 3D model has local Cartesian mapping as opposed to global Cartesian mapping within the 3D scene it is a part of. When a 3D model is first created, its origin often rests at coordinates 0 x, 0 y, and 0 z (0, 0, 0). So when you select an object in a larger 3D scene, the gizmo that appears in the center of that object is placed at that object's origin.

When using the Rotate tool, you can click any of the circular colored lines to rotate the object in that corresponding direction (see Figure 4.6). You can also click-and-drag the wider outside line to rotate the object in multiple directions at once, kind of like a "free rotate."

Figure 4.6
Circular axis
handles.

Remember to undo any changes you make to the model.

Scale Tool

The Scale tool, which has an icon button that looks like a tiny square with four rays exploding from its corners (see Figure 4.7), is used to shrink/enlarge objects.

Figure 4.7
The Scale tool.

Notice when you use the Scale tool and an object is selected, the directional handles are now shown as colored boxes, as in Figure 4.8. If you want to scale the object uniformly, you would need to click-and-drag from the gray center box. Conversely, if you only want to squash or stretch the object in one specific direction, you would click-and-drag on one of the directional handles. This is not really recommended when dealing with 3D models, however, as it will distort them (see Figure 4.9).

Figure 4.8
Square axis handles.

Figure 4.9
Scaling an object in only two directions makes it look squashed.

Scene Toggles

From left-to-right, look at the toggles at the top of the Scene pane and what their precise functions are.

Textured/Wireframe Toggle

The Textured drop-down menu lets you toggle between preview modes. You can choose Textured to view all objects with their corresponding colored texture maps or Wireframe to see all objects as they appear in see-through 3D mesh outlines (see Figure 4.10). To see both simultaneously, you can choose Tex-Wire (see Figure 4.11).

Figure 4.10
Wireframe view.

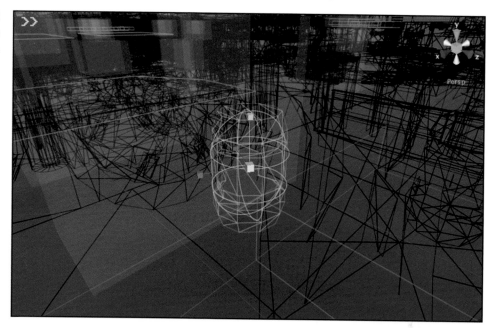

Figure 4.11
Tex-Wire view.

Color Range Toggle

The RGB drop-down menu gives you alternative ways to preview your scene. RGB, standing for "red, green, and blue," shows you the basic color preview. You can, instead, preview only the alpha transparency values by choosing Alpha and see a semi-transparent view by selecting Overdraw. These views are just for preview purposes and will not be visible in your game.

Lights Toggle

If you are using a computer with less video RAM than what is recommended, your Scene view may run slowly, or you may even notice lag. If this happens, you can toggle lights preview off. The button to toggle lights preview on/off is the sunshine icon to the right of Textured and RGB in the top of Scene. Then your system shouldn't struggle as hard to render the scene. By default, lights preview is set to on.

Camera Effects Toggle

On the other hand, if your computer has quite a bit of onboard memory, and you don't notice any lag, you can toggle camera effects preview on. The camera effects preview on/off button is the picture frame landscape icon to the right beside the toggle lights preview button. This will show you the different camera effects currently active in your scene.

Game Tab

The Game tab shows you a live view of what's going on in your game. Look at Figure 4.12.

Figure 4.12
The Game tab.

You can click-and-drag the Game tab out from being docked beside Scene. Many editors approve of customizing their workspace in this fashion, because you can set it up to see the view in-game (via the Game tab) while editing objects in preview mode (via the Scene tab). For the time being, however, keep the Game tab docked behind Scene.

Note

You can move, dock/undock, resize, and even close these panes at will. If you happen to close one that you didn't mean to, you can reopen it again by clicking the list arrow icon button in the top-right corner of that area. Select Add Tab and choose which tab you want to add.

Game Toggles

The Game tab offers four toggles at the top of its window, which you'll look at now.

Aspect Ratio Toggle

The first is a drop-down list toggle, which defaults to Free Aspect and can be used to toggle between the different video aspect ratios Unity can export to.

For instance, you select aspect ratio 4:3 from the drop-down list to make a game for a typical television screen and 16:9 for a widescreen television. You select Standalone (1024×768) for PC or Mac distribution. And you select Web (320×240) for the Unity Web Player, a plug-in that allows people to play your game embedded on a web page. You won't need to change the aspect ratio yet, so if you changed your aspect ratio, return to Free Aspect when you're done.

Maximize on Play Toggle

If you want to play-test your game in full-screen mode, click the Maximize on Play toggle button to turn it on. Now when you click the Play button at the top middle of the Unity interface, the Game pane will stretch to fill the entire Unity interface, hiding the other panes while you play-test your game (see Figure 4.13). Click the Pause button to pause the playtest, and click the Play button again to quit.

Turn off Maximize on Play for now, as it is off by default.

Gizmos Toggle

You can click the Gizmos toggle button to turn on/off the gizmos inside the Game pane. Gizmos include the wireframe mesh of your 3D models, positions of lights in your game world, and so on. Remember, though, that this is only a debugging tool and that as soon as you save and export your game to your desired platform, the gizmos will not be visible to other users when exploring your game.

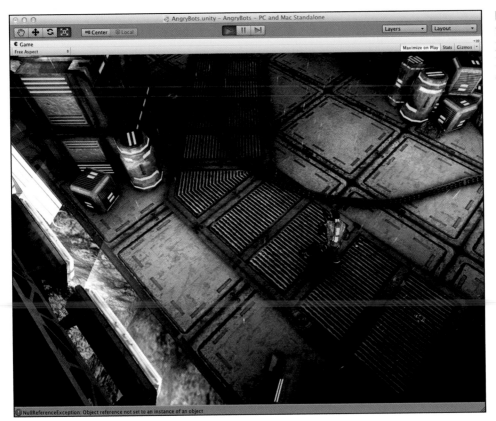

Figure 4.13
Using the
Maximize on
Play toggle
during playtest.

Stats Toggle

The Stats toggle switches on/off a small transparent pop-up pane that displays primary statistics about your game, including frame rate, number of vertices, textures used, screen resolution, video RAM being used, number of meshes and animations, and so on, as shown in Figure 4.14. This is important to see how fast 3D scenes are being rendered on your system and is a clear estimation of your game's current settings.

Animation Tab

The Animation tab in Unity is sometimes apparent by default and sometimes not. If you do not see Animation docked next to Scene and Game, you can open it by clicking on the list arrow icon button in the top-right corner of your Scene or Game view and go to Add Tab > Animation.

The Animation tab is used to create and modify animation clips directly inside Unity. This is meant to simplify your game building and be a powerful little tool to supplement the use of outside 3D animation programs. You can make simple animation clips and add animation events to animation clips that can call scripts at certain points in play.

As it's not needed for now, go ahead and leave the Animation tab hidden.

Figure 4.14

The Statistics
pop-up pane.

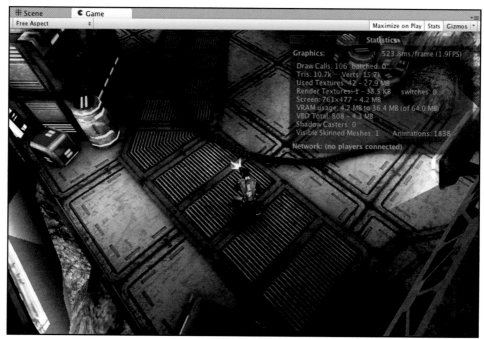

Hierarchy Tab

Hierarchy, which by default is in the top middle section of your Unity interface, holds
all the objects currently in your 3D scene. These objects might not be visible in 3D space,
or they might not be available in your current Scene view, which are two excellent reasons to have a Hierarchy view that shows all of them, as you can see in Figure 4.15.

Figure 4.15
The Hierarchy
tab.

The Hierarchy pane automatically updates to reflect all your current objects, even when playing your game, so that when you're in the middle of a playtest, for example, and you shoot your rifle at an enemy and a bullet is created aimed at an enemy, that bullet will appear in your Hierarchy pane. And when that bullet destroys your enemy and that enemy is removed from the game, both the bullet and enemy objects are automatically removed from your Hierarchy. This is an extremely efficient real-time utility.

In the Hierarchy pane, you can also click-and-drag objects around and even group them with each other. When a group has been constructed, a gray arrow will appear out beside the group name. An arrow pointing to the right indicates a group that has been collapsed, so you are aware there are sub-objects not currently being witnessed. An arrow pointing down indicates a group that is expanded, and you can see all of that group's sub-objects. Click on the gray arrow to toggle it between collapsed and expanded.

When it comes to programming, you can attach behavior scripts to single objects or to groups of objects.

Project Tab

The Project tab, which by default appears directly below Hierarchy in the middle of your screen, is a real-time representation of your current project assets you have on your hard drive, including files and subfolders you have imported or created (see Figure 4.16). These items might not be in the current scene you are working on, but you have access to them and can use them by dragging them into your scene if you desire their employment.

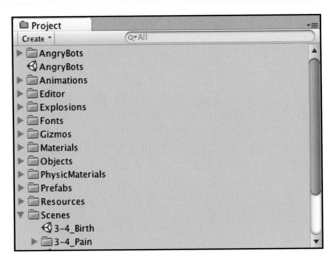

Figure 4.16
The Project tab.

You can right-click on an item in your Project pane and select Reveal in Finder (Windows users select Reveal in Explorer) to open a separate Finder window containing that item on your hard drive. If you were to make a new empty folder in this window and close it to return to Unity, the Project pane would update to show that new folder robotically. However, it is strongly recommended that most of the changes you make should be made inside Unity! To add assets to the Project tab, you can drag any file from your OS into the Project pane, or use Assets > Import New Asset. This way, Unity is in control of your project, and Unity is a lot more flexible when using contained elements, even though both are supported.

Scenes are also stored in your Project view. Scenes are like individual game levels. For example, the AngryBots scene (part of the AngryBots project) comes up in Unity when you first launch the program.

To create a new scene, use Cmd+N (Windows users press Ctrl+N/S). To save your current scene, use Cmd+S (Windows: Ctrl+N).

Inspector Tab

Last but not least is the Inspector tab. The Inspector tab, by default found on the right side of the Unity interface, displays all of the preconfigured properties relating to the object you currently have selected in any of the other tabs. These object properties may include the object's position (x, y, and z coordinates) in 3D space, its scale and rotation values, if there are any animations or scripts attached to it, and so on. Different properties will appear for different objects you select.

For instance, click on the First Person Controller Prefab in your Hierarchy tab and see that besides Transform properties, you also have an FPSWalker (Script), Character Controller, and Mouse Look (Script). Your screen should look similar to Figure 4.17.

There are a lot of very interesting and empowering actions you can take through the Inspector pane, even while the game is running, that will change your game in all sorts of ways. You will get to know more about the Inspector pane later.

> **Note**
>
> When experimenting with the layout of your tabs, if you find a workspace that feels comfortable to you that you want to continue using, you can save it. That way, every time you open Unity, you can switch to your favored layout. To do so, click the Layout button in the upper-right corner of the Unity interface (as shown in Figure 4.18) and, from the drop-down menu, click Save Layout. The program will prompt you to give your custom layout a name. After you do so, your layout will appear in the drop-down list when you click the Layout button.

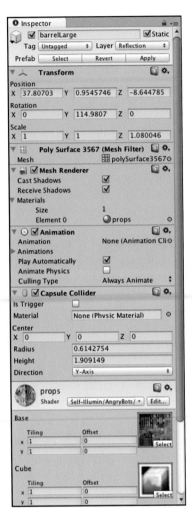

Figure 4.17
The Inspector tab.

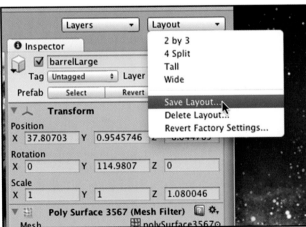

Figure 4.18
The Layout drop-down menu.

Navigating Scenes in Unity

This section discusses how you navigate in 3D space using Unity. Maybe you've already played around with other 3D software packages such as Blender, 3ds Max, Maya, or Lightwave. If so, you may have noticed that every 3D package is a little different when it comes to navigating around in them, although there are enough similarities so you don't get totally lost.

I hope to share some of those differences in Unity, so that it's easier for you to navigate around in your levels as you're building your games and you don't choke on a missed expectation.

Zooming In/Out

The scroll wheel on your computer mouse is used to zoom in and out. So when you scroll upward, you zoom in on a spot in 3D space and when you scroll downward, you zoom out. This is pretty standard to most 3D editors. What isn't standard is that you can also use your up and down keys to zoom in and out and your left and right keys to pan left and right, respectively. This is more like the navigation you'd expect in a video game.

Shifting Your Focus

You can also change your camera's focus so that you are looking where you want to. You do this by selecting an object in your Hierarchy and pressing the F key ("F" as in "focus"). Go ahead and try it:

1. Expand the Environment (static) group and select one of the crate_A objects from the Crates listed there.

2. Select the Scene tab by clicking on its name tab and press the F key on your keyboard, or go to Edit > Frame Selected. Your Scene view will jump to the crate object selected and centered in view (see Figure 4.19).

3. Now when you zoom in/out, notice how your focus will remain trained on the object you've just selected.

Orbiting Objects

To orbit around your camera's focal point in 3D space, press and hold the Option or Alt key and then click-and-drag with your mouse. As long as you have the Option/Alt key pressed and are clicking-and-dragging, you will rotate your camera around the current focal point. When you let go, you can continue navigating your scene, such as zooming in/out, and at any time, you can go back to orbiting by using the Option/Alt key and the click-and-drag method.

Figure 4.19
The Scene view is focused on the crate object.

Using the Scene Gizmo

There is a small directional axis view compass called a Scene Gizmo in the upper-right corner of your Scene view, with the red (x), blue (z), and green (y) axes visible, among others that are unmarked and gray (it's called out in Figure 4.20). You can quickly view your current 3D scene by clicking on one of the axes of the Scene Gizmo.

For instance, click on the green Y axis, and you will be immediately taken to a top-down angle, where you are looking down on your focal point on the map, as shown in Figure 4.20. Click on the other axes, and you will be taken to those angle views, too. Some of these angles are not very practical, such as when viewing from a side angle that has a mountain in the way or viewing from the bottom angle when you have ground in the way (see Figure 4.21), but they are available if you need them.

Figure 4.20
Looking down at the selected crate.

Figure 4.21
Looking at the crate from the side with a wall in the way.

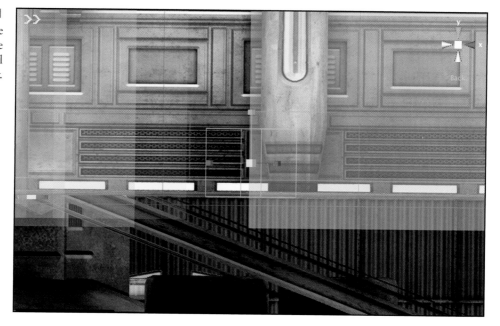

When you are done, click the large gray cube in the middle of the Scene Gizmo and you will be returned to the default perspective view where you last were before playing with the Scene Gizmo.

Selecting the Four-Split Layout

If you have ever worked in another 3D editor, you might be asking yourself, "Why only one perspective view?" You have others, but this is the default layout.

Actually, you can switch to a more typical 3D layout that has four concurrent views by clicking on the Layout button in the upper-right corner of the Unity interface and selecting 4 Split from the drop-down list. This will give you four Scene panes tiled where the one Scene pane sat previously. You can then press the F key when each view pane is active to center the views on the same focal point and use the axis view compass to alternate angle views, keeping one of the Scene panes at a perspective view. See Figure 4.22.

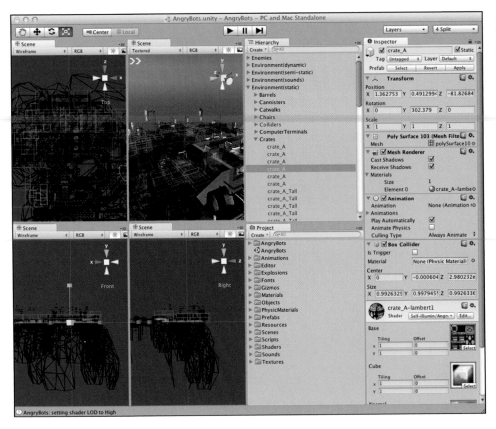

Figure 4.22
The 4 Split layout.

When you are done, switch back to the single Scene pane by clicking on Layout and selecting your favorite layout from the list (the default layout is Wide, by the way).

How Unity Works

Unity can be a little confusing in the way it is used to make 3D games if you don't under-stand the premise behind it. Basically, Unity's entire infrastructure rests on two elements: game objects and components. Game objects are the 3D models, shapes, light sources, cameras, and other things you place in the game scene. Components are items you attach to these objects that affect the way they behave and operate in the game, such as scripts, colliders, and more. Take a look at the way these two elements interrelate to form complex smooth-running video games.

Game Objects

The Hierarchy tab, as you've already seen, contains all the current objects in your game, and these objects are where your game starts. Unity is object-oriented, as is the program-ming logic behind it. You may have worked with OOP, or object-oriented programming, before—and if so, you will understand the flexibility this gives you as a game developer.

Start by opening a new Unity project and experimenting with objects from the GameObject menu.

You can create an empty game object by choosing GameObject > Create Empty from the main menu. An empty game object is basically a dot in 3D space, and this dot can be used as a starting point, like putting an empty game object in front of the barrel of a gun and using it to start a bullet shooting from that gun.

There are other types of game objects found if you point to GameObject > Create Other in the main menu, which you can review in the following sections.

Particle System

A particle system is basically a particle-creation engine within the game. For example, a particle system can be used in 3D space to create fire, smoke, rain, or even special effects such as magic spells and warp effects.

Camera

Cameras are extremely powerful and editable in Unity. Cameras are how 3D scenes can be seen. Cameras are how your 3D scenes are viewed during play. You can set one cam-era to look in one direction and another to look in a completely different direction—and switch dynamically back and forth between them in the code. You can set as many cameras in your game as you like. There is no limit to the number of cameras you can place in your game environments, besides practicality.

GUI Text

GUI, pronounced "gooey," stands for graphical user interface and is that part of the game interface that the user can see and read. For instance, a main menu, character select menu, inventory screen, or onscreen pop-up tip, are all part of a game's GUI. GUI text is the typographical component of these GUIs. Whatever you want written onscreen should be done though GUI text.

GUI Texture

The GUI texture is similar to the GUI text, except the GUI texture is a 2D graphical part of any onscreen GUI. For example, if you have an inventory screen where you can dress out your warrior character, you might have blocks for armor and headgear and boots, and each of these inventory items—and the background image—are GUI textures. You might also have a health bar that gets smaller as the player's health score drops. The health bar would be a GUI texture.

3D Text

3D text is pretty much the same as GUI text, except 3D text, as the name implies, exists in 3D space rather than 2D and thus can be panned, orbited, and zoomed around just like a 3D object. This is a uniquely powerful tool in Unity.

Lights

You have three types of lights you can place and use in Unity. With any of these lights, you can define the light's color to be any color in the color palette.

Point Light

Point lights are comparative to ball lights. They exist in a specified point in 3D space and have a radius defining the area they light up. Past that radius, their light diminishes, which is called a "fall-off." Point lights are useful for simulating the light coming from a manmade light bulb or campfire.

Spotlight

Spotlights are lights that share some traits of both point and directional lights. They exist in one spot and throw light in one direction but they have a "fall-off" range like the point lights.

Directional Light

Much like the sun's rays, directional lights keep going and going without diminishing. You can change the direction where a directional light is pointing, just like you can with a spotlight.

3D Shapes

You can make some basic 3D objects in Unity, such as cubes, spheres, capsules, cylinders, and planes.

- **Cube**—A cube is an object having six sides. Technically, each of those sides is supposed to be square matching sides, much like dice. But in 3D editors, you can stretch a cube out to make a rectangular box, too, and it is still considered a cube. See Figure 4.23.

- **Sphere**—A sphere is an object having all of its points the same distance from its center origin. The distance from the center to the surface of the sphere is its radius. Any cross-section of a sphere is a circle. See Figure 4.24.

- **Capsule**—A capsule is basically a cylinder capped at both ends with hemispheres. See Figure 4.25.

- **Cylinder**—A cylinder is an object that has two congruent circular bases that are parallel to one another with edges connecting their sides. A cylinder shape can make up a soda can or marble pillar. See Figure 4.26.

- **Plane**—A plane is a polygon connecting multiple edges. It often appears as a flat square having no real depth. See Figure 4.27.

Figure 4.23
Cube.

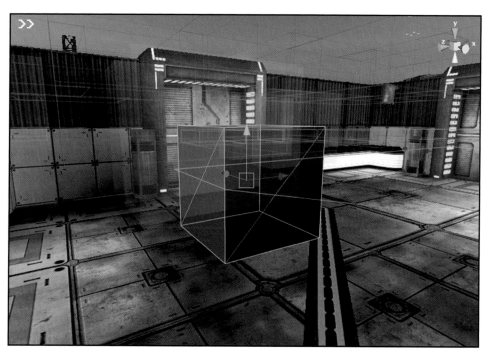

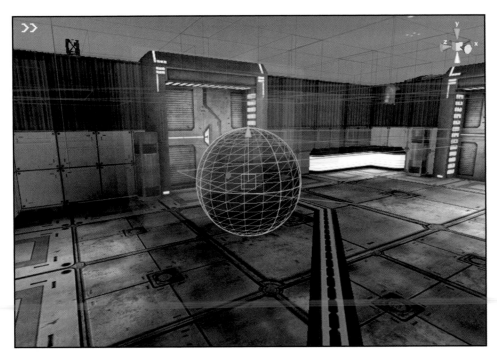

Figure 4.24
Sphere.

Figure 4.25
Capsule.

Figure 4.26
Cylinder.

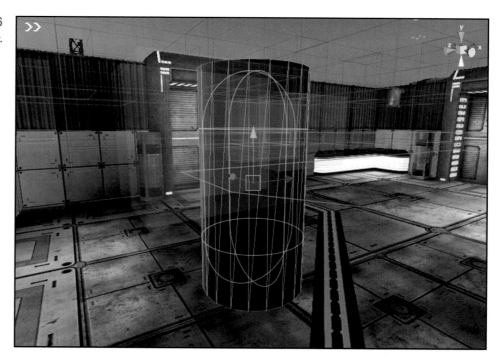

Figure 4.27
Plane.

Ragdoll

You have probably seen a video game where you shoot enemies and they die. After they die, their bodies flop around, so if you pull their arm, the rest of them will drag along, bouncing on the ground. This is because their limp lifeless bodies are not rigid anymore. Their bodies are being controlled by a complex physics algorithm referred to as a ragdoll, because they will respond to outside motions made against them much like a child's ragdoll would.

Imported 3D Models

You can also import 3D models into Unity. These 3D models can be created in any number of 3D model editors, which you'll look at later on. Once they are imported into Unity, they, too, become game objects. This is the preferred creation method of most of the objects you will see in video games. For example, in AngryBots, the robot shown in Figure 4.28 is a 3D model that has been imported into the Unity program.

Figure 4.28
This robot is an imported 3D asset.

Components

You can attach components to game objects. This includes any of the game objects found under GameObject on the menu bar as well as imported 3D models. When you have a game object selected in your Scene tab, that object's attached components will appear in the Inspector tab beneath its ID and Transform sections.

Components are found under Component on the main menu.

- **Mesh**—There are mesh attachments you can use. 3D meshes, also referred to as models, are the primary graphics primitive of Unity. These components help you render meshes.

- **Particles**—There are particle attachments you can use to control particle systems.

- **Physics**—There are physics you can attach to objects, such as Rigidbody, which can be attached to a crate to make it solid and give the player the ability to knock it around like you'd expect to do with a real crate. Other physics include colliders, which handle collisions between more than one object and objects with the terrain, and joints, which set up ways in which one object is affected by another in a parent-child relationship, much like the links in a chain.

- **Audio**—You can attach audio to game objects using audio components. For example, you might want a car to demonstrate a sound like an idling engine, so you'd use an audio component to do so.

- **Rendering**—Rendering components are unique ways to filter lights and camera views, such as lens flares, halo effects, and sky boxes.

- **Miscellaneous**—Miscellaneous components include those attachments not found elsewhere in the Components list, such as animations.

- **Scripts**—You can write your own scripts for Unity objects, but Unity ships with several prewritten scripts built-in to help you get your game up and running without having to do a whole lot of programming yourself.

- **Image effects**—Image effects are very similar to effects that you might have used in paint editors like Adobe Photoshop. There are blurs, glows, and other image morphing and toning effects that can change the look of selected objects in your game.

- **Camera controls**—As the name implies, camera controls are used to control how your cameras operate in-game.

What's Next?

You should be fairly familiar with how to get around in the Unity interface. The rest you can pick up as you go along. If you want to use hotkeys, which can be very useful in a minimalistic interface design like Unity has, see the following table for a list of the most commonly used hotkeys for Unity. You should also have learned how Unity depends on two elements, game objects and components, and how these two relate to one another. Now, you're ready to make your very first iOS game using Unity iOS.

Table 4-1: Unity's Shortcut Keys

Command	Hotkey
New Scene	Cmd/Ctrl+N
Open Scene	Cmd/Ctrl+O
Save Scene	Cmd/Ctrl+S
Save Scene As	Cmd/Ctrl+Shift+S
Build Settings	Cmd/Ctrl+Shift+B
Build & Run	Cmd/Ctrl+B
Undo	Cmd/Ctrl+Z
Redo	Cmd/Ctrl+Y
Cut	Cmd/Ctrl+X
Copy	Cmd/Ctrl+C
Paste	Cmd/Ctrl+V
Duplicate	Cmd/Ctrl+D
Delete	Del
Frame Selected	F
Find	Cmd/Ctrl+F
Select All	Cmd/Ctrl+A
Play	Cmd/Ctrl+P
Pause	Cmd/Ctrl+Shift+P
Step	Cmd/Ctrl+Option/Alt+P
Load Selection [0-9]	Cmd/Ctrl+Shift+[0-9]
Save Selection [0-9]	Cmd/Ctrl+Option/Alt+[0-9]
Refresh	Cmd/Ctrl+R
Create Empty (GameObject)	Cmd/Ctrl+Shift+N
Move To View	Cmd/Ctrl+Option/Alt+F
Align With View	Cmd/Ctrl+Shift+F
Scene	Cmd/Ctrl+1
Game	Cmd/Ctrl+2
Inspector	Cmd/Ctrl+3
Hierarchy	Cmd/Ctrl+4

(continued)

Table 4-1: Unity's Shortcut Keys (continued)

Command	Hotkey
Project	Cmd/Ctrl+5
Animation	Cmd/Ctrl+6
Move Tool	W
Rotate Tool	E
Scale Tool	R
View Tool	Q

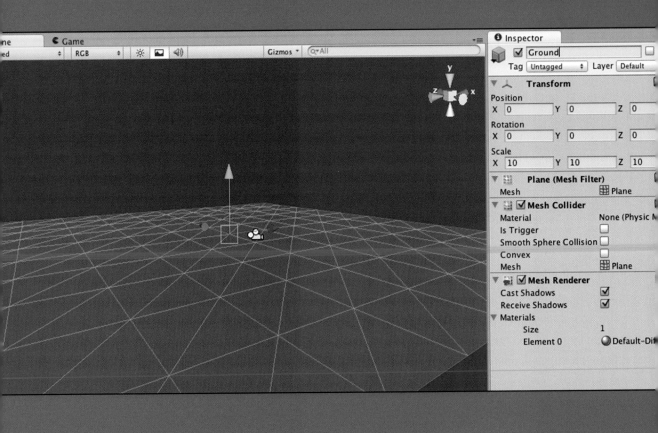

5

Crafting a Unity Game

You have had a brief introduction to Unity. You should know the basics of adding assets to scenes, positioning, rotating, and scaling them. You should understand which components can be attached to assets, as well as how to use the Inspector tab. Just being familiar with the Unity interface and where to find some of the tabs is enough for now, so it's time to push on!

You start by building a 3D action game with Unity that will work on an iPad. You will use basic scripts to set up iOS controls that capitalize on the touchscreen functionality of the iPad. You will also set up a game objective, or what is expected of the player. All this comes in handy later, when you finish building this as a multiplayer online game.

One of the great things about Unity is its flexibility when it comes to target platforms. It can be used to build games for the iPhone, iPod Touch, iPad, Mac, Wii, and more. In this book, you build games for the iPad, but Unity games you make for the iPad can be published to other target platforms with very little effort.

Initial Setup

Because you are targeting an iOS device, there are a few things you must do before going any further to help set up your project for building to the iPad.

In this section, you create a basic scene to start with and learn how to open it in your iPad.

First, you must set up your developer account a bit more in Apple's Provisioning Portal and create a provisioning profile that allows your iPad access to your Unity games. Thankfully, this can be done relatively quickly.

1. Open your web browser and log in to your Apple iOS Dev Center account before you click on the Provisioning Portal link.

2. Create and download a certification key, following Apple's step-by-step guidelines. Click on App IDs and create a new App ID. This should follow the template of *com.yourcompanyname.yourgamename* (replacing the names with your own). You might want to write this information down elsewhere, as you will use it later when defining settings in Unity.

3. Add the UDID of your test iPad to the device list (the UDID is a unique identifier you can find by launching iTunes, selecting your device from the list, going to the Summary tab, and clicking on Serial Number).

4. Create a provisioning profile using the certificate key, App ID, and all devices you are using to test with.

5. Connect your iPad to your Mac and open Xcode, which you should have installed after becoming an Apple iOS developer. Click on Organize and add the provisioning profile you just made. Close Xcode when you're through.

If you have never used Xcode before, I recommend you consider familiarizing yourself with it a little first. You can find a starter project with Xcode online at http://meand mark.com/xcodeintro.pdf and a list of Xcode keyboard shortcuts online at http://iphonedevelopertips.com/wp-content/uploads/2008/12/xcodelarge.png. For more information about Xcode, you might search the Apple developer website. You don't *have* to be familiar with Xcode to build Unity games for iOS devices, because for the most part, Unity builds out to Xcode for you.

Now create a game start in Unity:

1. Open Unity. Close the pop-up message window that greets you, and then go to File > New Project. Choose a directory somewhere on your computer and name your project **SorcerRun**, as it will be your first attempt at building a game in Unity. Make sure no packages are selected and click Create Project. Packages are sets of ready-made assets you can use to speed up development. You'll want to start from scratch for this lesson, but later you can experiment and play with packages. For instance,

you will use the Skyboxes package to create atmosphere for your game and Standard Assets (Mobile) to set up basic iOS game controls. Wait for Unity to reload with your new project at the ready.

2. Go to the Project panel and click the Create drop-down menu to choose Folder. A new folder will appear. Name this new folder **Scenes**. If you don't know how to do that, notice that the new folder name is surrounded by blue highlighting and a blinking text cursor has appeared to tell you it's ready for you to start typing. If you don't see this, click the folder name twice until you do. Type into that field the name **Scenes** before pressing the Return (or Enter) key.

3. Go to File > Save Scene in the main menu. Navigate to the directory you just created (SorcerRun/Assets/Scenes). If you cannot see where your Scenes folder went, such as shown in Figure 5.1, click the large blue down arrow beside the Save As field, and the pane will expand to show all options, as you can see in Figure 5.2. Save the new scene as **SorcerRun**. After saving your scene, go to your Project panel and expand your Scenes folder; you will see your new scene was added to the Scenes folder.

Figure 5.1
An example of
a minimized
Save As
window in
Unity.

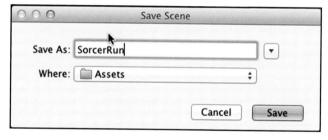

Figure 5.2
The same
window after it
was maximized.

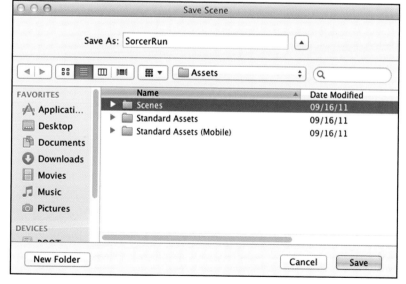

4. In the main menu, go to File > Build Settings. Click the Add Current button to add the currently selected scene to your project. You can view what's added in the small inset window. When you add your current scene, as shown in Figure 5.3, you will see it has an index of 0— which means it will be the first scene loaded whenever your game starts up.

Figure 5.3
Adjust the Build settings of your Unity project.

5. In the Platform list, select iOS and click the Switch Platform button. This option will not be available unless you have paid for the Unity iOS exporter. Click Player Settings and close the Build Settings window for now. You will see the Player Settings has opened in the Inspector view. Go there now to change some things.

6. In the Per-Platform Settings panel, double-check to make sure the tab showing an iPhone/iPad is highlighted. There are a lot of settings you can undertake in this panel. You can explore these in more detail on your own. Right now, go to Resolution and Presentation. Click the name bar once to rollout the options. Set it to Default Orientation and Landscape Left.

7. Roll out the options for Other Settings. Set your Bundle Identifier to the App ID you used in your provisioning profile (*com.yourcompanyname.yourappname*). The Bundle Version can be 1.0, since this is your first build.

8. Outside Unity, open Xcode, which you should have already downloaded after becoming an Apple developer. Close the Welcome screen and return to Unity. The reason to start Xcode is because having it running in the background helps tell Unity which version of Xcode to publish to.

9. In Unity, go to the File > Build & Run to reopen the Build Settings dialog box. Here, you want to click the Build and Run button. Inside your current project directory, create a new folder and name it **SorcerRunXcode**. Save your build project as **SorcerRun** inside that new folder.

10. After the project has been built out to Xcode, the Xcode window will pop up with your Unity project open. What happened is that Unity generated the source code of an Xcode project, and you now have this project ready to build and run from within Xcode. You will have two targets. Be sure your iPad is plugged in before selecting your project target and your iOS device. When you press the Run button, your Unity project should load within your iPad. If it does not, try repeating these steps. Of course, currently there's not a whole lot to see in your Unity project besides the loading screen, which is shown in Figure 5.4.

Figure 5.4
The default Unity loading screen.

Using Unity Remote

Unity Remote, which comes with most versions of Unity, is a software app that can make your iOS device act as a remote control for your Unity project. Some users have reported having difficulty setting up Unity Remote, and they use Xcode to play their Unity projects on their iOS devices, which works just as well. So think of Unity Remote as another option. If you want to use it, and it works well for you, by all means use it. Otherwise, do not worry about it.

If your version of Unity did not come with Unity Remote, you can download Unity Remote free from the App Store.

The following steps explain how to install Unity Remote from its source code.

1. First, switch to your iOS device and download the source code from the Unity website (unity3d.com). Unzip the download to your directory of choice. This contains a project you must launch with Xcode and build to install the Unity Remote on your iOS device.

2. Assuming you already created the provisioning profile at the beginning of this chapter, you just need to double-click the UnityRemote.xcodeproj in the UnityRemote folder of your Unity iOS install directory. This launches Xcode, where you then click Build and Go. After it finishes, Unity Remote will be installed on your iOS device.

3. Once installed, make sure your device is connected via WiFi to the same network as your development machine. Launch Unity Remote on your iPad while Unity is running on your computer, and select your computer from the list that appears. Now, whenever you enter Play mode in the Unity's editor, your iPad will act as a remote control you can use for developing and testing your game. You'll be able to control the application with the iPad wirelessly. You will even see a low-res version of the app on the iPad itself.

The main shortcoming to using Unity Remote is that the Unity editor cannot properly emulate iOS hardware. For instance, you won't be able to get the same behavior of graphics performance, touch responsiveness, sounds playback, and so on, that you would get on a real iOS device.

If your graphics are lagging or your connections appear slow, you should make sure that your Macintosh and iPad have Bluetooth turned off. Having Bluetooth off on both on your iPad and Mac should improve your ad-hoc network connection quality.

Building a Quick-and-Dirty Game World

In this section, you'll stage a death-match level for a game. A death-match level is one with no clear start or end, because the main play stays within the bounds of the level from beginning to end. This is the way classic *Doom* and *Quake* brawl levels were constructed back in the day, and the way that arenas are built for fighting games like *DOA* and *Mortal Kombat*.

1. In your SorcerRun scene, go to GameObject > Create Other > Plane to drop a flat plane object into the scene. A plane is like a giant square that has no depth.

2. In the Inspector view, adjust the Transform > Scale options to read 100 X, 100 Y, and 100 Z.

3. At the top of the Inspector view is a name field, which should say Plane. Rename this object **Ground**. Your scene should resemble Figure 5.5.

Figure 5.5
Create a ground plane so you have a little terra firma.

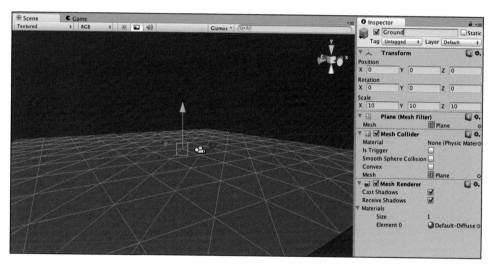

4. Go online to NOCTUA Graphics (www.noctua-graphics.de)—a free resource site by Herbert Fahrnholz—and click on your language's link. Then navigate to the Download page, where you will find a link to Textures. Go to the stone category (see Figure 5.6) and select an apt texture; I chose texture stone13. Click on the thumbnail of your texture to see the expanded image. Right-click on the image you see there and save it to your computer somewhere.

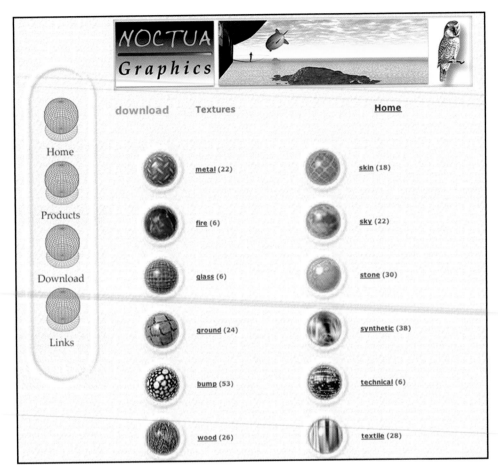

Figure 5.6
Visit
NOCTUA
Graphics to
find seamless
textures.

5. Return to Unity. In the Project tab, select your Scenes folder and click the Create > Folder button. This new folder should be nested inside your Scenes folder. Name it **Textures**.

6. Find where you saved your stone texture and drag-and-drop it into your new Textures folder. Your Project tab should resemble Figure 5.7.

Figure 5.7
Put your stone
image into a
Textures
subfolder.

7. Select your Ground object. Drag your stone image from your Textures subfolder in the Project tab and drop it onto your Ground object in your Scene view. Your texture will be automatically applied as a diffuse texture to your Ground object. What this means is that the stone image is now used as wallpaper to cover the surface of your primitive shape.

8. In the Inspector tab, with your Ground object still selected, look under the Materials rollout for X and Y fields for Tiling. Change these values so you have Tiling > X 5 and Y 5. This shrinks your texture and forms more consistent-looking wallpaper, as you can see in Figure 5.8. Of course, Herbert Fahrnholz' NOCTUA Graphics is a superb source for seamless textures, so you shouldn't be able to see any visible lines where the texture bumps up against itself. However, you won't be able to drag *any* common ordinary graphic off the Internet and apply it as a tiled texture and make it look good; you can only use seamless textures.

Figure 5.8
The Ground plane with the stone texture tiled over it.

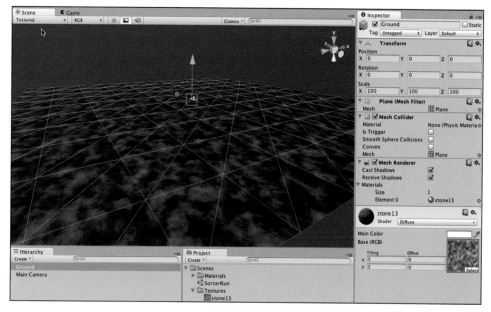

9. Now you need to add some walls. Go to GameObject > Create Other > Cube to drop a Cube object into the Scene view. Rescale the cube to be about X 24, Y 105, and Z 250. Rename it **Wall**.

10. Return to the NOCTUA Graphics website and browse the Wall category on the Textures page. Find one that appeals to you and save it to your computer. (I used tapete02.) Return to Unity and place the new graphic into your Scenes > Textures folder in the Project tab.

11. Select your Wall object. Next, drag your wall texture from the Project tab and drop it onto your Wall object to add it as a diffuse material. Set the Tiling field values as needed; if the texture looks too large, you can raise the Tiling values, and if the texture looks miniscule, you can lower the Tiling values.

12. Once you're finished with your Wall object, go to Edit > Duplicate to make a clone of it. Make multiple clones and move them around the Ground object in a circle, each one touching the other and passing slightly through the Ground object so there isn't a gap beneath or between. What you are trying to do, more or less, is fence the players in, so they cannot leave the area you are developing. (Yes, there will be a huge gap at the top, and I will cover that later.) You can press the F key to focus on each object as you're editing it. Be sure to use the Move and Rotate tools on the objects as you go, and switch between a top-down view (by clicking the green handle of the Scene Gizmo) and the perspective view. When you're done, your wall enclosure should resemble the one in Figure 5.9.

13. Create a point light in your scene to illuminate the area. In the main menu, go to GameObject > Create Other > Point Light. (*Point lights* provide a single light source with no discernible direction of light. They are used for ambient lighting in game areas.) Once the point light appears in the Scene view, use the Move tool to move the light up off the map. Usually, lights in game levels approximate where you place physical lights, so if you have a lamp, for example, you place a point light near the light bulb of the mesh object. However, you will not mess with physical light sources for now. Just leave your point light hovering in the air just a hair lower than the tops of your walls.

14. In the Inspector tab, set the Range of your light to 800 and the Color to some off-white color (you can see the yellowish off-white color I chose in Figure 5.10).

15. That's it for now! Next you need to create a player character.

Figure 5.9
Walls created to fence in the players.

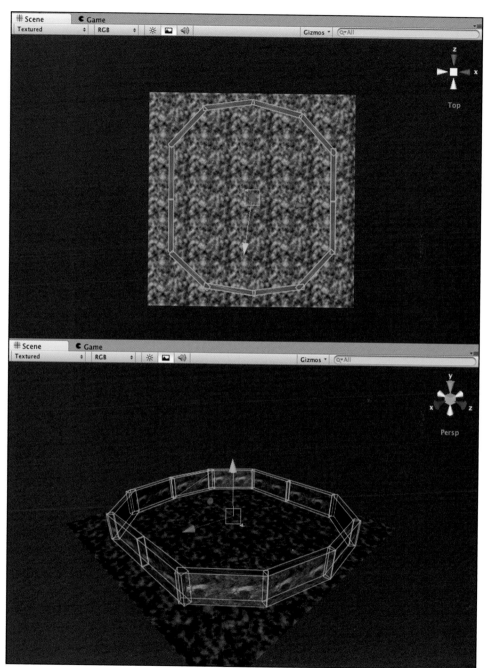

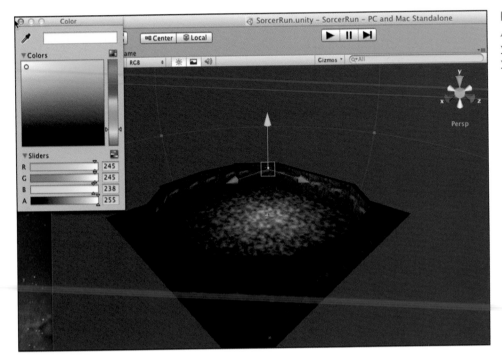

Figure 5.10
A light helps
you to see what
you're building.

Creating Your 3D Assets

Before you add the scripts that will run on game load, you need a visual framework to look at. Keep in mind that your game environment and game objects must be conservative when building for mobile gaming. There are some tricks to keep in mind to do so, which you will see.

For creating 3D assets, you'll have to step away from Unity for a little while. Now, take a look at what 3D assets are and how you can create them.

FBX Files

Unity has a preference for FBX file types for 3D objects. FBX is a file format owned and developed by Autodesk, the leading company in 3D modeling and animation. Autodesk, by the way, is the owner and developer of such 3D tools as 3D Studio Max and Maya, which are the two biggest-selling 3D tools on the market.

FBX is prevalent with Unity because FBX files provide interoperability between digital content creation (DCC) applications like Unity and many more; FBX is also very popular with XNA Studio developers who make games for the Xbox, and this popularity appears to be growing as more applications turn to FBX files for their 3D asset needs.

How to Create FBX Files

Of course, you could use Autodesk's 3D Studio Max or Maya programs to export to FBX, as long as you have the appropriate plug-ins. Many 3D artists do purchase these fine programs. However, at licensing costs of upwards of $3,000 (USD), this is not an easy decision and probably not one within your budget right now.

Another solution is to use Wings3D. Blender is a 100 percent free, open source 3D content-creation suite, and it is available for most operating systems. To read more about Wings3D, check out www.wings3D.com.

What If You Don't Have FBX Files?

Suppose, however, that you are a 3D artist already, but your chosen program does not export directly to FBX. First, you might want to conduct a web search to see if there is a plug-in you can install to your 3D art program that will allow you to export to FBX, because chances are great nowadays that you will find one. If not, then don't fear, because you're not stuck!

Imagine you have a whole library of 3D models you want to use, but most of them are in 3DS or OBJ file formats and not FBX. Again, there's hope!

Autodesk has released a standalone program called the FBX Converter, which you can download from its website at http://images.autodesk.com/adsk/files/fbx20121_converter_mac_enu.pkg.tgz.

If that link does not work, you might do a quick web search or search the Autodesk site directly to find the FBX Converter.

The FBX Converter is a neat little tool that enables you to convert OBJ, DXF, DAE, and 3DS files to or from multiple versions of the FBX format. You can also view FBX animation files in real-time with the built-in FBX Viewer, explore and compare FBX file contents with the FBX Explorer, and manage animation takes with the FBX Take Manager. And best of all, it's free!

You're Not a 3D Artist ... What Do You Do?

Not good with 3D art programs? Unsure of what a polygon is? I will show you in the next part of this lesson, of course, but if you have trouble with even this basic lesson, or decide that in the future you would rather hire a 3D artist, there are other options.

There are resource sites that share 3D assets for game development. Some of these sites are free and some are commercial in nature. Even the ones that are free usually do not give you unrestricted license to do whatever you want to with the 3D assets you download and incorporate into your game. Although this sounds restrictive, think about it from the artist's point of view: Would you like to spend hours adding fine detail to an elf model to have someone download it from the Internet and stick it into a porn video they happen to be making, without asking your permission first? Chances are your answer would be negative, and I don't blame you! So even if there aren't restrictions on what you use a 3D asset for, if somebody else made it and you are downloading it to use it, contact the artist and ask him/her if it is okay first. Plus, by contacting and networking with 3D artists directly, you might gain new and influential teammates! They might want to assist you in your future project needs.

The following lists show a sampling of noted websites (like the one in Figure 5.11) containing 3D assets for download or purchase.

Free resources:

- 3dmagicmodels.com
- archive3d.net
- opengameart.org
- www.3dsmodels.com
- www.3dvalley.com
- www.katorlegaz.com/3d_models/index.php

Commercial sites:

- developer.daz3d.com
- www.3dmedia.be/03/
- www.arteria3d.com
- www.creativecrash.com
- www.frogames.net
- www.gameprefabs.com
- www.nekotika.com

Mixed sites:

- unity3d.com/unity/editor/asset-store
- www.3drt.com
- www.dexsoft-games.com
- www.turbosquid.com

Figure 5.11
Frogames offers 3D art packages at a price.

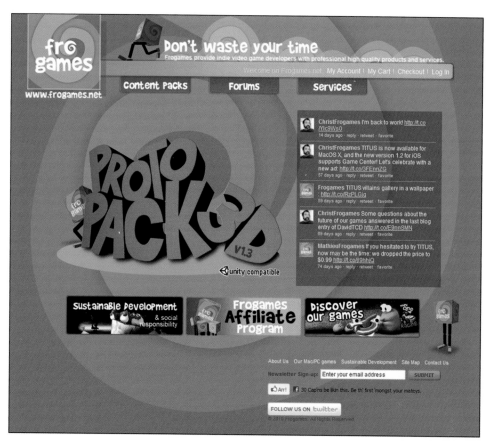

Note

If you plan to do a whole lot of 3D asset creation for Unity games, you should check out the book *Creating 3D Game Art for the iPhone with Unity* by Wes McDermott, published by Focal Press 2011. McDermott shares some exciting tips on using 3D programs modo and Blender to fine-tune your 3D assets.

A Primer on 3D Modeling

There are a few simple things you need to know about 3D modeling before you can get started. If you are already an accomplished 3D artist, you probably do not need to review this section and can skip to the section entitled, "Constructing a Player Model."

Most 3D programs, like Unity, share similar aspects. You can incorporate an orthographic, perspective, or isometric windows into your 3D scenes. *Orthographic* means that you are looking at two dimensions at once, such as X and Y. With perspective or isometric, you are viewing three dimensions at once (X, Y, and Z). Isometric is usually locked to one viewpoint that is equidistant from the intersection of X, Y, and Z.

3D objects are primitive shapes based on Cartesian geometry. Look at Figure 5.12 for an example as you go along.

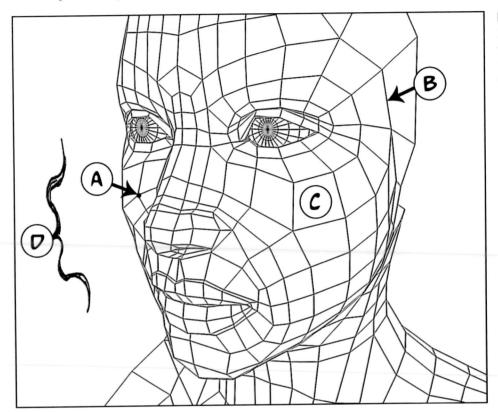

Figure 5.12
Examples of a vertex (A), edge (B), poly (C), and mesh (D).

First, you start with a point in space, which has a single coordinate set with integers for X, Y, and Z. A point in Cartesian space is often referred to as a *vertex*. Add another vertex and you can connect the two with a straight line, what is often referred to as an *edge* or *segment*.

Once you have lots of vertices and edges connecting them, you can start patching between them. A patch between three points in space that are connected by three lines is called a triangle, or simply *tri*. Two tris make up a polygon, or simply *poly*. Patches are often referred to as *faces*.

Once an entire object is constructed from faces, it will look like a statue made with chicken wire; this wire is referred to as a *mesh*. The mesh gets covered with a surface material, and artists can cover this material with a texture or bitmap image. There are other types of materials that can cover a surface, however, like bump-maps (which give the surface a bumpy texture) and specular maps (which render glossy highlights over the surface).

As you build 3D objects, you can tweak their various components, including vertices, edges, tris, and polys. Ways you tweak these involve transforming them (which means moving them from one place to another), rotating them from side-to-side, scaling them up or down, and extruding them (which is similar to yanking a pinch of clay away from the main ball of clay).

Constructing a Player Model

In this section, you will be making a player model for your game. This is a witch riding a broomstick. You can call her Fleura. Refer to Figure 5.13 to see the concept artwork for the character you are going to build. This is Fleura. She may appear difficult, but the actual building of her will be simple, as long as you have patience.

Figure 5.13
Fleura, the flying witch.

Using Wings3D for the First Time

You'll make the 3D assets using an application called Wings3D. Wings3D is a simple subdivision modeler, easy and intuitive to use, and is open source (free). The main drawback to Wings3D is that there is currently no built-in support for animation, and it does not natively export files to FBX; you will have to use the FBX Converter program to bridge the gap from Wings3D to Unity. As you are not going to get involved in animation, it is of no concern at this point that Wings3D lacks that ability. If, later on, you decide to develop animated objects for Unity, you might want to familiarize yourself with Blender instead.

Start by downloading and installing the latest stable version of Wings3D for your operating system from the following site: www.wings3d.com/.

1. Once you have it on your machine, open Wings3D. You will be greeted by a blank scene to work from, as seen in Figure 5.14. This is the Geometry window, which will be your 3D canvas. There are other windows, including an Outliner, Geometry Graph, Palette, New Geometry Window, and Console, which can be opened as well. But most of your work will occur in the Geometry window.

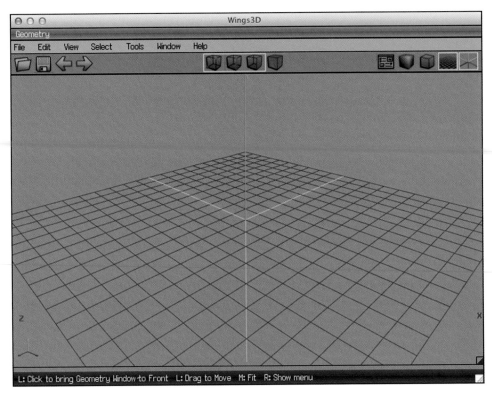

Figure 5.14
The first screen you will see in Wings3D.

2. Since you're not worrying about animation for the purposes of this lesson, you are going to model the witch sitting on her broomstick. Right-click in the blank scene and select Cube from the menu. It is not uncommon for Wings3D units and other 3D package units to be different in size. Therefore, you will need to experiment with the import/export sizing options to get suitably sized objects. In your case, 10 Wings3D units equal 1 Unity unit, so if you create a plane 1,000 units wide on all sides and import it into Unity, it will appear the same as a 100-units-wide plane. So base all your Wings3D modeling off 10 units. To define exact sizes of shapes in Wings3D, click the small window thumbnail beside your selected shape option and a size definition window will pop up. For instance, when you create a Cube, set its size to 10×10×10.

3. Selection modes are shown in the upper-middle portion under the main menu, as shown in Figure 5.15. The first icon is for vertex selection. The second is for edge selection. The third is for face selection. The fourth is for body selection, or selecting the whole object. Change to Body Selection mode.

Figure 5.15
Component
selection
modes, from
left to right:
vertex, edge,
face, and body.

4. Select your cube shape. Right-click on it after it turns red and select Absolute Commands > Scale Uniform. Move your mouse and you will see the percentage scale shift in the upper-left corner of your Geometry window. Move your mouse until the percentage is close to 60 percent and click your left mouse button to confirm your changes.

5. Zoom out from your scene using the middle mouse button/mouse wheel. If you do not have a middle mouse button/mouse wheel, you will have to set your preferences differently in Wings3D before continuing by going to Edit > Preferences > Camera Preferences and choosing the Two Button Mouse (Nendo camera mode) scheme. Then you can zoom by holding down the right mouse button (RMB) while moving the mouse forward and backward.

Blocking Out the Model

You are going to use Wings3D's Bridge function to connect the blocks of the model, but in order to do so, you have to build an artificial skeleton of blocks to connect. This part is a little tricky, so refer to Figure 5.16 and the screenshots as you continue.

1. Right-click on your cube shape and select Duplicate from the pop-up menu. Then select axis Y to move your new cube straight up above your first one about one-half cube distance apart. You can tweak its size and position later. As shown in Figure 5.17, make another cube copy until you have three cubes, stacked on one another. Select the bottom cube. To deselect other cubes, click on them until they are no longer red.

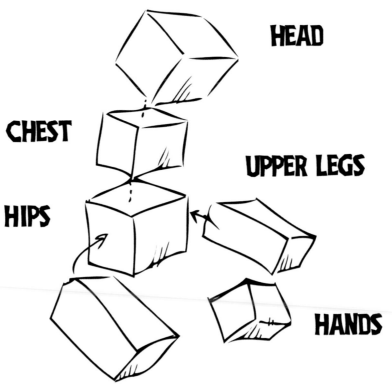

HEAD

CHEST

UPPER LEGS

HIPS

HANDS

Figure 5.16
Where you will place the blocks.

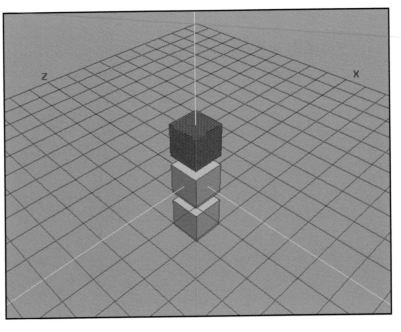

Figure 5.17
Make three blocks stacked on one another.

Note

Don't worry if you make a mistake! It's easy to undo. Do you see the large left and right arrows (shown in Figure 5.18) in the top-left of the Geometry window? Just like surfing the Internet in a web browser, the left arrow is the Undo button, which allows you to undo operations one step at a time. The right arrow is the Redo button, which allows you to redo those same operations. Be sure and take full advantage of these. If you take a step and realize it didn't turn out the way you'd hoped, don't press on anyway; immediately click the Back button and try something else.

Figure 5.18
The Undo and Redo buttons give you control over mistakes.

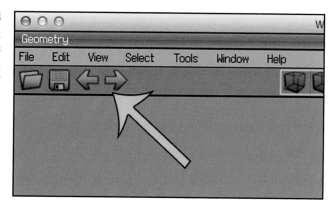

2. Pan by clicking the middle mouse button/mouse wheel (or tapping the Q key if you are using the Nendo camera mode). Now you can move your mouse to reposition the scene's camera and use the mouse wheel to move in/out. Position your camera up, looking straight down on your stack of cubes. As you can see in Figure 5.19, you should not be able to see the bottom cube you selected, because it will be underneath the others.

3. Right-click and select Duplicate > Axis Z. Move your new cube out to one side of the original copy, not quite touching it. With this new cube still selected, right-click and choose Duplicate > Axis Z again. Pull your duplicate cube out on the opposite side of the center column, as seen in Figure 5.20.

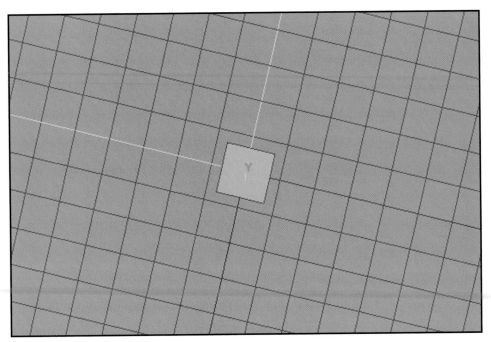

Figure 5.19
Looking down on the stack of cubes.

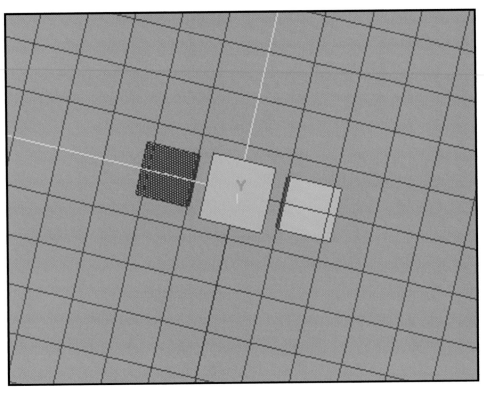

Figure 5.20
Drag duplicates of the bottom cube out to either side of it.

4. Pan your camera until you can see the center bottom cube again (the one you originally duplicated). Duplicate it again, moving the duplicate out in front of the column along axis X. See Figure 5.21.

Figure 5.21
Make another
duplicate of
the cube.

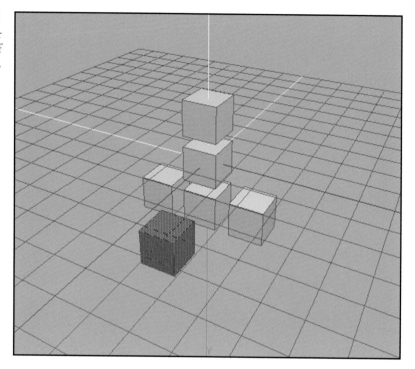

5. Now, rearrange these basic building blocks. Since the final duplicate block is still selected, you can start there. Right-click and choose Scale Uniform. Make this block approximately 60 percent of its original size. Next, right-click and choose Rotate and pick Axis Z. Rotate the cube until it's cocked up like in Figure 5.22 (mine approximated −60 percent).

6. Choose the center cube in the central column you built. Use Scale Uniform to shrink it to about 75 percent of its original size and use Rotate > Axis Z to cock it ever so slightly. Then choose Move and Axis Y to move the cube down until it almost touches the cube below it. Use Move and Axis X to reposition this cube to the very edge of the cube below it. Compare your placement to Figure 5.23.

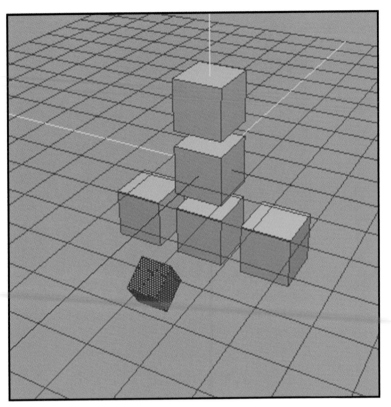

Figure 5.22
Rotate the front cube as shown.

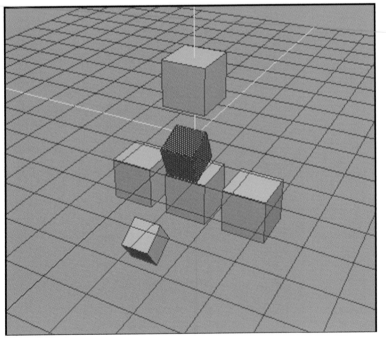

Figure 5.23
Stack your middle column cubes as such.

7. Select the cube right above that one, deselecting the other. Scale this cube uniformly to 85 percent of its original size. Rotate it along axis Z. Move it along axis X until it almost touches the cube below it. It should rest just off the forward-facing edge, as shown in Figure 5.24.

Figure 5.24
Your top cube should almost loom over the others.

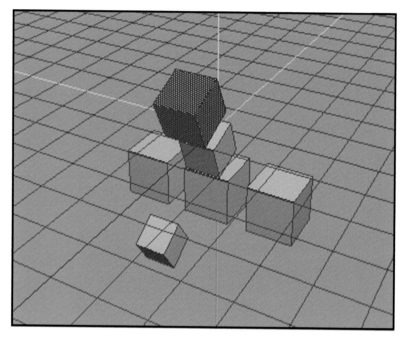

8. Now select one of the side cubes, deselecting the last cube you edited. This one will take a little more work. First, right-click on it and choose Scale Axis and pick Axis X. Then scale it so that it is almost rectangular in shape. After you commit that change, scale it uniformly so that it is 70 percent of its original size. Deselect everything by pressing the spacebar. Change to Face Selection mode and select the forward-facing face. Scale it until it is 65 percent of its original size.

9. With that same face still selected, right-click and choose Extrude > Axis X. Move your mouse until you make an extrusion that adds a whole other cube onto the front of your block, like in Figure 5.25. Deselect everything and pan your camera until you are looking at the underside of your new extrusion. Select the bottom face of your extrusion. Extrude this along axis Y (straight down), pulling down until you've added a whole new rectangle. With the face still selected, scale it uniformly to be half its size (see Figure 5.26).

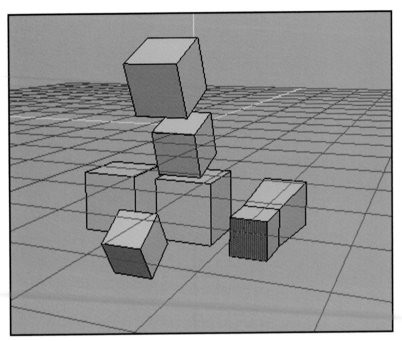

Figure 5.25
Make your side cube a rectangle and then extrude one end of it.

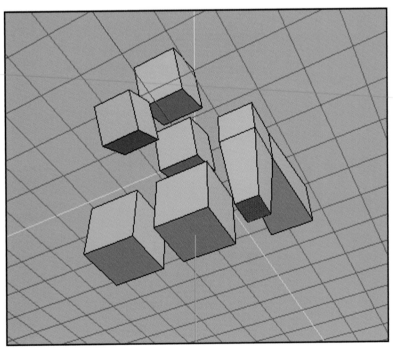

Figure 5.26
Extrude down to make the leg calf.

10. Switch to Body Selection mode. As soon as you do, note that your whole leg shape is automatically selected. If not, select it. Use axis Z to rotate it until it is half-cocked in the air, and then move it down axis Y until it is a little lower than the bottom block of the central column. Move it up along axis X until it is just in front of said block and along axis Z until it is almost touching it. Your result should appear similar to Figure 5.27.

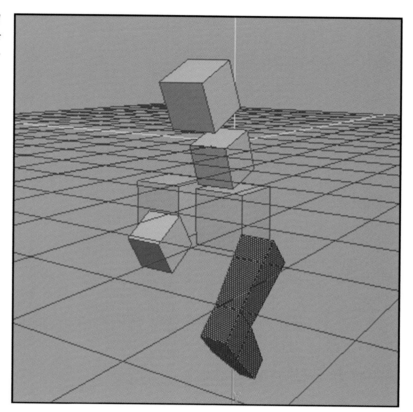

Figure 5.27
Rotate your leg.

11. Now you'll focus on the hands. That is what the middle front-facing tilted cube will be. Deselect everything first. Switch to Face Selection mode and select the face closest to the central column. Right-click on the face and select Plane Cut, and then right-click on axis Z. This brings up the Slice into Equal Parts window. Make sure that the Slice into Equal Parts window has the value 2 and click OK. The face has split into two equal-sized faces and your selection mode has changed to edge type, with the new edge separating these faces selected by default (see Figure 5.28).

Figure 5.28
Split the top
of the hands'
block in two.

12. Switch back to Face Selection mode. The two new faces should be selected by
default; if not, select them now. Right-click on them and select Bevel. Move your
mouse until you have beveled smaller faces out away from the hands. Extrude these
new faces three times to create the lower arms, elbows, and upper arms; the first
two extrusions should use axis X, and the last one should use axis Y. Compare your
work to Figure 5.29.

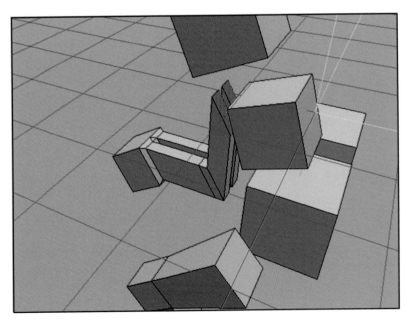

Figure 5.29
Bevel the tops
of the hands to
make wrists
and then
extrude them
to make arms.

13. Remember that second block opposite the leg you made and haven't touched yet? First, deselect all. Switch to Body Selection mode and select that block. Right-click on it and choose Delete. Select the leg you've been working on. Right-click on the leg and select Duplicate. Move the duplicate along axis Z so it is opposite the original leg.

14. Now you're ready to start connecting some of these bits and pieces. Select a face of the hip block (the center bottom cube) nearest a leg and bevel it outward, like you did with the faces on the hand cube to make the wrists. Do the same with the opposite face of the hip block. Try to make the beveled face the same approximate size on both sides of the hip block. Select both outward-facing faces of the hip block and move them down using axis Y. Deselect them and select the bottommost downward-facing face of the hip block and scale it uniformly until it's half its original size. Your final hip block should look like Figure 5.30.

Figure 5.30
Constructing
the hip block.

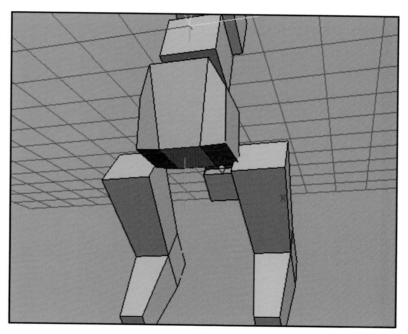

15. One at a time, move the legs up so they are almost touching the front bottom edge of the hip block's beveled sections. Deselect them and, on each, select the face at the top of the leg and the outward-facing face of the beveled sections of the hip block, as you see in Figure 5.31. Right-click and select Bridge. This closes the gap between the two faces with geometry.

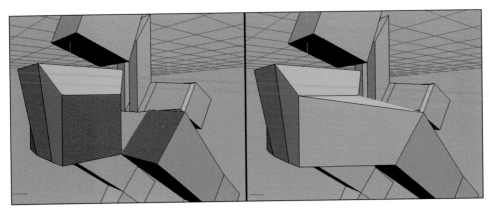

Figure 5.31
Using the Bridge command to construct new geometry between the selected faces.

16. Change to Edge Selection mode. Find the underside edge of the newly connected geometry and move it down. You can use the Free option or simply move along axis Y. See Figure 5.32.

Figure 5.32
Alter the underside of the thigh.

17. Deselect and change to Vertex Selection mode. There are two vertices sticking way out on the upper part of each thigh. You will need to select these one at a time and bring them in closer in line with the leg, so that there's still a little curve but not a pointy protrusion. Figure 5.33 shows what I mean.

Figure 5.33
Alter the top of
the thigh.

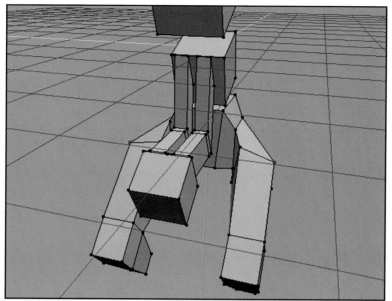

18. Deselect all by pressing the Spacebar. Switch to Face Selection mode and select the two faces between the hip block and the upper body block. Right-click on them and choose Bridge to create new geometry connecting the two. Change to Edge Selection mode and move two edges back a little: the one on the very back, and the one straight across from it above the belly, so the witch isn't bent in a weird way (see Figure 5.34). Finally, deselect those edges.

Figure 5.34
So the witch's
back isn't bent,
move a couple
of edges.

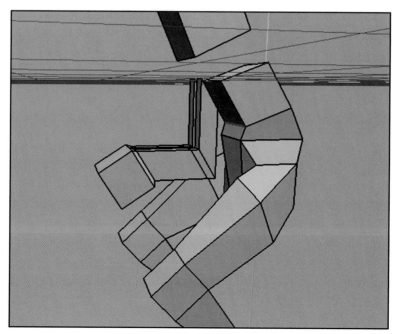

19. Change to Face Selection mode and select the front chest face. Right-click and select Plane Cut and right-click on axis Z to cut the chest into two equal-sized faces. Make sure you are in Face Selection mode. With both chest faces selected, right-click on them and pick Inset. Drag your mouse to create smaller inset chest faces and mouse click to commit your changes.

20. Select one of the new inset faces and the arm face closest to it. Right-click on them and select Bridge to connect the two. Switch to Edge Selection mode and select the top and bottom edges of the new geometry construction and move them down. Repeat this on the other arm.

21. Deselect all and switch to Face Selection mode. Select the faces making up the interior block of one elbow and move those faces outward. Repeat this on the other elbow as well, until your screen looks like Figure 5.35.

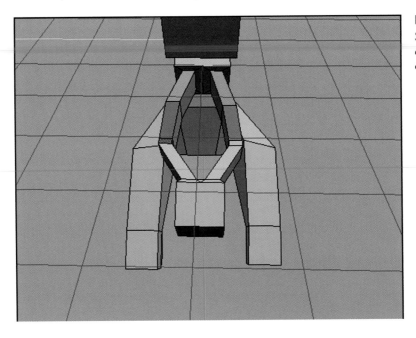

Figure 5.35
Shift the elbows outward.

22. Deselect all and then select the bottommost faces of the legs and move them up, under the thighs, rotate them along axis Z, and then extrude them. Once you've done that, scale them uniformly so they're 150 percent of their original size, as shown in Figure 5.36. Select each one individually, right-click on them, and pick Plane Cut along Axis Z to cut them in half. Select the vertices around the edges and move them incrementally, and then select the faces and rescale them so they're quite a bit larger. Look at Figure 5.37. Extrude these faces to give the feet more depth.

Figure 5.36
Start to create
the feet.

Figure 5.36
Start to create
the feet.

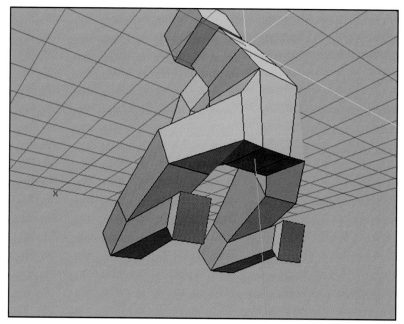

Figure 5.37
Finish the
shape of the
feet.

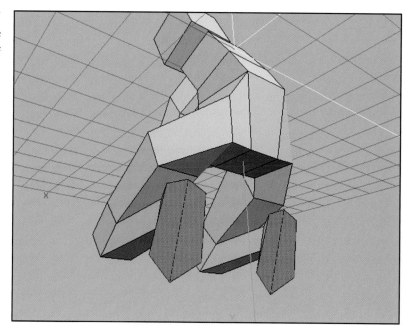

23. If you want to, pan the camera to one side. You can click-and-drag with your cursor to create a marquee to select by; whatever this marquee surrounds or touches will be selected. Use this method to select each foot independent from the rest of the model and move them closer to the center, so the toes are almost touching. This finishes the feet.

24. Select the top-most arm vertex after deselecting the rest. Right-click and choose Weld. If you receive the message "You can weld only one vertex," it's because you have more than one vertex selected. Make sure you only have the intended vertex selected before attempting a Weld. After clicking Weld, pick (left-click) the vertex you want to weld your original vertex to and right-click to execute the Weld. Do the same with the vertex on the bottom outside corner of the arm, so your screen resembles Figure 5.38. Repeat this with the arm.

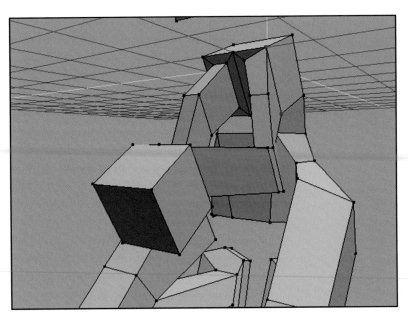

Figure 5.38
Attach the shoulder and armpit vertices to the body to make the shape more believable.

25. Select the face on the top of the body. Inset a new, smaller face and move it up axis Y. Do the same to the bottom face of the head block—use Inset and Move > Axis Y. Then move along axis X to move the inset face toward the back of the head block. With both new inset faces selected, right-click and choose Bridge to create a neck (see Figure 5.39).

Figure 5.39
Use the Bridge command to make a neck.

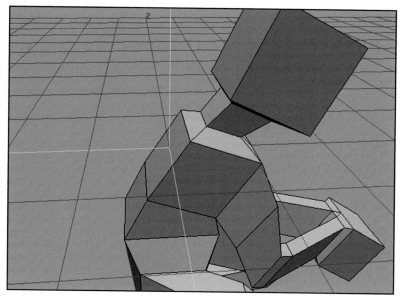

Creating the Character's Head and Hat

As you probably surmised, you are now leaving the body and moving to the head area. In this section, you'll also learn how to add a hat.

1. Select the left and right sides of the head block (where the ears would go) and inset faces and move the inset faces out along axis Z. This rounds the sides of the head. Now you have to work on the front face of the head, where the actual face would go. Select the front face, right-click, and choose Plane Cut. Right-click on the Axis Z option and, on the Slice into Equal Parts window, type in the number 4 to bisect the face into four separate but equal faces (see Figure 5.40).

2. Use the Vertex Selection mode to select and adjust the positioning of vertices around the front of the head block to shape into a letter U or shovel shape. Then select the middle two faces of the front of the head block and use Plane Cut on them. Right-click on the axis Y option and make sure to use a value of 4. When you click OK, you should see a view similar to Figure 5.41.

3. Select the top two new edges and move them down. Select the bottom two new edges and move them up, almost meeting the middle two, as shown in Figure 5.42. Then, shift the vertices of the nose and weld the two outside vertices on either side of the nose together. Tweak it until it looks more like Figure 5.43.

4. Now, move to the back of the head and create a shape for the hair. Select the back face of the head and use Plane Cut along axis Z to split it in two vertical pieces. Using your best guess, select and drag the vertices inward or outward following the outline shown in Figure 5.44 until you have a wedge of hair.

Figure 5.40
Split the face so you can alter it.

Figure 5.41
Cut the front faces so you can make a nose.

Figure 5.42
Move your new lines like so.

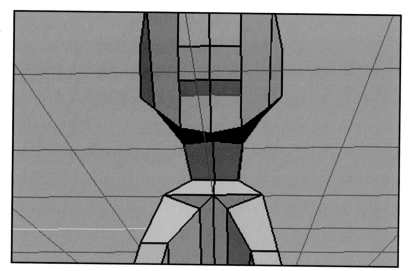

Figure 5.43
Complete the shape of the nose.

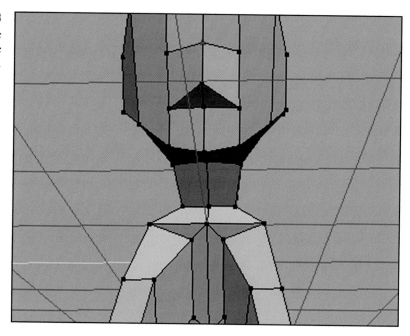

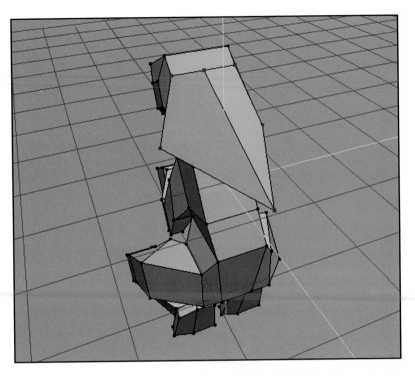

Figure 5.44
Extrude and reshape the geometry to form a chunky block for hair.

5. Move to the top of the head, where you need to add the witch's hat. Extrude the top face and scale it uniformly so it hangs wide over the top of the witch, like a hat brim would. Then, with it still selected, use Plane Cut along axis Z to split it by a value of 4. Then, in Vertex Selection mode, tweak the outline of the hat to appear more oval. Select the faces making up the top of the hat brim and extrude them upwards. Then scale them uniformly inward, so your hat appears like Figure 5.45. With the faces still selected, right-click and pick Collapse from the pop-up menu to condense the faces to a single vertex.

6. To add the conical top of the witch's hat you have to create a new shape, apart from the ones you've been working with. Add a cylinder and shrink it down so it is half as tall as it is wide. Move this cylinder to the top-center of the hat and rotate it so it is cocked at an angle and looks like it's sitting on the witch's head and coming off of the hat itself. In fact, you can sink it a quarter of the way into the hat shape to prevent gaps.

7. Extrude the top face of this cylinder three times, collapsing it to a point after the third extrusion by right-clicking and picking Collapse from the pop-up menu.

8. In Vertex Selection mode, use the click-drag marquee selection method to select each row of vertices. Make a joint in the hat one row at a time, rescale them smaller, and rotate them so the cone appears to get smaller and bent backward the farther up it you go. Use Figure 5.46 as a guideline.

Figure 5.45
Adding a hat to the top of the witch's head.

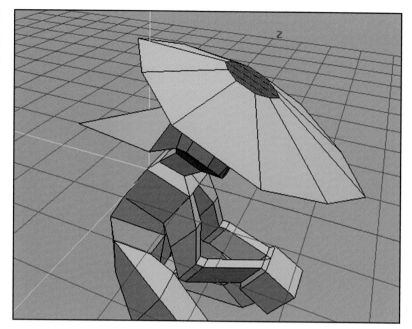

Figure 5.46
Create a sweeping conical hat top by extruding a single cylinder.

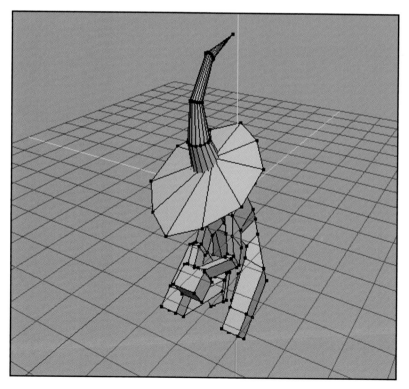

Creating the Broomstick

Feel like you're getting the hang of this program? Hopefully so, because you have one last item to add to the scene: the witch's broomstick!

1. You'll start by adding a new cylinder shape and scaling it vertically so it looks long. Add some joints just as you did with the witch's hat by extruding it, rotating it slightly, and scaling uniformly. By adding joints along the broom and not making it look perfectly straight, you will make the broom look more realistic.

2. At the bristle part of the broom, continue extruding, scaling, and rotating as you move out, out again, and then narrow in, slowly swelling out for six more joints. On the seventh joint, use the Collapse command to bring it to a point. Your broom will look different, based on how you make it, but you can use Figure 5.47 as an example.

Figure 5.47
Extrude, scale, rotate, and move each cap as you take an ordinary cylinder and make it into a broomstick.

3. Rotate the broom along axis Z and move it under the witch, so she has a hold of it in her hands and appears to sit on it. See Figure 5.48.

Figure 5.48
Finally, put the witch on her broom!

Adding Final Polish

The last thing to do before adding a texture is to tweak the vertices to get the best result out of your design. This is something usually done in the final polish stage and is a vertex-by-vertex minor adjustment. Use your best judgment.

Something I should have noticed from early on was that I built my character upside-down. To check yours, go to View > Reset View in the main menu. This forces the camera back to its default position, which is the right way to look at the scene. My character was upside down when I did so, so I had to rotate my objects to move them into correct position.

Adding Image Maps to Texture Your Character

The witch is one solid color: gray! This is a bit drab, so you might want to make her look like a real witch. You need to put some color on her.

To do so, you'll use UV mapping and a 2D paint editor. Because UV mapping is a difficult and sometimes misunderstood task, take it slow and be patient with any mistakes that happen. You might also want to read this handy Wings3D UV mapping tutorial online at www.pagodaproductions.com/tiki/Wings3D%20UV%20Mapping.html.

1. Using Object Selection mode, select the entire model. Right-click and choose Combine from the pop-up menu. This combines the object.

2. Right-click on your witch model and choose UV Mapping. An AutoUV Segmenting window opens. This window contains the object selected. In this window, change to Edge Selection mode. What you will do is take the object and cut it out along its edges in order to lay it out flat, so that you can apply a 2D image map to texture it. It's a lot like what many elementary kids do with paper in art class. Select the outermost edges around major sections you want to cut away separate (see Figure 5.49). Especially cut away the face as a separate part, almost like a mask. Other sections to cut edges for include the cone of the hat, the pole of the broomstick, the straw end of the broomstick, the legs, arms, feet, and soles of the feet, the torso, hat brim, neck and ears, and the clump where the hair goes. Along cylinders like the hat cone and broomstick, all you have to do is ring the caps and select a single line of segments down one side.

Figure 5.49
Select the edges you want to cut your UV mapping from.

3. With all these edges selected, right-click and pick Mark Edges for Cut. Then right-click and pick Continue > Unfolding. The AutoUV Segmenting window closes, and a new window, called AutoUV, opens. It shows the object unwrapped against a multicolored alphabet image map (a default way to preview image mapping).

4. Press the Spacebar to deselect all of these objects. Click on them one at a time to select and deselect them. Right-click on the unfolded UVs and see that you can move, scale, and rotate them in ways similar to 3D shapes. Get used to how you can arrange these shapes. Take care in their placement in the AutoUV window so that none overlap or cover any others. You can preview the size and layout of the multicolor pattern on the 3D model by checking the Geometry window from time to time as you work (see Figure 5.50).

5. Once you have all the unfolded UVs ready, right-click in the AutoUV window somewhere and select Create Texture. A Draw Options window will pop up. Choose a larger size than default, just because you might need the added color resolution. I picked a 1024×1024 pixel image. You can specify a color for background, but the default is set to white, and that's fine for what I'm doing. Make sure that in the Render section, however, you see a Draw Edges in the stack order; if not, add one, because this is the command that draws the edges on the texture so you can see what to paint later.

Figure 5.50
This is the
patchwork
witch, but she
won't stay that
way.

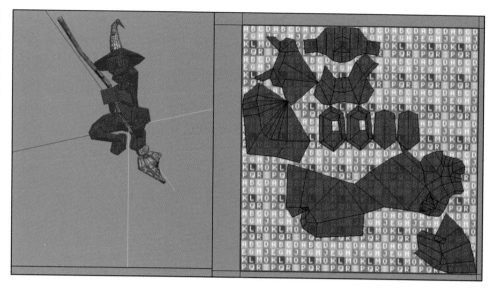

6. When you've finished, go back to your Geometry window and click Window > Outliner to bring up your Outliner window. This shows you the objects you've created and which materials are applied. The new texture appears with a checkerboard thumbnail next to it, as you can see in Figure 5.51. Right-click on the image thumbnail beneath it and choose Make External to export the texture image. Save it somewhere on your computer so you can easily find it and open it within your chosen 2D paint editor.

Figure 5.51
The Outliner
window.

7. In your paint editor, you can see the edges of your objects. Refer back to Wings3D if you forget what each section is or what it should look like. You can paint simply with basic colors if you are not an accomplished digital artist, or you can work your texturing mojo if you're more experienced. I used Photoshop; you can see the before-and-after texture image map in Figure 5.52. You might also look at the accompanying sidebar for an example of how UV map painting can be done in GIMP, which is a free 2D image editor.

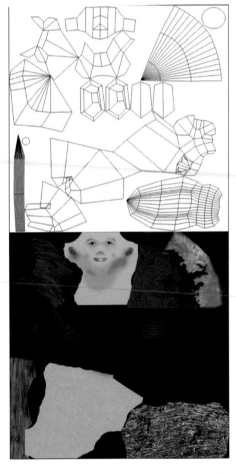

Figure 5.52
The texture map image before and after editing in Photoshop.

8. Along the way, or when you think you're done, do a Save As from your paint editing program and save your file with the same name you named your image when you performed the Make External command in Wings3D, overwriting your original (it's always nice to create a back-up first, though, just in case!). Then return to Wings3D and in the Outliner window, find your texture image map. Right-click on the image thumbnail and choose Refresh. Wings3D will find the latest changes you've made to your model and sync it. If you do so iteratively during painting, you can preview your texturing job as you go.

The finished model is shown in Figure 5.53.

Figure 5.53
Multiple angles of Fleura. This is with the soft shading preview turned on.

Using GIMP to Paint a UV Map

In this quick example, I will show you how you can use the free 2D image editor GIMP to paint UV maps for Wings3D. To download GIMP, go to www.gimp.org/downloads/.

First, create a cylinder shape in Wings3D, just to have something simple to paint. This will be an explosive barrel, one of the most clichéd game objects. After creating the cylinder (see Figure 5.54), select it, right-click, and pick UV Mapping. This opens the segmenting window, where you use Face Selection mode to select the top and bottom faces. Then switch to Edge Selection mode so the edges ringing the top and bottom faces are automatically selected. All you have to do then is select one edge running down the side of the cylinder to complete your edge selection. See Figure 5.55 to see the selections I made.

(continued)

Using GIMP to Paint a UV Map (continued)

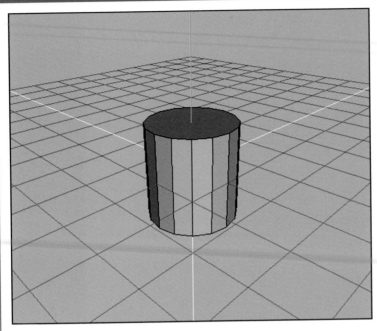

Figure 5.54
Creating a basic cylinder in Wings3D.

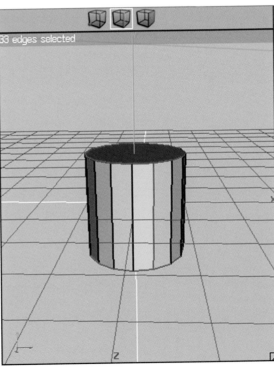

Figure 5.55
Select the edges or seams you want to cut your UV map along.

(continued)

Using GIMP to Paint a UV Map (continued)

Figure 5.56
Creating a UV map of your cylinder.

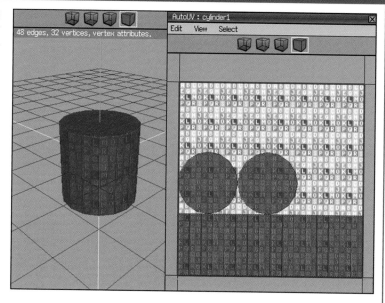

With these edges selected, right-click and pick Mark Edges for Cut and right-click again and pick Continue > Unfolding. This gives you the default UV map in the AutoUV window pane, as you see in Figure 5.56. Right-click on the UV map and pick Create Texture, and then go to Windows > Outliner to see your texture map thumbnail shown there. Select the texture name, right-click on it, and pick Make External. Then save the texture file on your desktop somewhere. After that, minimize Wings3D and open the texture file in GIMP.

The first thing you do here is look at your Layers in the floating panel on your right. Create a new layer by clicking the New Layer button (see Figure 5.57), leaving the new layer's settings to default, and then drag the new layer beneath the Background layer. Select the Background layer. Use the Layers panel Opacity slider to set the Background layer's opacity to about 60%. Then lock that layer by putting a check in the Lock checkbox.

Open your web browser and go to www.nordicfx.net/?portfolio=barrel-texture-001. Download the free barrel texture on this page. Unzip the file and open barrel_001_nordicfxnet_diffuse.jpg in GIMP. Select the whole image by pressing Ctrl/Cmd+A and copy it to by pressing Ctrl/Cmd+C. Return to your UV map image and paste into it by going to Edit > Paste As > New Layer on the main menu. This pastes the barrel side image as a new layer. Make sure this new layer is sandwiched between the background and bottom layer.

(continued)

Using GIMP to Paint a UV Map (continued)

Select the Move tool from the Toolbox (see Figure 5.58) and move your pasted image so that its bottom-right corner matches the bottom-right corner of your UV map. Use the Scale tool from the Toolbox to make the barrel side image fit the outline of the side of your cylinder and press Enter/Return to commit your changes (or click the Scale button in the Scale window).

Do the same with the barrel_lid_001_nordicfxnet_diffuse.jpg image, pasting it as a new layer and scaling it to fit the size of either the top or bottom circle on your UV map. However, this time you will duplicate the layer by pressing the Duplicate button on the Layers panel (see Figure 5.59) and use the Move tool to move your duplicate to fill the empty circle on your UV map; be sure Move the active layer is selected in your Toolbox, else you will move unwanted layer selections. The reason it is so ghostly-looking is because of the 60% opacity background layer. When you're through, right-click on the background layer and pick Delete to remove it. Your final placement should look like Figure 5.60.

(continued)

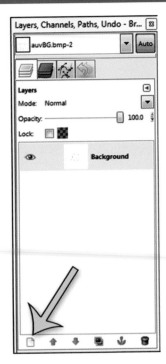

Figure 5.57
The New Layer button can be found at the bottom of the Layers panel.

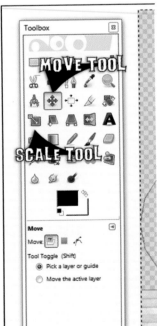

Figure 5.58
The Move and Scale tool can be found in the Toolbox.

Using GIMP to Paint a UV Map (continued)

Figure 5.59 The Duplicate button can be found at the bottom of the Layers panel.

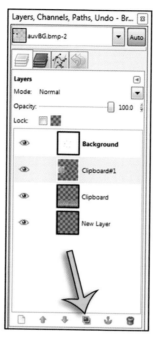

However, first add some personal touches to your barrel. In my case, as seen in Figure 5.61, I used the Text Tool to type the letters "T.N.T." and then played with the Rotate tool and filters to blend it in. I also chose the bottom layer in the Layers panel, which had previously been left empty, and went to Edit > Fill with Background Color (which was default white).

Figure 5.60 Place your texture elements like you see here.

(continued)

Using GIMP to Paint a UV Map (continued)

Figure 5.61
Personalize
your barrel as
you desire.

Save your finished image to your desktop, overwriting your original (speaking of which, it always helps to duplicate your original, renaming it with the suffix "_original" so you always have a backup copy just in case). Close GIMP and return to Wings3D. In the Outliner window, right-click the texture name and pick Refresh. Your texture should "pop" onto your 3D model, as you see in Figure 5.62.

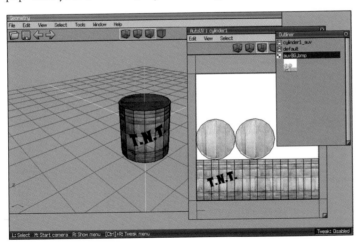

Figure 5.62
Importing the
edited UV
map.

(continued)

Using GIMP to Paint a UV Map (continued)

That should give you a basic understanding of how editing a UV map in GIMP should work. The same principle extends to Photoshop and other 2D image editors. The trick is to use layers so you can preview your outline while working on the underlying texture.

Saving and Exporting Your Model

When you are done, be sure to save your original Wings3D file in the WINGS native file format. That way, if you ever have to reopen and edit it again, which will happen when you least expect it, you have a workable file to use. Then choose one of the export options—3DS, DAE, or OBJ—any of these should translate in the FBX Converter tool just fine.

Now you need to open the FBX Converter app, import your file, preview it, and export it as an FBX file. If you get stuck using FBX Converter, refer to Autodesk's video tutorial, which is online at http://youtu.be/g9DkHAkvW1c or search YouTube for "FBX Converter" if that video or link does not work for you. The video can show you not only how to operate the application but also how to preview, compare, and do batch conversions of your FBX files.

Likewise, you might experiment with exporting 3DS, DAE, and OBJ file types from Wings3D directly into Unity. I discovered that, although I had substantial difficulties getting 3DS files to import correctly, I had no problem directly importing OBJ files I'd made in Wings3D. To import any 3D file into Unity, you can go to Assets > Import New Asset in the main menu.

You will import and start using your witch model in-game later in Chapter 7, "Mixing the Brew Together."

Custom Icons and Splash Images

The splash screen is customized in the Per-Platform Settings window, under the iOS tab. Roll out the Splash Image section to find your override options for splash screen (see Figure 5.63). Your options are limited by which version of Unity you currently own.

(continued)

Custom Icons and Splash Images (continued)

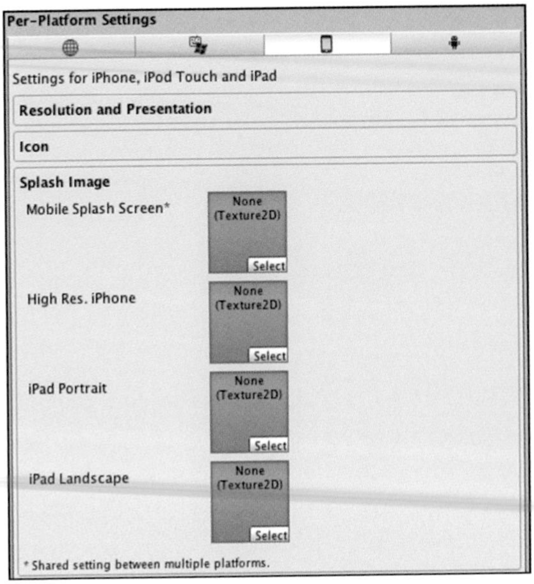

Figure 5.63
Viewing Splash
Image settings.

The standard splash screen size varies with the output device:

- 320×480 pixels for first through third generation iOS devices
- 640×960 for fourth generation iOS devices
- 1024×768 for iPad Landscape; 768×1024 for iPad Portrait

Textures that do not match these sizes are automatically resized to fit. You need only specify the ones applicable to your target output device.

Slightly less important is your game icon. You can customize which icon your project will have after it's built. This icon is a square shown in many places within your target devices to refer to and provide a link to open your game. To override the default icon for your project, go to the Icon rollout under iOS tab in Per-Platform Settings. Icons are generally texture sizes like 24×24, 56×56, and so on.

Remember to leave the Prerendered Icon option unchecked, so that iOS applies the special sheen and bevel effects to the application icon.

Even if you don't have a Pro version of Unity, there is an optional way to sneak in your game logo through scripting. Here is how you would do it:

1. In your 2D paint editor program, create an image that's 256×128 pixels. Type the name of your game and your name as its creator, if you so choose. Add some frills to it, if you like, to make it stand out more. Lastly, depending on which 2D paint editor you're using, add a glow effect that surrounds your words, so that they stand out even more. Save your image as a targa (TGA) file.

(continued)

Custom Icons and Splash Images (continued)

2. Back in Unity, import your TGA file you just created as a new texture.

3. Add a new empty GameObject and name it **MyMenu**. Then add GUITexture component to MyMenu. For the texture, select the Texture file you just imported.

4. Set the Pixel Inset values. These differ based on screen and texture sizes. For the file you've just created, for instance, the Width is 256 and the Height is 128. X and Y determine where the top-left corner of the image starts.

5. Create a new JavaScript file and name it **ControlMyMenu**. Add it as a component of the MyMenu object. Open it and enter the following script:

```
function Update () {

  if (Input.touchCount > 0 ) {

    for(var i : int = 0; i< Input.touchCount;i++) {

        var touch : Touch = Input.GetTouch(i);

        if ( touch.phase == TouchPhase.Began &&

                        guiTexture.HitTest(touch.position)) {

            guiTexture.enabled = false;

        }

      }

    }

  }
```

6. This script relies in large part on the touchscreen functionality of the iOS device. It checks to see if the player touches the game logo. If the logo has been touched, it disables the GUITexture. The reason why you need to iterate over each touch is to determine if the game has started yet and to do a test with GUITexture. If the game has started and the player touches the logo, GUITexture is disabled and the logo disappears.

What's Next?

You have learned how to set up a new Unity project, construct a basic scene to fence the player in, and model 3D assets using the Wings3D program. In addition, you've learned how to create UV map textures. These are all skills that will be important in making an iPad game.

In the next chapter, you will see how to program a networked online game using Unity. Networking is vital to making a multiplayer online game.

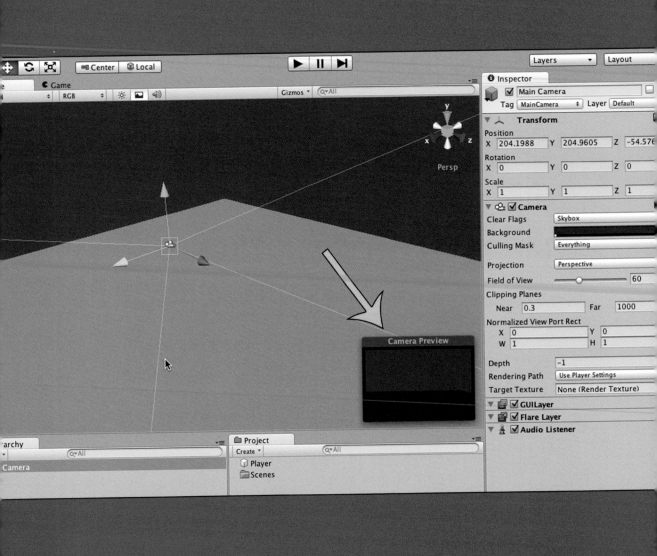

6

Crafting a Multiplayer Online Game with Unity

In this chapter, you will look at what it takes to set up a simple multiplayer application using Unity. This first attempt will be nothing fancy. In fact, you've already done harder things in Unity. Here, you'll run a test to move some basic objects over a shared network, a feat in and of itself, because it involves multiple areas of coding and getting hardware to sync up correctly. It mostly comprises a handshake going on between client (the end user device) and server (where you house your game).

This example uses the Unity components Network, NetworkView, and Direct Connect for connection between the client and the server. Unity, by the way, has the following network capabilities:

- Unity supports .NET 1.1 and 2.1.

- You can disable or enable networking in Unity by choosing Edit > Project Settings > Player > Enable/Disable Unity Networking.

- Unity networking supports WiFi, 3G, and GSM connections.

- You can connect between multiple types of Unity targets; for instance, you can connect from a desktop version of Unity to Unity iPad or from Unity Web Player (over the Internet) to Unity iPad. This means that more players can connect, from multiple versions of the same game, as long as you've set them up to talk to one another.

Running in the Background

Multiplayer games aren't a whole lot of fun to program or debug, partly because the programming is more complex than making a basic game and also because you have two concurrent instances of your game running, the server and client versions.

It helps to run the server in the Unity Editor's Game tab and run the client from your mobile device. It also helps to set your project settings for each project you want to make multiplayer, so your server won't go to sleep. So make sure your project's option to Run in Background is on. This will keep your server's game running in the background and helps to avoid unexpected server shutdown issues. You can access this option (seen in Figure 6.1) from Edit > Project Settings > Player in the Editor's main menu. Remember to do this with each new multiplayer project you create.

Player Settings (Player Settings)	
Company Name	YourCompany_tutorial
Product Name	M2H_Networking_Tutorial
Default Screen Width	1024
Default Screen Height	768
Default Web Screen Width	800
Default Web Screen Height	600
Display Resolution Dialog	Enabled
Default Is Full Screen	☐
Use Alpha In Dashboard	☐
Run In Background	☑
Capture Single Screen	☐
Always Display Watermark	☐
Resolution Dialog Banner	None (Texture 2D)
First Streamed Level With Resources	0

Figure 6.1
Toggling the Run In Background option to on.

The networking code examples in this chapter and the next are courtesy of Unity programmer Andrius Kuznecovas, author of *iPhone Multiplayer Tutorial.*

Creating a Basic Scene to Use

In this section, you start by making a plain, ordinary scene that you can use to test your code:

1. Create a new project and call it **Test**. Once your empty project appears, create a new folder in your Project tab and name it **Scenes**.

2. Make a new prefab object by going to the main menu and selecting Assets > Create > Prefab. Rename this new prefab **Player**. It will look like a white box, as shown in Figure 6.2.

Figure 6.2
Your new prefab object, called Player.

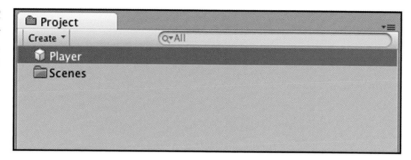

3. Create a plane in your scene by going to GameObject > Create Other > Plane. In the Inspector view, adjust the Transform > Scale options to read 100 X, 100 Y, and 100 Z. You will have to grab and move your Main Camera above the plane. This is easier than you think, because while dragging the Main Camera, the editor will show you a Camera Preview so you know you've positioned it correctly. See Figure 6.3. Rename your plane **Floor** (by typing **Floor** into the topmost field of the Inspector tab while your plane is selected).

Figure 6.3
Use the Camera Preview to make sure your positioning is correct.

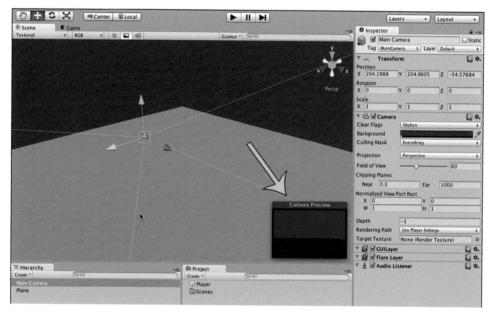

4. Create a capsule in your scene by going to GameObject > Create Other > Capsule in the main menu. It will look like a pill standing up on end. Press the F key or go to Edit > Frame Selected to zoom in so you can see your capsule, as seen in Figure 6.4.

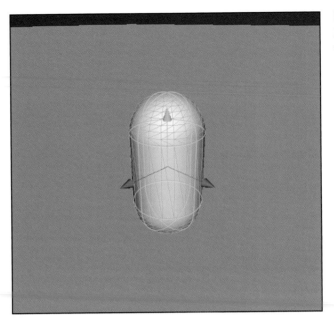

Figure 6.4
Zoom in to see
the capsule.

5. Drag your capsule from the Hierarchy view to your player prefab in the Project view. Then delete your capsule from the scene. What you have done is link the two, so now the player prefab is a capsule.

6. Create a light in your scene. Go to GameObject > Create Other > Directional Light. Light parameters need to be set to Position (0, 15, 0), Rotation (25, 0, 0), and Scale (1, 1, 1).

7. Save your scene as **MyGame** by going to File > Save Scene in the main menu. Save this scene in your Scenes folder. You should see it appear under the Scenes folder in your Project tab, as shown in Figure 6.5.

Figure 6.5
Save the scene
as MyGame
within the
Scenes folder.

Adding Scripts

Now you need to know how to create the server and client, instantiate the scene and its objects on the network, and so on. You'll start with the most important part first: creating the server and client.

1. Go to Assets > Create > JavaScript to create a new JavaScript. Unity uses two script file types, the most common one being JavaScript. If you know JavaScript already, programming Unity games will be easy. If not, you can brush up on JavaScript at www.webreference.com/javascript/reference/core_ref/contents.html (an online reference guide to core JavaScript). Name your new JavaScript **ConnectionSetupGUI**.

2. Drag this file and drop it on the Main Camera object in the Hierarchy view to connect the two. Open the file, delete everything that's there by default, and type these variables into it:

```
var remoteIP = "127.0.0.1";

var remotePort = 25000;

var listenPort = 25000;

var useNAT = false;

var yourIP = "";

var yourPort = "";
```

3. It is now time to set up the interface using Unity GUI. Unity GUI is Unity's own GUI class that allows manual positioning. Add the following script below your variables (lines starting with // are comments for you to understand what is going on inside the script):

```
function OnGUI () {

    // Check to see if you are connected to the server

    if (Network.peerType == NetworkPeerType.Disconnected)

    {

        // If you are not connected

        if (GUI.Button (new Rect(10,10,100,30),"Connect"))

        {

            Network.useNat = useNAT;

            // Connect to the server

            Network.Connect(remoteIP, remotePort);

        }
```

```
if (GUI.Button (new Rect(10,50,100,30),"Start Server"))

  {

    Network.useNat = useNAT;

    // Create a server

    Network.InitializeServer(32, listenPort);

    // Notify the objects that the level and the network is ready

    for (var go : GameObject in FindObjectsOfType(GameObject))

      {

        go.SendMessage("OnNetworkLoadedLevel",

        SendMessageOptions.DontRequireReceiver);

      }

  }

  // Fields to insert IP address and port

  remoteIP = GUI.TextField(new Rect(120,10,100,20),remoteIP);

  remotePort = parseInt(GUI.TextField(new

  Rect(230,10,40,20),remotePort.ToString()));

}

else

  {

    // Get your IP address and port

    ipaddress = Network.player.ipAddress;

    port = Network.player.port.ToString();

  GUI.Label(new Rect(140,20,250,40),"IP Address: "+ipaddress+":"+port);

    if (GUI.Button (new Rect(10,10,100,50),"Disconnect"))

      {

        // Disconnect from the server

        Network.Disconnect(200);

      }

  }

}
```

4. Finally yet importantly, add the following function to the tail of your scripts. This script is vital, because this is called whenever someone successfully connects.

```
function OnConnectedToServer () {

    // Notify your game objects that the scene and network are ready

    for (var go : GameObject in FindObjectsOfType(GameObject))

    go.SendMessage("OnNetworkLoadedLevel",

    SendMessageOptions.DontRequireReceiver);

}
```

5. You can test your server and client. But first change the game settings, similar to what you did in Chapter 5.

6. Go to File > Build Settings. Click the Add Current button to add the current scene to your project. In the Platform list, select iOS and check the Switch Platform button. Choose Player Settings and close the Build Settings window for now.

7. Go to Player Settings in the Inspector view. Make sure the iPhone/iPad tab is highlighted. Click the Resolution and Presentation bar to roll out those options. Set it to Default Orientation and Landscape Left. Roll out the options for Other Settings. Put your Bundle Identifier and Bundle Version into those fields.

8. Outside Unity, open Xcode, and then return to Unity. Go to File > Build & Run in the Unity main menu to reopen the Build Settings window.

9. Click the Build and Run button. Inside your current project directory, create a folder and name it **MyFirstNetworkGameXcode**. Save your build project as **Test** inside that new folder.

10. After the project finishes its build, the Xcode window will pop up with a project opened in it. Be sure your iPad is plugged in before selecting your project target and your iOS device. When you click the Run button, your Unity project should load within your iPad.

11. Create a server in the Unity Editor. Try to connect to the server using the IP address you find on the server screen. If everything goes according to plan, you will see a Disconnect button and your IP address will appear on both output screens. Note that both applications must be running on the same network for everything to work correctly (WiFi should be acceptable, too, depending on your iPad's settings).

Adding Network Instantiation

Now that you know the network can connect your game from server to client, you must add network instantiation to your game objects, specifically your player (sphere).

1. Select your player prefab. With it selected, go to Components > Miscellaneous > NetworkView.

2. When NetworkView appears on your player prefab, change the State Synchronization parameter to Reliable Delta Compressed. This is to show your synchronized transformations to all users, so that if your player moves two tics to the left and raises her make-believe sword, other players connected on the network can see that player moving and respond accordingly.

3. With Player still selected, go to Prefab > Component > Physics > Rigidbody. This makes the players physical, so they can't go through walls or fall through the Floor you've set up.

4. Create a new empty GameObject and name it **Spawn**. Set its parameters to Position (0, 5, 0), Rotation (0, 0, 0), and Scale (1, 1, 1). What you have done is set a place for the player to spawn at upon game load. The Player Scale is set to be 1 times their original object scale.

5. Create a new JavaScript file. Name this new file **NetInstantiate**. Open it and add the following scripts:

```
var TestPlayer : Transform;

function OnNetworkLoadedLevel () {

    // Instantiating TestPlayer when network is loaded

    Network.Instantiate(TestPlayer, transform.position, transform.rotation, 0);

  }

function OnPlayerDisconnected (player : NetworkPlayer) {

    Network.RemoveRPCs(player, 0);

    Network.DestroyPlayerObjects(player);

  }
```

6. Select your Spawn object and go to Component > Scripts > NetInstantiate in the main menu to connect the script you just made to the Spawn object. With your Spawn object still selected, change the Player parameter to Player (Transform) by selecting your player prefab from the list.

7. Test your game now, if you like. Remember to build your game, create a server, and attempt to connect to it from your iOS device. However, to see the true beauty in this, you'll set up a control script so you can make multiple players in the Test game.

8. Create a new JavaScript and name it **NewPlayer**. You'll use this script to handle the creation of new player spawn positions. Open this JavaScript file and type the following script inside it:

```
function OnGUI() {

    if(GUI.Button(new Rect(20,100,50,50),"up"))

    {

        //Clone the Player and place it at a new location,

        //so they're not right on top of one another

        GameObject.Find("Player(Clone)").transform.position

                = new Vector3(0,5,0);

    }

}
```

9. Select your Spawn object and go to Component > Scripts > NewPlayer to add your new JavaScript to your Spawn object.

10. Build your project and create a server again to test this out. Now you can see that multiple player objects can exist within the same game and can move independently. All that remains is adding actual gameplay, but these are the basics.

Other Network Solutions

So far, you used just one type of Unity networking. In the next chapter, you'll look at two other options. For now, take a look at some third-party solutions that might work better for you. You have to find the one that works consistently every time for your application.

Incorporating Third-Party Solutions

Unity's integrated network solution is not your only recourse. There are third-party options to consider, too. This book will not focus them, but you might want to consider them in the future. They include

- **SmartFox**—www.smartfoxserver.com
- **NetDog**—http://netdognetworks.com
- **Photon**—www.exitgames.com

Using SmartFox's Network Solution

SmartFox was designed specifically to target Flash Player games, but due to its popularity, it quickly gained interest among other utilities, including Java, Director, Unity, and more.

Pretend you're going to use SmartFox to expand your game into a multiplayer online game. Here is how you go about using it:

1. Start by downloading the Unity assets from SmartFox. These files are usually embedded in a free demo project. You'll also need the SmartFox server, the Pro version. At the time of this writing, you don't have to pay for a license to download it.

2. Put the files where they belong. Take the essential files out of the SmartFox demo and place them into your Unity project directory.

3. Look inside the Games > Scenes folder for the Login scene; this is the first scene that should load on game start. It contains some important GUI class data. It checks for IP and port number. Upon successful connection, it will ask the user for a nickname and proceed, by default, to load a scene named Room_1 that is in the root of your Assets folder.

4. You can change this by editing LoginGUI.cs, which can be found under Games > Scripts > Chat. The value for this IP is set to 127.0.0.1. If you are planning on hosting your server elsewhere, reference the IP here. Default port number is 3000, but it can be made to work with whatever port number you insist. If you suffer errors such as failed connection attempts, make sure your router isn't blocking that port.

5. Ensure that config.xml inside the Server folder of your SmartFox directory is set to port 3000. You can edit the XML file by opening it in Notepad or BBEdit.

6. Then check to make sure you can connect to your server. Navigate to where you installed SmartFox and run the file called start.bat. A small console window should open, and SmartFox should begin setting up the server process for you. After it finishes, it should sit idle with a line saying "Internal event received: server ready."

7. Load the Login scene found in Game > Scenes in your Unity Project tab. Go to File > Build Settings and add the current scene to the list, making sure it is set to value 0 so it loads first. Then close the Build Settings window.

8. Press Play and click the Connect button in the Login scene. If all goes well, you should be asked for a nickname. If you are unable to connect, double-check the config.xml file and your router; if you still cannot connect, you cannot continue. However, even if it accepts your nickname and you continue, you won't go anywhere, because you don't have the scene Room_1 that it defaults you to upon entry. You can change what scene it loads in the script file or by renaming your main scene Room_1. The choice is up to you.

9. In your main scene, you need to do some network instantiation things before going much further. From inside the NetworkPrefabs folder of the Project tab, drag the localPlayer object into your Hierarchy tab. This adds an FPS (first-person shooter) controller to your scene.

10. Delete the Main Camera from your Hierarchy tab, as you'll use the FPS camera instead.

11. Create an empty GameObject named **Network Controller**. Drag the NetworkController and PlayerSpawnController scripts from Game > Scripts > Network in your Project tab onto your new Network Controller object.

12. Drag the ChatController found in Games > Scripts > Chat onto the Network Controller object, too.

13. Lastly, from Network Prefabs, drag the FPS object to your Hierarchy tab.

14. Make sure your Network Controller object is still selected so that its parameters appear in the Inspector tab. Drag the localPlayer object from your Hierarchy tab and drop it under the PlayerSpawnController field of the Player Spawn Controller (Script) rollout in the Inspector tab. Set your Spawn Points to 1.

15. Drag the GUI skin from Game > Skin in the Hierarchy tab and drop it on the empty slot of the Chat Controller (Script) in the Inspector tab.

16. To add your own custom character model to the player object, drag your imported 3D asset and drop it onto the remotePlayer prefab found in the Project tab's networkPrefabs folder. Add the following scripts to the remotePlayer entity:

    ■ NetworkTransformReceive (Game > Scripts > Network)

    ■ AnimationSynchronizer (Game > Scripts > Network)

    ■ BubblePopUp (Game > Scripts > Chat)

17. Add a GUI skin to the BubblePopUp script (one can be found in Game > Skin called Skin). You will need to add three assignable animations to your custom character: Idle, Walk, and Jump.

There's more to it than that, but that's enough to get you started if you decide to use SmartFox in the future. Also, be sure to try NetDog and Photon, which are both excellent choices as well.

What's Next?

Now, if you were to take this blank slate and make it into a real game, you'd probably want to remove the sphere and make it a static mesh object instead, so your players would have something to look at besides a simple geometric pill shape. Another important upgrade would be to add an actual environment, besides the plain, ordinary floor you've made so far. And lastly, you might want to add some playability. What are the players' goals supposed to be?

But you don't have to do any of that. This was just a test to get your network application building skills up to speed. In the next chapter, you will be taking the game you've already started creating in Unity and finish building it into an online multiplayer game for the iPad.

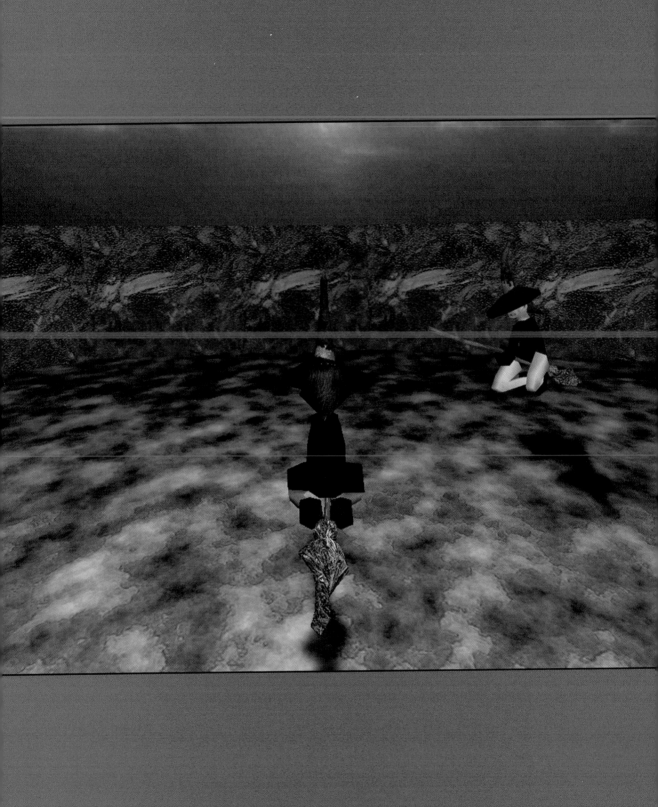

7

Mixing the Brew Together

In Chapter 5, "Crafting a Unity Game," you learned how to use the Unity application to make your video games. In Chapter 6, "Crafting a Multiplayer Online Game with Unity," you learned about clients and servers and how network instantiation worked. In this chapter, you'll put it all together and take your Unity game to the next level by making it a more refined online game. All it takes are a few tweaks and some server setup.

Also, you'll learn more Unity networking methods. You don't have to use all three. Find the one that works for your game project and strip the others away at your discretion.

Editing SorcerRun for Network Compatibility

You will make more changes here later, but it's always best to start with the basics:

1. Open your SorcerRun project and select your SorcerRun scene.

2. Import your FBX file for your witch model that you made earlier. Name this new 3D asset **witchFBX** and move it to your Hierarchy tab.

3. Add a NetworkView component by going to Component > Miscellaneous > NetworkView in the main menu.

4. Go to GameObject > Create Empty to create a new GameObject and name it **Spawn**. Set its Transform parameters to have Position (0, 30, 11), Rotation (0, 0, 0), and Scale (1, 1, 1). Later if you notice that your witch model spawns in the wrong position, adjust the Position values, and if she appears too small, adjust the Scale values; for instance, if she appears mouse-sized, you might try two times her size or setting Scale (2, 2, 2).

5. You need to give the witch some physical substance for accurate collision detection. Create two new folders: NetworkFiles for new scripts and Plugins for your C# files, which should be pre-compiled.

6. Create a C# file and name it **NetworkRigidbody**. C# is particularly useful for creating harder programmed objects for your game, which is why you should use it for rigidbody construction.

7. Move NetworkRigidbody to the Plugins folder. Open the C# file to edit it. By the way, this script is fairly universal, so you can use it anywhere you have need to for rigidbody objects.

> **Note**
>
> Lines starting with // are for comment purposes only, so you can better understand the script, and you do not have to type them. Also, every command line ends with a semicolon (;) to show the computer what to execute. If you leave a semicolon off, it will cause program errors. For further help with understanding the C# language and how it applies to Unity, go online to www.unifycommunity.com/wiki/index.php?title=CSharp_Unity_Tutorial.

```
using UnityEngine;

using System.Collections;

public class NetworkRigidbody : MonoBehaviour {

    public double m_InterpolationBackTime = 0.1;

    public double m_ExtrapolationLimit = 0.5;

    internal struct State
```

```
    {
      internal double timestamp;

      internal Vector3 pos;

      internal Vector3 velocity;

      internal Quaternion rot;

      internal Vector3 angularVelocity;

    }
// Store twenty states with "playback" information
State[] m_BufferedState = new State[20];
// Keep track of what slots are used
int m_TimestampCount;
void OnSerializeNetworkView(BitStream stream, NetworkMessageInfo info) {
    // Send data to server
    if (stream.isWriting)
      {
        Vector3 pos = rigidbody.position;

        Quaternion rot = rigidbody.rotation;

        Vector3 velocity = rigidbody.velocity;

        Vector3 angularVelocity = rigidbody.angularVelocity;

        stream.Serialize(ref pos);

        stream.Serialize(ref velocity);

        stream.Serialize(ref rot);

        stream.Serialize(ref angularVelocity);

      }
    // Read data from remote client
    else
      {
        Vector3 pos = Vector3.zero;

        Vector3 velocity = Vector3.zero;

        Quaternion rot = Quaternion.identity;

        Vector3 angularVelocity = Vector3.zero;
```

```
stream.Serialize(ref pos);

stream.Serialize(ref velocity);

stream.Serialize(ref rot);

stream.Serialize(ref angularVelocity);

// Shift the buffer sideways, deleting state 20

for (int i=m_BufferedState.Length-1;i>=1;i--)

  {

    m_BufferedState[i] = m_BufferedState[i-1];

  }

// Record current state in slot 0

State state;

state.timestamp = info.timestamp;

state.pos = pos;

state.velocity = velocity;

state.rot = rot;

state.angularVelocity = angularVelocity;

m_BufferedState[0] = state;

// Update used slot count; however, never exceed the buffer size

// Slots aren't actually freed so this just makes sure the buffer

// is filled up and that uninitialized slots aren't used.

m_TimestampCount = Mathf.Min(m_TimestampCount + 1,

m_BufferedState.Length);

// Check if states are in order; if not you can reshuffle or

// drop the out-of-order state. Nothing is done here

for (int i=0;i<m_TimestampCount-1;i++)

  {

    if (m_BufferedState[i].timestamp <

            m_BufferedState[i+1].timestamp)

      Debug.Log("State inconsistent");

  }
```

```
    }

}

// You have a window of interpolationBackTime where you play

void Update () {

    // This is the target playback time of the rigidbody

    double interpolationTime = Network.time - m_InterpolationBackTime;

    // Use interpolation if target playback time is present

    // in the buffer

    if (m_BufferedState[0].timestamp > interpolationTime)

      {

        // Go through buffer and find correct state to play back

        for (int i=0;i<m_TimestampCount;i++)

          {

            if (m_BufferedState[i].timestamp <= interpolationTime ||

                    i == m_TimestampCount-1)

              {

                State rhs = m_BufferedState[Mathf.Max(i-1, 0)];

                State lhs = m_BufferedState[i];

                double length = rhs.timestamp - lhs.timestamp;

                float t = 0.0F;

                if (length > 0.0001)

                  t = (float)((interpolationTime - lhs.timestamp) /

                    length);

                transform.localPosition = Vector3.Lerp(lhs.pos,

                                        rhs.pos, t);

                transform.localRotation = Quaternion.Slerp(lhs.rot,

                                        rhs.rot, t);

                return;

              }

          }

      }
```

```
                  // Use extrapolation

                  else

                    {

                      State latest = m_BufferedState[0];

                      float extrapolationLength = (float)(interpolationTime -
                                                          latest.timestamp);

                      if (extrapolationLength < m_ExtrapolationLimit)

                        {

                          float axisLength = extrapolationLength *
                                  latest.angularVelocity.magnitude * Mathf.Rad2Deg;

                          Quaternion angularRotation =

                            Quaternion.AngleAxis(axisLength,latest.angularVelocity);

                          rigidbody.position = latest.pos + latest.velocity *
                                  extrapolationLength;

                          rigidbody.rotation = angularRotation * latest.rot;

                          rigidbody.velocity = latest.velocity;

                          rigidbody.angularVelocity = latest.angularVelocity;

                        }

                    }

                }

          }
```

8. Save the C# file when you're finished and return to your Unity editor.

9. Select witchFBX in the Hierarchy tab (not in the Project tab). Add NetworkRigidbody.cs to your FBX file by going to Component > Scripts > NetworkRigidbody.

10. Disable the NetworkRigidbody component in the Inspector tab for now by removing the checkmark from the component. You'll enable it again later.

11. In the NetworkView pop-up, set the Observed parameter to witchFBX (NetworkRigidbody).

12. Create a new JavaScript file by going to Assets > Create > JavaScript in the main menu. Name your new JavaScript file **RigidAssign**. Assign it to your witchFBX object and open it to type the following:

```
function OnNetworkInstantiate (msg : NetworkMessageInfo) {

    if (networkView.isMine)

      {

        var _NetworkRigidbody : NetworkRigidbody =
                GetComponent("NetworkRigidbody");

        _NetworkRigidbody.enabled = false;

      }

    else

      {

        name += "Remote";

        var _NetworkRigidbody2 : NetworkRigidbody =
GetComponent("NetworkRigidbody");

        _NetworkRigidbody2.enabled = true;

      }

  }
```

13. Save your file and return to the Unity editor.

14. Create a new prefab and name it **WitchPlayer**.

15. Drag witchFBX from the Hierarchy tab and drop it onto your WitchPlayer prefab in the Project tab. Delete witchFBX from the Scene view.

16. Go to Edit > Project Settings > Tags and create a new tag named **WitchPlayer** for your WitchPlayer prefab. Select your WitchPlayer prefab again and assign the new tag to it. Click on Untagged and select WitchPlayer.

17. In the main menu, go to Assets > Create > JavaScript and name your new JavaScript file **Instantiate.js**. Drag and drop your new JavaScript file onto the Spawn object in the Hierarchy tab. It will be used to instantiate your player objects over the network. Open the JavaScript file and edit it like so:

```
var WitchPlayer : Transform;

function OnNetworkLoadedLevel () {

  // Instantiate WitchPlayer when the network is loaded

  Network.Instantiate(WitchPlayer, transform.position, transform.rotation, 0);

  }

function OnPlayerDisconnected (player : NetworkPlayer) {
```

```
// Remove player if the network is disconnected

Debug.Log("Server destroying player");

Network.RemoveRPCs(player, 0);

Network.DestroyPlayerObjects(player);

}
```

18. Select the Spawn object in your Hierarchy tab and set its WitchPlayer parameter to WitchPlayer (Transform); you'll have to select your WitchPlayer prefab from the list.

19. Select the Main Camera object in the Hierarchy. Add a new JavaScript named **SmoothFollow**; then assign it as a component of the Main Camera. This script sets up the camera actions, so the camera floats directly behind the witch object and gives the player a decent third-person view. Edit the SmoothFollow.js file to read as follows:

```
var target : Transform;

var distance : float = 10.0;

var height : float = 5.0;

var heightDamping : float = 2.0;

var rotationDamping : float = 3.0;

function LateUpdate () {

    if(GameObject.FindWithTag("WitchPlayer"))

      {

        if (!target)

        target = GameObject.FindWithTag("WitchPlayer").transform;

        // Calculate current rotation angles

        var wantedRotationAngle : float = target.eulerAngles.y;

        var wantedHeight : float = target.position.y + height;

        var currentRotationAngle : float = transform.eulerAngles.y;

        var currentHeight : float = transform.position.y;

        // Damp the rotation around the y-axis

        var dt : float = Time.deltaTime;

        currentRotationAngle = Mathf.LerpAngle (currentRotationAngle,

        wantedRotationAngle, rotationDamping * dt);

        // Damp the height
```

```
        currentHeight = Mathf.Lerp (currentHeight, wantedHeight,

                        heightDamping * dt);

        // Convert the angle into a rotation

        var currentRotation : Quaternion = Quaternion.Euler

                        (0, currentRotationAngle,0);

        // Set the position of the camera on the x-z plane to:

        // distance meters behind the target

        //transform.position = target.position;

        var pos : Vector3 = target.position - currentRotation

                * Vector3.forward * distance;

        pos.y = currentHeight;

        // Set the height of the camera

        transform.position = pos;

        // Always look at the target

        transform.LookAt (target);

    }

}
```

20. With the Main Camera object still selected in Hierarchy, add a new JavaScript file called **PlayerControls**; then assign it as a component of the Main Camera. This script uses input from an iOS device (don't let the references to iPhone fool you; it works for iPads just as well) so the players can steer the witch's actions in-game. This becomes hard to test on your Mac or PC. You can only test this properly on an iOS device or emulator. Edit the PlayerControls.js file to read as follows:

```
var turnSpeed : float = 3.0;

var maxTurnLean : float = 70.0;

var maxTilt : float = 50.0;

var sensitivity : float = 0.5;

var forwardForce : float = 5.0;

var guiSpeedElement : Transform;

var craft : GameObject;

private var normalizedSpeed : float = 0.2;

private var euler : Vector3 = Vector3.zero;
```

```
var horizontalOrientation : boolean = true;

function Awake () {

    if (horizontalOrientation)

      {

        iPhoneSettings.screenOrientation =

        iPhoneScreenOrientation.LandscapeLeft;

      }

    else

      {

        iPhoneSettings.screenOrientation =

        iPhoneScreenOrientation.Portrait;

      }

    guiSpeedElement = GameObject.Find("speed").transform;

    guiSpeedElement.position = new Vector3 (0, normalizedSpeed, 0);

  }

function FixedUpdate () {

    if(GameObject.FindWithTag("WitchPlayer"))

      {

        GameObject.FindWithTag("WitchPlayer").rigidbody.AddRelativeForce(0, 0,

                  normalizedSpeed * (forwardForce*3));

        var accelerator : Vector3 = iPhoneInput.acceleration;

        if (horizontalOrientation)

          {

            var t : float = accelerator.x;

            accelerator.x = -accelerator.y;

            accelerator.y = t;

          }

        // Rotate turn based on acceleration

        euler.y += accelerator.x * turnSpeed;

        // Since we set absolute lean position, do some extra smoothing on it

        euler.z = Mathf.Lerp(euler.z, -accelerator.x * maxTurnLean, 0.2);
```

```
        // Since we set absolute lean position, do some extra smoothing on it

        euler.x = Mathf.Lerp(euler.x, accelerator.y * maxTilt, 0.2);

        // Apply rotation and apply some smoothing

        var rot : Quaternion = Quaternion.Euler(euler);

        GameObject.FindWithTag("WitchPlayer").transform.rotation =

                Quaternion.Lerp(transform.rotation, rot, sensitivity);

        }

    }

    function Update () {

        for (var evt : iPhoneTouch in iPhoneInput.touches)

        {

            if (evt.phase == iPhoneTouchPhase.Moved)

            {

                normalizedSpeed = evt.position.y / Screen.height;

                guiSpeedElement.position = new Vector3 (0, normalizedSpeed, 0);

            }

        }

    }
```

21. With Main Camera in Hierarchy selected, go to the Player Controls script pop-up and set the following parameters: Turn Speed (3), Max Turn Lean (70), Max Tilt (50), Sensitivity (0.5), and Forward Force (2.0).

> **Note**
>
> If you happen to play-test your game level and you see that the witch model is not facing the right way or direction, this is often a mishap between the model editor where you created your 3D model, the FBX Converter, or the import into Unity. Some programs do not store Y and Z coordinates the same. The answer to fixing this is simple: Return to the 3D model editor, rotate it, and save over your original file. Then update your witchFBX asset in Unity.

This is just one example of initializing game controls. There are lots more, or you can program your own. You can find basic controls already included in the Standard Assets (Mobile) package that ships with Unity. Or you can purchase many more from GamePrefabs (www.gameprefabs.com). GamePrefabs has lots of ready-made assets, including script files, for Unity game projects.

There are two more things you must do to complete the game level's look, and they are minor cosmetic changes. Read on!

Adding a Skybox to Your Game

You can add a skybox to give your player something to look at in the sky. Skyboxes (like the one shown in Figure 7.1) are essentially wrappers you can place around your entire scene that display the vast horizons of your world. Skyboxes come with the Standard Assets package in any Unity project.

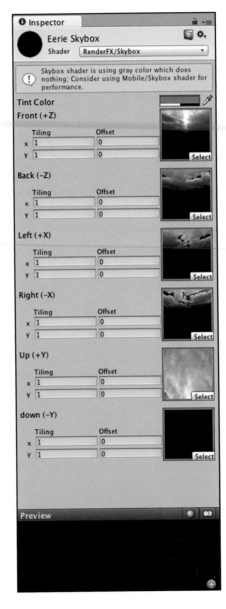

Figure 7.1
An example of a skybox.

Skyboxes render before anything else in the scene in order to give the impression of complex scenery at the horizon. Each is a virtual box of six textures, one for each primary direction.

To enable a skybox, follow these steps:

1. First of all, you must import Unity's built-in skyboxes. Right-click in your Project tab and select Import Packages > Skyboxes. Choose to import them all.

2. Once you have the skyboxes imported into your Project tab, select your Main Camera in the Hierarchy tab. Go to Component > Rendering > Skybox to add the component to the Main Camera; it will appear in the Inspector tab.

3. Drag one of the skyboxes (the shiny sphere ones, not the textures themselves) from the Project tab and drop it on the Material field of the Skybox component in the Inspector tab. I chose Eerie Skybox in this example.

4. That's it! When next you play-test your scene, you will see your skybox in action.

Adding a Ceiling to Your Game

Another thing you might notice about your level is your players can fly right out of the arena, if they so choose. To prevent this, you have to add another object on top of the walls to act as a cap or ceiling. I suggest making one from a cylinder sized to fit the area, as shown in Figure 7.2. I set my cylinder's parameters in Transform to Scale X (1000), Y (5), and Z (1000). You want the ceiling to just barely touch the tops of your walls.

Figure 7.2
In Unity, create a cylinder and cap your arena with it.

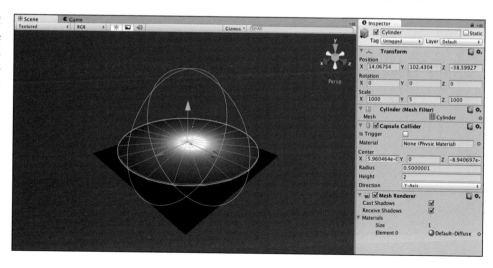

However, you don't want this object to get in the way of the player viewing the skybox, so you need to set it to transparent.

> **Caution**
>
> Using transparent objects in your game can be tricky, as there are traditional graphical programming problems that can present sorting issues in your game. For this reason, you should use transparent objects sparingly and only when they're necessary.

To set your cylinder to transparent, follow these steps:

1. Start by adding a material to your cap object. Go to Assets > Create > Material in the main menu. Once the material has been created, apply it to your object by dragging the material from the Project tab onto the selected object in the Scene view or Hierarchy tab.

2. Select your material's shader from the drop-down list in the Inspector tab. Pick Transparent > Diffuse, which makes geometry partially or fully transparent by reading the alpha channel of the main texture. In alpha, pure black (0) is completely transparent, whereas pure white (255) is completely opaque. If your main texture does not have an alpha channel, the object will appear completely opaque.

3. You don't have to add a texture map. Just set your main color to pure black (0). You should see your ceiling block vanish in the Scene view, and if you play-test your game, you'll see that you can still collide with it, even though you can't see that it's there. If your block doesn't disappear, you need to select your cylinder and, in the Inspector tab, look at the Mesh Renderer pop-up to see if your new material appears in the Materials section; if not, drag and drop your new material from the Project tab onto the field where it says "Default-Diffuse" in the Materials section to overwrite the default material. That's it!

Letting Players Shoot Bubbles

If you were to play the game now, all you'd have is a witch that flies around the level you built based on the direction she's facing. She doesn't really do anything besides that. You're now going to allow her to shoot bubbles and hit obstacles with them. This technique is used in a multiplayer shooter so players can shoot one another.

1. In Wings3D or your chosen 3D art editor, create a sphere and paint it any color you like (pink or green are great suggestions). You can apply a texture to it if you want. That's up to you. What you do want to do is make it appear transparent. Most modeling programs have a material editor allowing you shift opacity of the object's material. (In Wings3D, this is found in the Outliner window; right-click on the default material and pick Edit Material from the pop-up menu; then set the Opacity to half, or 0.5, as shown in Figure 7.3.) When you're done, save your sphere as **Bubble**. Export it to 3DS, OBJ, or DAE, and then convert it to FBX with the FBX Converter.

Figure 7.3
Set a
transparent
material on
your bubble.

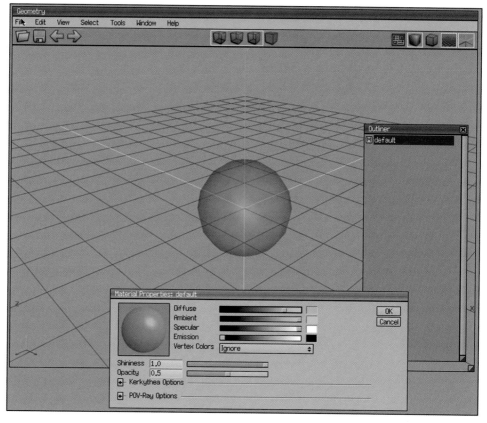

2. Import your Bubble file into Unity and name your new 3D asset **bubbleFBX**. Move it to the Hierarchy tab.

3. Create a new prefab and name it **bubblePrefab**. Attach bubbleFBX to your bubblePrefab. Then delete the bubbleFBX instance in your Scene view, if you still have one.

4. Add a new JavaScript file called **BubbleLauncher** to your Main Camera object in the Hierarchy tab. Edit your new script as follows:

```
var bubble : GameObject;

var timer : int = 0;

function FixedUpdate() {

    timer++;

 }

function Update () {

    if ((Input.GetMouseButtonDown (0))&&(timer>10))

        {
```

```
// check if WitchPlayer exists

if(GameObject.FindWithTag("WitchPlayer"))

  {

    var position : Vector3 = new Vector3(0, -0.3, 0.5) * 10.0;

    position =

      GameObject.FindWithTag("WitchPlayer").transform.TransformPoint

                           (position);

    // instantiating the bubble object

    var thisBubble : GameObject = Network.Instantiate

       (missile, position,

        GameObject.FindWithTag("WitchPlayer").

        transform.rotation,0) as GameObject;

    Physics.IgnoreCollision(thisBubble.collider,

            GameObject.FindWithTag("WitchPlayer").collider);;

    timer = 0;

  }

 }

}
```

5. Save your file and return to Unity. With Main Camera selected, go to the Inspector tab and set the Bubble parameter of the BubbleLauncher pop-up to bubblePrefab.

6. Go to Edit > Project Settings > Tags and create a new tag called **Bubble** and assign it to bubblePrefab.

7. Add a new JavaScript called **BubbleTrajectory** to your bubblePrefab and open the BubbleTrajectory script to edit it as follows:

```
var explosion : GameObject;

function OnCollisionEnter(collision : Collision) {

    if(GameObject.FindWithTag("WitchPlayer"))

      {

      if(((collision.gameObject.tag == "Untagged")||(collision.gameObject.tag

          == "WitchPlayer"))&&(collision.gameObject.tag != "Bubble"))

        {
```

```
            var contact : ContactPoint = collision.contacts[0];
            Instantiate (explosion, contact.point + (contact.normal * 5.0) ,
                              Quaternion.identity);
            if (collision.gameObject.tag == "WitchPlayer")
              {
                Instantiate (explosion, contact.point + (contact.normal * 5.0)
                            ,camera.main.transform.rotation);
                collision.gameObject.transform.position =
                        GameObject.Find("Spawn").transform.position;
              }
            Destroy (gameObject);
          }
        }
    }

function FixedUpdate () {
    if(GameObject.FindWithTag("Bubble"))
      {
        rigidbody.AddForce (transform.TransformDirection (Vector3.forward +
                              Vector3(0,0.1,0)) * 720.0);
      }
    }
}
```

8. Select the bubblePrefab prefab and set the Transform > Scale parameters to (6, 6, 6). You can resize the bubble if you think it looks too small or too large after play-testing.

Now you have the start of a great game! You can fly your witch around the level, shoot bubbles, and if you had anything to shoot at, you could blast it with bubbles. The next thing to do, then, is to give the witch some targets to shoot. In order to do that, you have to set up the game as an online game that can be played with others.

Setting Up the Server for Gameplay

What you need to do next is set up the server. In this section, you'll be adding three types of servers. Why use more than one, you might ask?

First of all, it's vital to provide as much compatibility to your end users as possible. Yes, you are only making an iPad game. That in itself is limiting your target audience. However, you could just as easily publish the game you made in Chapter 5 to the Unity web player or to another platform device. When you consider making a multiplayer online game, you want to offer your players as many options as possible so as not to exclude anybody wanting to play.

Also, you don't have to use all three methods. You could learn to use just one and be done with it. But in case you get curious or want to know how another method works, I will show you three methods upfront so you can decide which one is right for you.

Here are the three server setup methods you'll be using:

- **Master Server**—Unity's Master Server is a meeting place for games actively seeking clients and clients who want to connect to them. Its purpose is also to hide IP address and port details and perform technical tasks around network connection setup that might be otherwise difficult for developers, such as handling firewalls.

- **UDP Server**—UDP stands for User Datagram Protocol. The client sends a datagram to the server, which then processes the information and returns a response accordingly. (A *datagram* is a basic transfer unit associated with a packet-switched network and consists of header and data areas, containing source and destination addresses.) When setting up a UDP broadcast connection, you are basically setting up a server program that waits for datagrams from clients. When it receives a datagram, it returns the requested game data to the client.

- **Direct Connect**—Unity's Direct Connect is what you used in Chapter 6. It requests that the client type in the IP address of the server they are attempting to reach. Both client and server should also be on the same network when using Direct Connect.

Creating Separate Scenes for Each Server Setup

To better handle each server setup, you should create a separate scene for each. That way, you can turn them on/off as needed.

1. First, create a new scene (choose File > New Scene). Name it **ServerMenu**. Nothing has to go in this scene for now, but go ahead and save your scene. This scene will be used by the players to select server connection type.

2. Now create another new scene and save it as **ServerMaster**. This scene will be used for the Master Server.

3. Create another scene and same it as **ServerUDP**. This scene will be used for UDP broadcast connection.

4. Create one more scene. Name this one **ServerDisconnect**. You'll use this scene when the players disconnect from their chosen servers. It will clean up back-end files before establishing a new connection.

5. Add all the scenes you've just created to a new folder in your Project view. Name this folder **ServerScenes**. Then add these scenes to your project's Build Settings by going to File > Build Settings > Add Open Scene from the main menu.

6. Your scene ServerMenu must be first in the list of scenes, with a value of 0, so that it loads first whenever the player starts the game.

Editing the ServerMenu Scene

Now you must create an actual menu whereby the players choose which server connection they desire. Having some instruction as to what each connection option means would be nice, but you won't add that level of detail at this point. Consider this something you can add in your next iteration.

1. Open the ServerMenu scene.

2. Go to Assets > Create > JavaScript in the main menu to create a new JavaScript file and name it **MainMenu**.

3. Drag and drop the MainMenu script onto the Main Camera in your Hierarchy view and add the following code:

```
function OnGUI() {

    GUI.Label(new Rect((Screen.width/2)-80,
            (Screen.height/2)-130,200,50),"SELECT CONNECTION TYPE");

    GUI.Label(new Rect((Screen.width-220),(Screen.height-30),220,30),
            "SORCERRUN MULTIPLAYER DEMO");

    if(GUI.Button(new Rect((Screen.width/2)-100,
            (Screen.height/2)-100,200,50),"Connect to Master Server"))
    {
        Application.LoadLevel("ServerMaster");
    }

    if(GUI.Button(new Rect((Screen.width/2)-100,
            (Screen.height/2)-40,200,50),"Direct Connect"))
    {
        Application.LoadLevel("Sorcerrun");
    }

    if(GUI.Button(new Rect((Screen.width/2)-
            100,(Screen.height/2)+20,200,50),"Connect to UDP"))
    {
```

```
        Application.LoadLevel("ServerUDP");

    }

}
```

Editing the ServerMaster Scene

With that out of the way, you can start building the server connections. The first, and possibly most important, is the Master Server.

1. Open the ServerMaster scene.

2. Go to Assets > Create > JavaScript in the main menu to create a new JavaScript file. Name it **NetLoad**. You'll use this script for loading the SorcerRun scene and objects to the network.

3. Create a new empty GameObject and name it **ConnectionGUI**.

4. Add the NetLoad script to the ConnectionGUI object. Open it to insert the following script:

```
// Keep track of the last level prefix (which is incremented

// each time a new level loads)

private var lastLevelPrefix = 0;

function Awake () {

    DontDestroyOnLoad(this);

    networkView.group = 1;

    Application.LoadLevel("ServerDisconnect");

}

function OnGUI () {

    // When network is running then display the level SorcerRun

    if (Network.peerType != NetworkPeerType.Disconnected)

      {

        if (GUI.Button(new Rect(350,10,100,30),"SorcerRun"))

          {

            // Make sure there are no remaining remote procedure calls.

            // Then send the command to load the level.

            Network.RemoveRPCsInGroup(0);

            Network.RemoveRPCsInGroup(1);
```

```
                // Load the level with an incremented level prefix

                // (for NetworkViewID).

                networkView.RPC( "LoadLevel", RPCMode.AllBuffered, "SorcerRun",

                                    lastLevelPrefix + 1);

            }

        }

    }

@RPC

function LoadLevel (level : String, levelPrefix : int) {

    Debug.Log("Loading level " + level + " with prefix " + levelPrefix);

    lastLevelPrefix = levelPrefix;

    Network.SetSendingEnabled(0, false);

    Network.isMessageQueueRunning = false;

    // Each network view loaded from a level gets its own prefix.

    // This prevents old updates from clients leaking into

    // newly created scenes.

    Network.SetLevelPrefix(levelPrefix);

    Application.LoadLevel(level);

    yield;

    yield;

    Network.isMessageQueueRunning = true;

    // Now the level has loaded and you can start sending out data again.

    Network.SetSendingEnabled(0, true);

    // Notify the objects the level and network are ready

    var go : Transform[] = FindObjectsOfType(Transform);

    var go_len = go.length;

    for (var i=0;i<go_len;i++)

      {

        go[i].SendMessage("OnNetworkLoadedLevel",

        SendMessageOptions.DontRequireReceiver);

      }
```

```
    }

function OnDisconnectedFromServer () {

    Application.LoadLevel("ServerDisconnect");

    }

@script RequireComponent(NetworkView)
```

5. Make sure this script has added a NetworkView automatically. If it has not, you have to add NetLoad by choosing Component > Scripts > NetLoad from the main menu.

6. Create a new JavaScript file and name it **MasterServerGUI**. With this script, you will actually set up the Master Server connection. You can read more about this type of setup on Unity's website at http://unity3d.com/support/documentation/Components/net-MasterServer.html.

7. Add the MasterServerGUI JavaScript file to the ConnectionGUI object. Then open the JavaScript file to edit it, like so:

```
DontDestroyOnLoad(this);

// Your gameName must be unique to your project.

var gameName = "John Does Game";

var serverPort = 25002;

private var timeoutHostList = 0.0;

private var lastHostListRequest = -1000.0;

private var hostListRefreshTimeout = 10.0;

private var natCapable : ConnectionTesterStatus =

            ConnectionTesterStatus.Undetermined;

private var filterNATHosts = false;

private var probingPublicIP = false;

private var doneTesting = false;

private var timer : float = 0.0;

private var windowRect = Rect (Screen.width-300,0,300,100);

private var hideTest = false;

private var testMessage = "Undetermined NAT capabilities";

// Enable this only if you're not running a client on the server machine:

// MasterServer.dedicatedServer = true;

function OnFailedToConnectToMasterServer(info: NetworkConnectionError) {
```

```
    Debug.Log(info);

  }

function OnFailedToConnect(info: NetworkConnectionError) {

    Debug.Log(info);

  }

function OnGUI () {

    ShowGUI();

  }

function Awake () {

    // Start connection test

    natCapable = Network.TestConnection();

    // What kind of IP does this machine have?

    if (Network.HavePublicAddress())

      Debug.Log("This machine has a public IP address");

    else

      Debug.Log("This machine has a private IP address");

  }

function Update() {

    if (!doneTesting) {

        TestConnection();

      }

  }

function TestConnection() {

// Run a test connection, report the results, and react to the results.

    natCapable = Network.TestConnection();

    switch (natCapable) {

        case ConnectionTesterStatus.Error:

          testMessage = "Problem determining NAT capabilities";

          doneTesting = true;

          break;
```

```
case ConnectionTesterStatus.Undetermined:

  testMessage = "Undetermined NAT capabilities";

  doneTesting = false;

  break;

case ConnectionTesterStatus.PrivateIPNoNATPunchthrough:

  testMessage = "Cannot do NAT punchthrough, filtering

                  NAT-enabled hosts for client connections,"

  +" local LAN games only.";

  filterNATHosts = true;

  Network.useNat = true;

  doneTesting = true;

  break;

case ConnectionTesterStatus.PrivateIPHasNATPunchThrough:

  if (probingPublicIP)

      testMessage = "Non-connectable public IP address

                      (port "+ serverPort +"blocked),"

      +" NAT punchthrough can circumvent the firewall.";

  else

      testMessage = "NAT punchthrough capable.

                      Enabling NAT punchthrough now.";

  Network.useNat = true;

  doneTesting = true;

  break;

case ConnectionTesterStatus.PublicIPIsConnectable:

  testMessage = "Direct connection by public IP address.";

  Network.useNat = false;

  doneTesting = true;

  break;

case ConnectionTesterStatus.PublicIPPortBlocked:

  testMessage = "Non-connectable public IP address

                  (port " + serverPort +"blocked),"
```

```
                 +" running a server is impossible.";

             Network.useNat = false;

             if (!probingPublicIP)

               {

                  Debug.Log("Testing if firewall can be circumvented");

                  natCapable = Network.TestConnectionNAT();

                  probingPublicIP = true;

                  timer = Time.time + 10;

               }

             else if (Time.time > timer)

               {

                  probingPublicIP = false; // reset

                  Network.useNat = true;

                  doneTesting = true;

               }

            break;

          case ConnectionTesterStatus.PublicIPNoServerStarted:

           testMessage = "Public IP address correct but server not initialized."

             +"Server must be started to check accessibility.

                     Restart test when ready.";

            break;

          default:

            testMessage = "Error in test routine, got " + natCapable;

      }

    }

function ShowGUI() {

    if (GUI.Button (new Rect(100,10,120,30),"Retest connection"))

      {

        Debug.Log("Redoing connection test");

        probingPublicIP = false;
```

```
    doneTesting = false;

  natCapable = Network.TestConnection(true);

}

if (Network.peerType == NetworkPeerType.Disconnected)

{

  // Start a new server

  if (GUI.Button(new Rect(10,10,90,30),"Start Server"))

    {

      Network.InitializeServer(32, serverPort);

      MasterServer.updateRate = 3;

      // Below requires some unique data on your part:

      // gameName is already set for you

      // "Summary" should be a brief subject heading for your game

      // "Description" should be a short few-words tagline for your game

      MasterServer.RegisterHost(gameName, "Summary", "Description");

    }

  // Refresh host list

  if (GUI.Button(new Rect(10,40,210,30),"Refresh current server list")||

      Time.realtimeSinceStartup > lastHostListRequest +

      hostListRefreshTimeout)

    {

      MasterServer.ClearHostList();

      MasterServer.RequestHostList (gameName);

      lastHostListRequest = Time.realtimeSinceStartup;

      Debug.Log("Refresh Click");

    }

  var data : HostData[] = MasterServer.PollHostList();

  var _cnt : int = 0;

  for (var element in data)

    {
```

```
              // Hide NAT enabled games if we cannot do NAT punchthrough
          if ( !(filterNATHosts && element.useNat) )
            {
              var name = element.gameName + " " + element.connectedPlayers +
                        " / " + element.playerLimit;
              var hostInfo;
              hostInfo = "[";
              for (var host in element.ip)
                {
                  hostInfo = hostInfo + host + ":" + element.port + " ";
                }
              hostInfo = hostInfo + "]";
              if (GUI.Button
                (new Rect(20,(_cnt*50)+90,400,40),hostInfo.ToString()))
                {
                  Network.useNat = element.useNat;
                  if (Network.useNat)
                    print("Using NAT punchthrough to connect");
                  else
                    print("Connecting directly to host");
                  Network.Connect(element.ip, element.port);
                }
            }
        }
    }
else
  {
    if (GUI.Button (new Rect(10,10,90,30),"Disconnect"))
      {
        Network.Disconnect();
```

```
        MasterServer.UnregisterHost();

    }

  }

}
```

8. Now you can test your project using the Master Server. Save your project first. Then build out your project to Xcode, after first initializing Xcode, and open your project in your iPad, as you've been doing. Run the Server scene in the Unity editor.

9. Click on Connect to Master Server in the Unity editor and on your iPad.

10. Click on Start Server in the Unity editor window. The server should appear on your iPad. If not, click on Refresh Current Server List. Connect to the server from your iPad.

11. Click on the SorcerRun button in the editor or on the iPad to run the game. You're done! Disconnect and return to the Unity editor when you're through testing.

Editing the ServerUDP Scene

Now you need to create a second major server connection type, the UDP broadcast connection:

1. Open your ServerUDP scene.

2. Create a new C# file; name it **UDPConnectionGUI**. Move the UDPConnectionGUI file to the Plugins folder.

3. Create a new empty GameObject. Name this new object UDPServerInit. With your UDPServerInit object selected, go to Component > Scripts > UDPConnectionGUI to assign the script file to the UDPServerInit object.

4. Assign a NetworkView component to the UDPServerInit object and change the Observed parameter in the Inspector view to UDPServer (Transform).

5. The last thing you want to assign to the UDPServerInit object is the NetLoad Script file.

6. Once you're done assigning all of that, open the UDPConnectionGUI script file and type the following:

```
using UnityEngine;

using System.Collections;

using System.Net;

using System.Net.Sockets;

using System.Threading;

public class UDPConnectionGUI : MonoBehaviour {
```

```csharp
private UdpClient server;

private UdpClient client;

private IPEndPoint receivePoint;

private string port = "6767";

private int listenPort = 25001;

private string ip = "0.0.0.0";

private string ip_broadcast = "255.255.255.255";

private bool youServer = false;

private bool connected = false;

private string server_name = "";

private int clear_list = 0;

public void Update() {

    if(clear_list++>200)

      {

        server_name = "";

        clear_list = 0;

      }

  }

public void Start() {

    Debug.Log("Start");

    LoadClient();

  }

public void LoadClient() {

    client = new UdpClient(System.Convert.ToInt32(port));

    receivePoint =

      new IPEndPoint(IPAddress.Parse(ip),System.Convert.ToInt32(port));

    Thread startClient = new Thread(new ThreadStart(start_client));

    startClient.Start();

  }

public void start_client() {
```

```
        bool continueLoop =true;
        try
          {
            while(continueLoop)
              {
                byte[] recData = client.Receive(ref receivePoint);
                System.Text.ASCIIEncoding encode =
                       new System.Text.ASCIIEncoding();
                server_name = encode.GetString(recData);
                if(connected)
                  {
                    server_name = "";
                    client.Close();
                    break;
                  }
              }
          } catch {}
        }
    public void start_server() {
        try
          {
            while(true)
              {
                System.Text.ASCIIEncoding encode =
                       new System.Text.ASCIIEncoding();
                byte[]  sendData  =  encode.GetBytes(Network.player.
                    ipAddress.ToString());
                server.Send(sendData,sendData.Length,ip_broadcast,
                       System.Convert.ToInt32(port));
                Thread.Sleep(100);
              }
```

```
                } catch {}

        }

void OnGUI() {

    if(!youServer)

      {

          if(GUI.Button(new Rect(10,10,100,30),"Start Server"))

            {

                youServer = true;

                Network.InitializeServer(32, listenPort);

                string ipaddress = Network.player.ipAddress.ToString();

                ip = ipaddress;

                client.Close();

                server = new UdpClient(System.Convert.ToInt32(port));

                receivePoint = new

                              IPEndPoint(IPAddress.Parse(ipaddress),

                              System.Convert.ToInt32(port));

            Thread startServer = new Thread(new ThreadStart(start_server));

                startServer.Start();

            }

        if(server_name!="")

         {

            if(GUI.Button(new Rect(20,100,200,50),server_name))

              {

                 connected = true;

                 Network.Connect(server_name, listenPort);

              }

         }

      }

    else

      {
```

```
            if(GUI.Button(new Rect(10,10,100,30),"Disconnect"))

                {

                    Network.Disconnect();

                    youServer = false;

                    server.Close();

                    LoadClient();

                }

            }

        }

    }
```

7. Test this connection, if you like. Do the same thing you did before. Save your project. Then build your project to Xcode and open it within your iPad.

8. Play the ServerUDP scene in the Unity editor. Then start the server from the editor by clicking Start Server.

9. Connect to the server from the iPad when the IP address button appears. Eureka! You have completed your UDP broadcast server connection setup. When you are through testing, disconnect and close the program.

Editing the SorcerRun Scene for Direct Connect

Now you need to create the last connection type, the Direct Connect. This should seem pretty familiar if you have completed Chapter 6.

1. Open the SorcerRun scene.

2. Go to Assets > Create > JavaScript to create a new JavaScript file and name it **ConnectionGUI**.

3. Assign the ConnectionGUI JavaScript file to the Main Camera. Then open the JavaScript file and type the following:

```
var remoteIP = "127.0.0.1";

var remotePort = 25000;

var listenPort = 25000;

var useNAT = false;

var yourIP = "";

var yourPort = "";

function Awake() {
```

```
        if (FindObjectOfType(MasterServerGUI))
            this.enabled = false;
        if(FindObjectOfType(UDPConnectionGUI))
            this.enabled = false;
    }
function OnGUI () {
    if (Network.peerType == NetworkPeerType.Disconnected)
      {
        // If not connected
        if (GUI.Button (new Rect(10,10,100,30),"Connect"))
          {
            Network.useNat = useNAT;
            // Connect to the server
            Network.Connect(remoteIP, remotePort);
          }
        if (GUI.Button (new Rect(10,50,100,30),"Start Server"))
          {
            Network.useNat = useNAT;
            // Create a server
            Network.InitializeServer(32, listenPort);
            // Notify the objects the level and network are ready
            for (var go : GameObject in FindObjectsOfType(GameObject))
              {
                go.SendMessage("OnNetworkLoadedLevel",
                SendMessageOptions.DontRequireReceiver);
              }
          }
        remoteIP = GUI.TextField(new Rect(120,10,100,20),remoteIP);
        remotePort = parseInt(GUI.TextField(new
        Rect(230,10,40,20),remotePort.ToString()));
      }
```

```
      else

        {

          // If connected fetch your IP address and port number

          ipaddress = Network.player.ipAddress;

          port = Network.player.port.ToString();

         GUI.Label(new Rect(140,20,250,40),"IP Address: "+ipaddress+":"+port);

          if (GUI.Button (new Rect(10,10,100,50),"Disconnect"))

            {

              // Disconnect from the server

              Network.Disconnect(200);

            }

        }

    }

function OnConnectedToServer() {

    // Notify the objects the level and network are ready

    for (var go : GameObject in FindObjectsOfType(GameObject))

    go.SendMessage("OnNetworkLoadedLevel",

    SendMessageOptions.DontRequireReceiver);

    }

function OnDisconnectedFromServer () {

    if (this.enabled != false)

      Application.LoadLevel(Application.loadedLevel);

    else

      {

        var _NetLoad : NetLoad =

        FindObjectOfType(NetLoad);

        _NetLoad.OnDisconnectedFromServer();

      }

    }
```

4. Test your Direct Connect setup. Save your project first. Then build your game to Xcode and open it within your iPad. Open the Unity editor and go to the SorcerRun scene, if you're not already there. Play the SorcerRun scene.

5. Click on Direct Connect in the Unity editor and on your iPad. Start the server from the Unity editor by clicking Start Server.

6. On your iPad, enter the IP address shown to you on the editor's Play screen.

7. Click Connect. You should be able to launch the game successfully! When you are through testing, disconnect and close the program.

Tidying Up Your Server Connections

If any of these instructions have appeared confusing, read back through them carefully. Especially double-check your script files for code errors if you are unable to connect to a server successfully. It might also help to make sure your iPad is using the same network connection as your computer and is not behind a firewall (even though there are workarounds for those things built into the code listed in this chapter).

Now that you see how each of these connection types work, you can strip away connection types at your discretion. Find the one that works best for you, usually one that appears consistently stable and expeditious of the three, and remove the rest. To remove a connection method, simply edit the MainMenu.js script file in your ServerMenu and delete the button instance launching the server connection scene you want to delete. Then delete that scene from your project file. Test your game to make sure you've removed these items correctly.

For example, say you don't like the UDP connection and want to delete it. You simply open MainMenu.js and delete the following lines of code:

```
if(GUI.Button(new Rect((Screen.width/2)-100,(Screen.height/2)+20,200,50),"

    Connect to UDP"))

    {

        Application.LoadLevel("ServerUDP");

    }
```

If you want to, you can follow along and delete your ServerUDP scene and then test your changes to make sure you haven't fouled up anything. That's it! So find what works and what doesn't and refine your game's client/server framework as needed.

Figure 7.4
Your finished game should look something like this.

What's Next?

This concludes the making of your first action multiplayer game for the iPad. Your in-game screenshot should look similar to Figure 7.4. It is okay if your game is a little different than the one depicted.

Now you can carry on and make this game better. Consider, for example, adding a bubble splat instead of an explosion graphic or a more complex death match arena that players can explore and navigate. Or you can make your own multiplayer iPad game that has nothing to do with this concept. With the skills you've learned working in Unity and 3D art editors, you can make all kinds of different games. You can make whatever you set your mind to, with varying degrees of effort.

Join Us **LOG IN**

RocketHub BETA

HOME | LEARN MORE | EXPLORE | OPPORTUNITIES | ABOUT US | BLOG

Search Projects

Your Creative Launchpad

Welcome to the crowdfunding revolution.

Learn more about how to make creative projects fly.

FEATURED IN:
THE WALL STREET JOURNAL | **SXSW** | *American Songwriter* | The Economist | *VARIETY* | n p r

 TAKE AN OPPORTUNITY

 LAUNCH A PROJECT

Featured Opportunity:

8

What's Next

This final chapter contains no source code, and I won't even talk much about Unity or the iPad. Instead, this chapter focuses on where you can go after you've read this book. It will discuss publishing and distributing your games online.

One of the best places I have found that can give you all the indie game design tips you might need when running your own business, and a site where you can advertise your work, is at Pixel Prospector (see Figure 8.1). You can find it at www.pixelprospector.com/indie-resources/.

Figure 8.1
Pixel
Prospector.

You can find a lot of site links, including online merchant account sites, game stores, and crowd-funding sites, at Pixel Prospector. They also have business tips, so if you want to go from being a hobbyist to being an indie game entrepreneur, Pixel Prospector can help you get started.

Don't Stop Here!

It's an oft-repeated but no less true statement: Your first few games will not be worth a whole lot. Game design is a skill, and any skill requires constant practice to perfect. You would not buy a Leonardo da Vinci drawing from when he was two years old, because it would be little better than a scribble; you'd wait until he was in his prime to purchase a piece by him. The same is true of your games. The first ones you develop are going to be buggy, rough around the edges, and not worth selling to anyone. They're practice games.

This also applies to games you make when converting to new platforms or experimenting with new technologies. The initial tests won't be worthy to be played except as a goof. Your later, more refined designs, however, should definitely be seen by the public eye, and these are the ones you should market.

So after completing the tutorial project in this book, make more games. Play with the technology. Use your talents to build something of great and lasting value, something you know you can market, something you know lots of people want to play.

Getting Your Game Out There

Now that you have a game you want to share with the world, take a look at the ways and means of doing so.

Working with a Game Publisher

In the old days of game programming, developers would single-handedly copy their game code to floppy disk and shrink-wrap it to sell it to local computer stores or advertise and sell it through magazine distribution and pay-by-mail. Those days are long, long gone. With the increasing complexity of video games, publishers took on the task of distributing and marketing the games. This model has become standard operating procedure for the last couple of decades or so. However, digital content (like the apps you see on the iPad) has had an increasing influence over the game industry in recent years, in part driven by new technologies such as Xbox Live Arcade, Steam, and Apple's App Store. Now, more and more game developers are turning to self-publishing again. So why would you want to work with a publisher?

The main reason is money. If you find yourself short of funds, signing a contract with a publisher is a lot like opening a bank account. Everything is ready-made for you, and you just have to fill in the blanks. You will be given capital funds to complete your iPad game development within the limitations set by the publisher.

Another reason is technical support and testing. Publishers are eager to make sure every game they release to the public is bug-free and has polished gameplay value. If you're not used to this process, which involves the intense editorial scrutiny of a quality-assurance team, you'll be in for a surprise, and it may not always be a pleasant one. Yet it will force you to work with an attention to details that's all too often neglected or dismissed by hobbyist developers. And in the end, you know your game will be a better game for it. It will receive more favorable reviews by press and players alike and thus increase your sales.

The last reason is the street cred that having a publisher can give you, especially an established publisher that has released many respected games before. It will make you stand out in a crowd.

On the downside, however, you will give up a certain amount of creative freedom, and you need to live with it and trust the publisher to do the best job it can for you. For example, if the publisher asks you to change direction completely ("let's make this a science fiction game about biological weaponry instead of a fantasy, because our polls show that will sell more"), you should seriously listen to them and consider their suggestions. Most publishers know what they're talking about, and they also know what works and what doesn't.

It is true, unfortunately, that with iPad games being such a new and rising commodity these days, publishers have a tendency to grasp at proven feature sets over other risky but innovative ones. But in exchange for giving up your freedom, they'll reward you by marketing your iPad game along proven channels and direct feeds to review websites and the press.

So if you get the chance to cooperate with a publisher, my advice is to go for it at least once, to better understand the industry. There are several publishers you might consider approaching. For an iPad game, there are two main publishers that come to mind:

- **Chillingo**—www.chillingo.com (see Figure 8.2)

- **ngmoco**—www.ngmoco.com

Figure 8.2
Chillingo's web portal.

Crowd-Funding

If you find that you can't possibly finance the whole iPad game on your own dime but won't approach a publisher for investment, your focus immediately should shift from programming and creating game content to marketing your game. You should create only enough game content to show your game idea in one form or another, as long as it creates interest or industry buzz. A fun-to-watch teaser trailer is one option.

Remember, you are marketing something that doesn't exist yet, except in your dreams and in your mind. If you have written game design documentation and have concept art, so much the better! Then what you do is advertise your game to the world and beg for investments from other people for your project. This takes a certain amount of chutzpah and dedication on your part, because when people invest in a plan, they expect to see rewards. If they invest in your game, you cannot quit or give up on the project, change the direction of the project so it's entirely different from what you originally advertised, or use the capital funds to pay off debts not connected to the game project.

Crowd-funding, as this is called, is becoming a popular vehicle in this economy to help kick-start many motion pictures, concerts, and indie games. The basic principle is you start with something for people to look at and read about. Then you ask for them to donate to the project. Once they make donations, you can take the capital funds to produce your game. Along the way, it is ideal to show your investors your progress toward completing game production.

Here are some things you should bear in mind about crowd-funding:

- Be realistic with the amount of funds requested as well as with the production time.

- Have a decent game that is authentic, is original, and tells a story.

- Have some early gameplay footage that looks promising.

- Include great rewards for your investors.

- Show who you are and what you've already accomplished.

- Thank your supporters personally. Make them feel like stars.

On the last one, here are some ideas of rewards you could bestow on your supporters:

- Donor appears as a character in the game

- Free copy of the game soundtrack

- Free download copy of your game

- Free poster featuring your game art (made and sold on Shutterfly at www.shutterfly.com)

- Free T-shirt with the game logo on it

- Hi-res copy of cover art for the game

- Limited 3D printed sculpture of the game character (made and sold on Ponoko at www.ponoko.com)

- Limited and signed DVD-ROM version of the game and full-color manual

- List the donor's name in the credits and on the website

Here are several sites you can use to poll, promote, and beg for investments for your game project.

- **GamesPlant** (www.games-plant.com)—An innovative crowd-funding platform for indie game projects. Their slogan is "…where fans make it happen."

- **IndieGoGo** (www.indiegogo.com)—Anyone can raise money with IndieGoGo, which boasts that it has helped raise millions of dollars for over 40,000 campaigns and across 201 countries.

- **Kickstarter** (www.kickstarter.com)—Focuses on creative projects being built by collective funds, including comics, games, movies, books, and more.

- **PayPal** (https://personal.paypal.com/us/cgi-bin/marketingweb?cmd=_render-content &content_ID=marketing_us/fundraise)—Offers fun and easy fundraising tools, so you can start collecting donations from friends, family, co-workers, or anyone you can reach over the Internet.

- **Pledgie** (http://pledgie.com)—A fundraising community for all kinds of projects, including art, education, health, charity, and creative goals (which is where games would fall).

- **RocketHub** (www.rockethub.com)—A Launchpad and community site for indie artists and entrepreneurs with a vision (see Figure 8.3).

Figure 8.3
RocketHub is a community for creative individuals who want to raise funds and foster awareness of their endeavors.

Hiring Talent

If you believe in your game development and have the funds to do so, you might consider hiring freelancers to help you finish your projects. Freelance talent can include artists, programmers, writers, voice actors, sound editors, and more.

There are plenty of websites offering outsourcing services. Most of them work on the same principle. You post a job offer, which could be anything from a small task ("I need someone to create a 3D model of a warthog") to an entire project ("I need a fantasy online game programmed in under four months"). You'll receive proposals from candidates, from which you can pick one or more to accomplish the job you set. Once you've received, reviewed, and approved the work, the freelancers get paid. You'll even find some sites that can hook you up with freelancers close to where you live.

I'll refer you to ones I know have a proven track record:

- **eLance** (www.elance.com)—Helps businesses hire and manage talent and helps qualified professionals find work online.

- **Guru** (www.guru.com/pro/index.aspx)—Has over a million registered members and is the largest online marketplace for freelance talent and employers to connect.

Marketing Your Game

Once you've come up with a game, people will still need to find out about it, and this is where marketing and advertising come into play.

One effective way to increase your chances is to make a game that's very presentable and cool looking, with colorful graphics, so that it looks fun to play based on screenshots alone. With the low barrier to entry on mobile devices due to low pricing, great-looking games with little in terms of play depth will more often than not outperform and out-sell a more complex game and hours of potential game depth.

If you browse game reviews, you'll see that people give the most attention to prominent screenshots of action scenes, usually with lots going on at the same time. This has become an art form in and of itself; professional developers even develop special tools to stage scenes so they can take the best possible action screenshots. You can consider that, too. Outstanding presentation is an important buy-in when talking to publishers, looking for investors, and selling your game to players.

On the Web

The moment you begin working on a game, you should also get a website up and running, posting development notes and some work-in-progress screenshots. This should be your first step to advertising your game. If you don't have web design skills, you can hire someone who does or find a web host with built-in layout tools. Some of the most popular hosts to look at for this reason are

- **DoodleKit** (http://doodlekit.com/home)—Features everything you need to build your site, including validated code layouts, cross-browser compatibility, inter-changeable themes, and designs to personalize your site, and more.

- **Handzon Sitemaker** (www.handzon.com)—Lets you build your site using the Handzon Online site builder using a simple drag-and-drop functionality that's great for beginners.

- **Moonfruit** (www.moonfruit.com)—A great option for artists who are more comfortable using a single site editor with a vast library of backgrounds, images, templates, and animations.

- **Wix** (www.wix.com)—Easily and quickly create a free Flash website using any of their available Flash templates (see Figure 8.4).

- **Yola** (www.yola.com)—Create a fast, free site by picking a type, answering a few questions, and picking a look and feel for your site. Then you're ready for web traffic to come in.

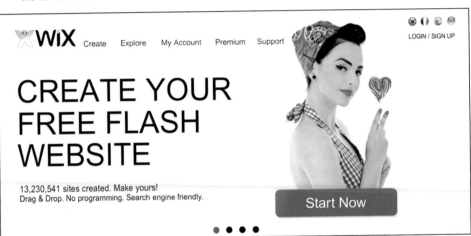

Figure 8.4
The Wix website lets you easily build Flash sites from dozens of templates.

On Social Network Sites

Besides having a website, you should also consider social network sites for promotional tools. Once you have something to tell the world, you'll be happy to reach out to dozens, hundreds, if not thousands, of your followers at once. The most popular social network sites you should consider are

- **Facebook**—www.facebook.com

- **Myspace**—www.myspace.com

- **Twitter**—twitter.com

Not only should you have a developer profile for each of these accounts, but generally you can create a profile for your game product as well; in Facebook, you can even post a flag, which is any product you recommend so that others can "like" it. Remember that, besides updating your website often, you should make regular updates to your social network profiles and especially post dev notes like "Worked on player control script for most of today" and "12% closer to completing the project." This makes your workflow transparent to people who want to follow it, which encourages press and players alike.

What you say is an important piece for marketing yourself. Your updates should be your public face, so it should be you who's talking. Don't put on a mask and try to sound like a big corporation, because you're not. Don't come across as cocky but likewise don't belittle yourself. You may be a humble beginner, but you're learning, so focus on what you've learned. And remember to put your best skills upfront and avoid writing about your weaknesses. You may not know it all, but you can learn it.

Press Releases

Build a press kit for your game. What's a press kit, you ask? A *press kit* is a collection of the best screenshots and videos from your game, bundled together with a succinct, yet punchy, description of your game, along with anything else you feel represents your game in the best light.

There are press release services specifically designed for indie game developers, and they cost a fraction of what a professional public relations (PR) agent would charge you. And writing a press release isn't that difficult, as long as you follow the rules. The following press release services tap directly into the right channels for game players and developers:

- **Game Press Release Submission Service** (www.mitorahgames.com/Submit-Game-Press-Release.html)—Their service will, for a fee, distribute your game press release to over 200 of the top games publications.

- **Games Press** (www.gamespress.com/about_howtosubmit.asp)—Whether you choose to e-mail your press release to them, register to post your own press releases as a trusted member, or build and host your website with them for maximum exposure, you can rely on Games Press to help you get the word out.

- **Indie Press Release Service** (www.gamerelease.net)—A press release distribution service for indie game developers to promote their own products. (Requires that you join the GameProducer.net Insiders group first.)

Game Reviews

Befriending a few iPhone/iPad game reviews sites prior to the launch of your game is a great way to get extra eyeballs on your game and is an effective way to build community anticipation. If you send a test built exclusively to a site or two, not only will they like you for providing them with a unique piece of content to talk about, but you'll get people reading about your game before it's even finished. The top review site to consider is Touch Arcade at www.toucharcade.com.

Selling Your Game Online

If you want to sell your indie game creations, you might consider using a payment processor like the ones listed next. They will host your games, send out the download links, and handle collection and payment management for your tax recording purposes. They become your merchant of record, so the taxes are their responsibility.

- **BMT Micro** (http://bmtmicro.com)—Offers a turnkey solution for selling your software product online.

- **eSellerate** (www.esellerate.net)—An e-commerce site that provides you the tools you need to sell, protect, and manage your software product.

- **Fastspring** (www.fastspring.com)—Helps you sell your software, games, e-books, and other digital content using a customizable hosted online store.

- **PayPal** (www.paypal.com/webapps/mpp/merchant)—You can use PayPal to accept credit cards online, track what you're paid through their online invoicing tool, and even set up a shopping cart.

- **Plimus** (http://home.plimus.com/ecommerce/)—A total service platform that helps e-commerce merchants through the use of marketing, networking, payment, affiliates, and more great tools.

How Much Should You Charge?

What price should your game go for? The answer is ambiguous.

Jeff Vogel, founder of Spiderweb Software and professional game writer, says, "Suppose the market for my retro RPGs is ten thousand people. If I charge each of them one or three dollars for a game, I go bankrupt in one year."

As most assessors know, niche products tend to cost more than those with broad markets. With indie entertainment (including video games, movies, and music), this statement does not hold true. For one thing, there's a perception that indie entertainment is cheaper-made and therefore inferior. And if you judge strictly by scope and production value, you are probably right. This still bugs me and frustrates anyone who is trying their best to sell their homemade game.

For instance, if you try selling your game in iTunes for more than a dollar, you might get some complaints about how expensive your game is.

Jeff Vogel proposes a separation of indie games based not on production value, but on content quality, into two major groups:

- The first category he calls "casual and disposable." These games are short, simple, and easy to learn. They lend themselves to quick play sessions and aren't deeply embedded in any one genre to gather enough of a following. You buy them for a small amount of money, have a bit of fun, and move on. Prices in this category should be between 99 cents and $5. Most iPad games fall into this category.

- The second indie game category Vogel calls "hardcore and deep." These games take longer to get the full experience, have a more complicated rules system, and belong to a niche market. These games, Vogel debates, should be more expensive because they are written for a small, dedicated fan base and therefore must extract more revenue to remain solvent. Prices in this category should be between $15 and $30. There are very few iPad games that actually meet this category, simply because complex games usually take up vast amounts of resources, which iPads do not bestow, and players are more accustomed to paying lower prices for iPad apps.

Of course, this forces a third category, a sort of middle-ground, of games that are short and sweet and that can be purchased for anywhere between $6 and $14. *Plants vs. Zombies* falls into this third category, and at a going iPad app price of $6.99 per download, players feel very satisfied that they get what they pay for.

To give you an indication of pricing, review the following list of iPad game prices as of March 2011:

- **Dead Space**—$6.99

- **Need for Speed Hot Pursuit**—$4.99

- **Scrabble**—$3.99

- **Sim City Deluxe**—$2.99

- **Ultimate Mortal Kombat**—$2.99

Submitting Your App to the App Store

Submitting your app to the App Store is a lengthy process the first time that you do it. You can find information about how to distribute your app to the App Store on Apple's iOS Dev Center, specifically in the Distribution section of the Provisioning Portal (see Figure 8.5). This information changes and is updated often, so you should start there, wherein you will find step-by-step instructions for the first task, which is to obtain your iOS Distribution Certificate.

Figure 8.5
The Provisioning Portal in iOS Dev Center is where you go to create Provisioning Profiles, especially for distribution purposes.

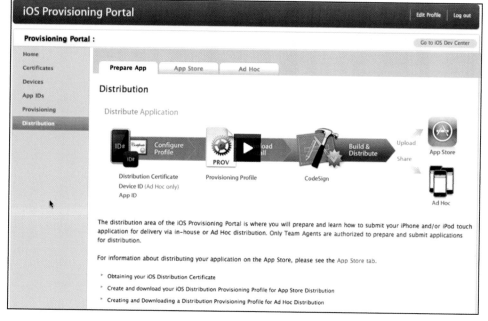

Once you have an iOS Distribution Certificate, you will have to create and download your iOS Distribution Provisioning Profile used for App Store distribution. To successfully build your app with Xcode for distribution via the App Store, you need this App Store Distribution Provisioning Profile; this is different from the Development Provisioning Profile in that Apple *only* accepts apps built with an App Store Distribution Provisioning Profile.

Creating a Distribution Provisioning Profile

This requires you to log into the iOS Dev Center as your Team Agent, which is typically the account you created when you first joined the iOS Dev Center. You can create your Distribution Provisioning Profile by following these steps:

1. Navigate to the Provisioning section of the iOS Dev Center and click on the Distribution tab. Click the New Profile button to start creating a new iOS Distribution Provisioning Profile (see Figure 8.6).

2. Make sure the App Store radio button is selected and give your profile a unique name like **App Store Provisioning Profile**. Then load your App ID. If you don't already have an App ID, which is an integral part of iOS development and is a unique 10-character string, you can create one in the App IDs section of the Provisioning Portal.

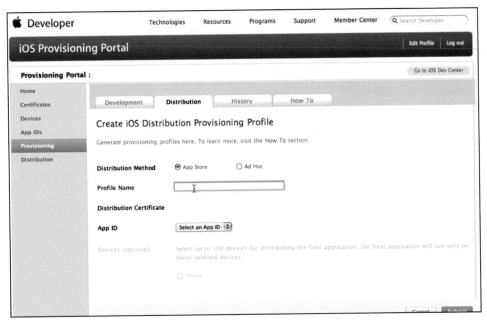

Figure 8.6
Creating a new Distribution Provisioning Profile.

3. After creating your App Store Distribution Provisioning Profile, click the Download button (see Figure 8.7).

4. Once the program is installed, open it in Xcode by double-clicking on it from whatever directory you installed it to.

Figure 8.7
Download your
App Store
Distribution
Provisioning
Profile.

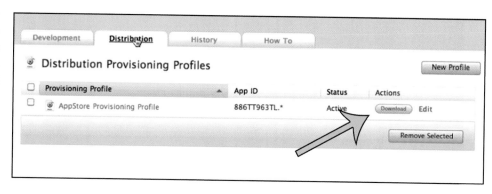

Duplicating Your Distribution for the Xcode Build

Now that you have an iOS Distribution Certificate and an App Store Distribution Provisioning Profile, you need to build your application with Xcode for distribution. Refer to the step-by-step guide in the Distribution section of iOS Dev Center's Provisioning Portal if you get lost or confused. Essentially, you have to duplicate the configuration first.

1. Go to the Unity project built out to Xcode in the Organizer. Right-click on your project file and select Get Info.

2. Go to the Configurations tab. Select Release, click the Duplicate button, and name your new copy of release **Distribution** (see Figure 8.8).

3. Go to the Build tab. Select Distribution as the active configuration from the drop-down list seen in Figure 8.9.

4. Before leaving the Build tab, scroll down to the Code Signing pop-up and find the Code Signing Identity section. Select the App Store Distribution Provisioning Profile you just created.

5. Upon closing the info pane, go to Targets, right-click on your Unity iOS device under Targets, and select Get Info.

6. In the info pane, go to the Properties tab to make sure (see Figure 8.10) Unity has included your company and product names correctly. This should correspond to the company and product name, which you can set in Unity in the Player Settings (see Figure 8.11). Close the info pane when you're done.

7. Back in Xcode's Organizer, set the active build to be Distribution. You do this through the top-left drop-down box.

Figure 8.8
Copy Release
and name it
Distribution.

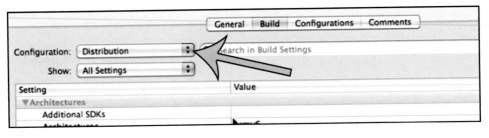

Figure 8.9
Select
Distribution as
your active
configuration.

Figure 8.10
Check your
Properties
tab to make
sure names
correspond
to your app
correctly.

Figure 8.11
Unity's Player
Settings is
where you set
your company
and product
names.

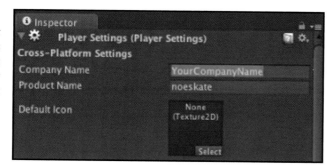

8. Then go to Build > Build in the main menu. Once your app is built, you can find it under Products. You can get to it by right-clicking on its list name and selecting Reveal in Finder.

9. At this point, you will want to zip your app up. So, in the Finder window, right-click on your app, and choose Compress. Your computer will zip the app up, and your zipped app will be ready to submit to the App Store.

Submitting the Zipped File to the App Store

To submit your app to the App Store, follow these steps:

1. Go to itunes.connect.apple.com.

2. As shown in Figure 8.12, you might need to log in again. Once in, click on Manage Your Apps to manage your applications and click on Add New App to begin (see Figure 8.13).

3. For the SKU Number that Apple requests in the form, use any unique identifier. If you have specified an App ID for this profile, add it as your Bundle ID. The Bundle ID Suffix should match the Bundle Identifier you set in Unity.

4. Next, you'll want to set the date the app will be available. You don't know for certain when Apple will approve the app, so set the Availability Date for some time in the future.

5. You can choose what pricing tier you want your app to belong to, but it's best to select Free your first time. Continue to fill out the form as accurately and fully as possible. When you get to Apple Content Descriptions (shown in Figure 8.14), be as honest as you can in describing your app content.

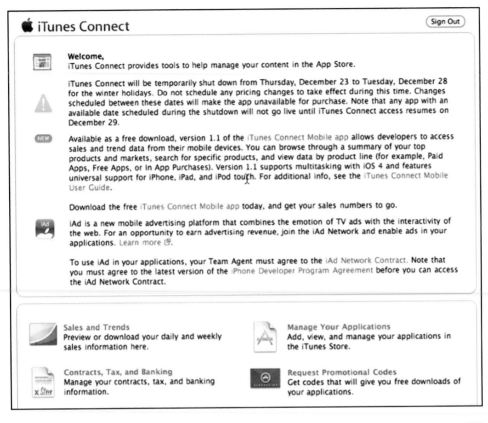

Figure 8.12
Go to iTunes Connect.

Figure 8.13
Then enter Manage Your Apps.

Tip

In filling out the submission information, be as transparent as possible to Apple, because Apple reviewers must verify your application in detail and providing the information required ahead of time will enable your application get through the review process quicker.

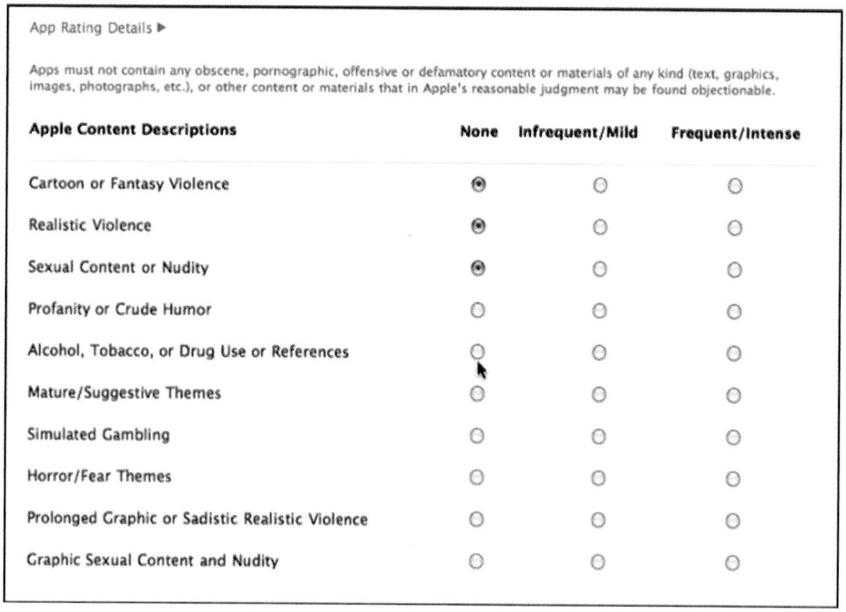

Figure 8.14

Be sure to be
as transparent
and honest as
you can when
entering
information
about your
app.

6. Next, you'll need to select a 512×512 pixel icon and iPad screenshots for your app. If you don't have these, go ahead and make them. You can use any image editing program to paint or modify an image for your icon, keeping the image size at 5123512 pixels. You can capture screenshots from in-game using Command+ Shift+4+Spacebar and clicking on the window pane you want to capture. Or you can open the Unity editor, set your Game tab to an appropriate iPad resolution, start play, and use Command+Shift+4 to click-and-drag a marquee over your targeted screen. Both methods will save a screenshot to your desktop, where you can edit, rename, and upload the images from.

7. You don't use any encryptions, so skip that section of the form. Go ahead and finish the form, saving your app description. Afterward, you can check the status of your app. The status should tell you it's waiting for app upload.

8. To upload your app, return to Xcode and navigate to and run the Application Loader (found in Utilities). Here (see Figure 8.15), you'll need to log in again with your iOS developer account. Select the app you want to upload and choose the zipped app file you built previously. Press Send and watch it upload.

9. All you have to do now is await Apple to review your app, and if successful, Apple will add it to the App Store. You can return to Manage Your Apps on iTunes Connect to check the status of your app until then. When your app appears in the App Store, you can advertise it to whomever you so choose.

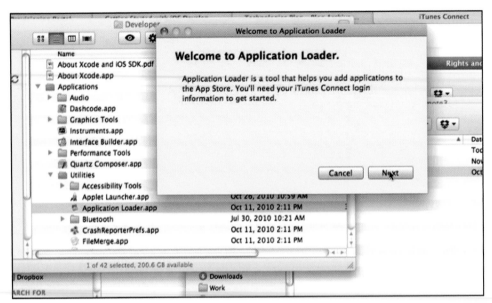

Figure 8.15
Use Xcode's
Application
Loader to
upload your
app.

Adding Your Game to Another Game Store

Besides the App Store, there are multiple online game stores that do very well. If you can get your game listed on their site, they will sell your game for you. Most of them won't publicly tell you how much of a commission they take until you've signed up with them, but the standard rate for each transaction is usually around 20 to 30 percent.

- **Beamdog** (www.beamdog.com)—A digital distribution service for PC and Mac games.

- **Desura** (www.desura.com)—A developer-driven and community-run digital distribution service for games.

- **Direct2Drive** (www.direct2drive.com)—A huge game download catalog whereby users can purchase PC and Mac games and play them over the Internet.

- **Game Tree Mac** (http://gametreemac.com/indie-mac-games/)—A distribution site for indie Mac games.

- **Gamers Gate** (www.gamersgate.com/casual/indie-games/)—A digital distribution site for PC and Mac games.

- **Get Games** (www.getgamesgo.com)—A UK-based digital distribution site for PC and Mac games.

- **Impulse** (www.impulsedriven.com/publisher/independent/)—Part of the GameStop retail store network, Impulse helps indie developers get their games in front of more people.

- **Mac Game Store** (http://macgamestore.com)—A place to advertise and sell your Mac game.

- **Steam** (http://store.steampowered.com)—A digital distribution site for PC and Mac games that has a dynamic community component running on cloud server technology (see Figure 8.16).

Figure 8.16 The Steam store allows you to download and play games, share your achievements with your friends, and play online games seamlessly through the cloud.

Appendix

Online Resources

This appendix contains the web links listed elsewhere in the book, as well as other significant sites you might find helpful during your journey building games for the iPad.

iPad game editor sites:

- **Cocos2D for iPhone**—www.cocos2d-iphone.org
- **GameSalad**—gamesalad.com/products/creator
- **iTorque**—www.garagegames.com/products/torque-2d/iphone
- **Unity iOS**—unity3d.com

Apple iOS and Unity setup sites:

- **Apple iOS Developer Center**—developer.apple.com/programs/ios
- **Apple iOS Provisioning Profiles**—developer.apple.com/iphone/manage/provisioning profiles/howto.action
- **Unity Licenses (Description)**—unity3d.com/unity/licenses/
- **Unity Shop**—https://store.unity3d.com/shop/

2D art and editor sites:

- **All CG Textures**—www.allcgtextures.com
- **Archive Textures**—www.archivetextures.net
- **Aviary Phoenix (Image Editor)**—www.aviary.com/tools/image-editor

- **Aviary Raven (Vector Editor)**—www.aviary.com/tools/vector-editor
- **CGTextures**—cgtextures.com
- **Dave Gurrea's Texture Library**—www.davegh.com
- **GIMP**—www.gimp.org
- **GoodTextures.com**—www.goodtextures.com
- **Mayang's Free Textures**—mayang.com/textures/
- **Mega-Tex High-Quality Textures**—www.mega-tex.nl/highqualitytextures/
- **MorgueFile**—www.morguefile.com
- **NOCTUA Graphics**—www.noctua-graphics.de
- **Paint.NET**—www.getpaint.net
- **Photoshop Express**—www.photoshop.com
- **Picnik**—www.picnik.com
- **Pixlr**—pixlr.com
- **Urban Textures**—www.urban-textures.com

3D art and editor sites:

- **3D Magic Models**—3dmagicmodels.com/
- **3D Media**—www.3dmedia.be/03/
- **3D Valley**—www.3dvalley.com
- **3drt**—www.3drt.com
- **3DS Models**—www.3dsmodels.com
- **Archive 3D**—archive3d.net
- **Arteria 3D**—www.arteria3d.com
- **Blender**—www.blender.org
- **Creative Crash**—www.creativecrash.com
- **DAZ3D**—developer.daz3d.com
- **Dexsoft Games**—www.dexsoft-games.com
- **FBX Converter**—images.autodesk.com/adsk/files/fbx20121_converter_mac_enu.pkg.tgz
- **Frogames**—www.frogames.net
- **GamePrefabs**—www.gameprefabs.com

- **Kator Legaz 3D Models**—www.katorlegaz.com/3d_models/
- **Nekotika**—www.nekotika.com
- **Open Game Art**—opengameart.org
- **Turbosquid**—www.turbosquid.com
- **Unity Asset Store**—unity3d.com/unity/editor/asset-store
- **Wings3D**—www.wings3d.com

Audio editors sites:

- **Audacity**—audacity.sourceforge.net
- **Aviary Myna (Audio Editor)**—www.aviary.com/tools/audio-editor
- **Aviary Roc (Music Creator)**—www.aviary.com/tools/music-creator
- **Video Game Music Archive**—www.vgmusic.com

Networking sites:

- **SmartFox**—www.smartfoxserver.com
- **NetDog**—netdognetworks.com
- **Photon**—www.exitgames.com

Game biz sites:

- **Chillingo**—www.chillingo.com
- **Gamasutra**—www.gamasutra.com
- **Game Press Release Submission Service**—www.mitorahgames.com/Submit-Game-Press-Release.html
- **Game Studies Archives**—gamestudies.org/0901/archive
- **Gamedevmap**—www.gamedevmap.com
- **Games Press**—www.gamespress.com/about_howtosubmit.asp
- **Indie Press Release Service**—www.gamerelease.net
- **ngmoco**—www.ngmoco.com
- **Pixel Prospector**—www.pixelprospector.com/indie-resources/
- **Touch Arcade**—www.toucharcade.com

Crowd-funding sites:

- **GamesPlant**—www.games-plant.com

- **IndieGoGo**—www.indiegogo.com

- **Kickstarter**—www.kickstarter.com

- **PayPal**—https://personal.paypal.com/us/cgi-bin/?cmd=_render-content&
  content_ID=marketing_us/receive_money

- **Pledgie**—pledgie.com

- **RocketHub**—www.rockethub.com

Freelance talent sites:

- **eLance**—www.elance.com

- **Guru**—www.guru.com

Web hosts and social network sites:

- **DoodleKit**—doodlekit.com/home

- **Facebook**—www.facebook.com

- **Handzon Sitemaker**—www.handzon.com

- **Moonfruit**—www.moonfruit.com

- **MySpace**—www.myspace.com

- **Twitter**—http://twitter.com

- **Wix**—www.wix.com

- **Yola**—www.yola.com

Online merchant account sites:

- **BMT Micro**—http://bmtmicro.com

- **eSellerate**—www.esellerate.net

- **Fastspring**—www.fastspring.com

- **PayPal**—https://paypal.com

- **Plimus**—http://home.plimus.com/ecommerce/

Game store sites:

- **Beamdog**—www.beamdog.com

- **Desura**—www.desura.com

- **Direct2Drive**—www.direct2drive.com

- **Game Tree Mac**—http://gametreemac.com/indie-mac-games/

- **Gamers Gate**—www.gamersgate.com/casual/indie-games/

- **Get Games**—www.getgamesgo.com

- **Impulse**—www.impulsedriven.com/publisher/independent/

- **Mac Game Store**—http://macgamestore.com

- **Steam**—http://store.steampowered.com

Glossary

This glossary defines terms used within this book and others you might encounter in your use of the software found herein.

3D graphics: Virtual realistic scenes created from 3D polygon primitives rather than flat 2D vector or bitmap images; 3D graphics have become a big potential selling point for video games and are quickly dominating the console market.

A

accelerometer: As it refers to the iPad's accelerometer, this is a device like a gyroscope that measures proper accelerations of frames of reference to detect the position of the device and provide for screen display (portrait or landscape).

action games: Games where the player's reflexes and hand-eye coordination make a difference in whether she wins or loses.

adventure games: Games that traditionally combine puzzle-solving with storytelling; what pulls the game together is an extended, often twisting narrative, calling for the player to visit different locations and encounter many different characters.

algorithm: A set of instructions, listed out step-by-step, issued to your computer, to make it do what you want it to do.

animated sprite: A 2D rectangular image that will be animated, like a character walking across the screen or a waving flag on a pole. An example, prior to animation, is shown in Figure G.1. *See also* sprite.

Figure G.1
An animated sprite of a fighter running and jumping.

antagonist: Another word for the villain or dark force at work in a story. *See also* protagonist.

App Store: As it refers to the iOS App Store, this is Apple's official online distribution platform for iPad, iPhone, and iPod Touch mobile devices.

application: In computer science terms, this can refer to any computer program with a user interface or one that has been designed for a specific task.

archetype: An original model of a person, ideal example, or a prototype after which others are copied, patterned, or emulated.

audio compression: A process that restricts the range of sound by attenuating signals exceeding a threshold.

Audio Listener: A Unity component that acts as a microphone-like device; it receives input from any given Audio Source in a scene and plays sounds through the computer speakers. For most games, it makes the most sense to attach the Audio Listener to your camera.

Audio Source: An object that plays back an audio clip in your Unity scene. If the audio clip is a 3D clip, the source is played back at a given position and will attenuate over distance. The audio can be spread out between speakers (stereo to 7.1) and morphed between 3D and 2D. This can be controlled over distance with falloff curves.

avatar: The player's character in a game; often the hero or protagonist of the game narrative. Some games offer player expression by providing avatar customization, as seen in Figure G.2.

Figure G.2
This character
customization
interface lets
you choose the
hero's skin tone
and hair color.

B

back story: The events that take place before the game narrative actually starts.

bit: The smallest measure of digital data that comes from the phrase "binary digit," and is either a 1 or a 0. *See also* byte.

bitmap: A fixed-resolution image, generally a scanned painting or drawing, composed of tiny squares of color information called pixels. *See also* pixel.

blood lock: A type of lock mechanism in which the player is trapped within a single area until he or she beats all oncoming enemies.

boss encounter: A more difficult enemy battle that represents a major shift in the game narrative.

byte: The next smallest measure of digital date and is composed of eight bits. *See also* bit.

C

cameras: Just as cameras are used in motion pictures to capture the visuals and display the story to your audience, cameras in Unity are used to display the game world to the player. You will always have at least one camera in each scene, but you can have more than one. Multiple cameras can give you a two-player split screen or create advanced custom effects. You can animate cameras or control them with physics. Practically anything you can imagine is possible with cameras.

casual gamer: A person who plays for the sheer satisfaction of the experience and is less intense about the games he or she plays (as opposed to a core gamer). *See also* core gamer.

Character Controller: A Unity component mainly used for third-person and first-person player controls that do not make use of Rigidbody physics. *See also* Rigidbody.

class: A script file defines a class in Unity. For example, the file MyScript.js defines a class called MyScript.

class function/variable: Whereas normal functions can only access functions and variables attached to their objects (unless you provide a particular reference elsewhere), class functions and variables are shared between all objects of the declared class. If one object changes a class variable, and another one reads that value, it will see the value set by the other object instead of its own personal copy.

class member: Any method, variable, or other value belonging to a class.

coin-op game: A coin-operated game, often enclosed in a box and set in an arcade.

collision detection: A method in game programming used to make sure that when objects come in contact with one another, they behave with causal response as they would in the real world.

component: The functional piece of every GameObject; you attach components to GameObjects to tell the engine what the GameObject can and cannot do. For example, without a Transform component attached to your GameObject, your GameObject wouldn't have a location in the game world.

computer graphics: Anything of a visual nature that artists create using the computer as a tool.

constructor: A constructor's job in Unity is to initialize all the members of an object in an appropriate way before anything gets a chance to call functions to it. In Unity, this functionality is handled by implementing Awake or Start events.

core gamer: A person who routinely plays lots of games and plays for the thrill of beating games (as opposed to a casual gamer). *See also* casual gamer.

core/game mechanics: The particular rules by which a player plays a specific video game.

crowd-funding: A relatively new practice of fundraising for the development of motion picture or video game production. You basically beg for donations from web users to make your product with.

crunch time: The more intense period of game production as developers get closer to deadline time, resulting in overtime and working obscene hours to hurry and get a project finished on time.

cut-scene: A brief cinematic that progresses the narrative of a video game while removing the player from gameplay temporarily. As Figure G.3 shows, cut-scenes are supposed to provide expositional information to help the player make informed decisions in-game.

Figure G.3
This cut-scene from the *Pocket RPG* iPad game reveals details the players would not otherwise know.

D-E

dialogue tree: A set of text dialogue common to RPGs, the dialogue tree has branching outcomes based on the player's choices.

Easter egg: An industry name for a secret reward in a game, something few people but core gamers will find. Game designers sometimes hide treasure chests in hard-to-reach places in the game environment, knowing casual gamers might not spot them.

edge: The straight line making up a ray between two vertices and the side of a polygon.

emotioneering: A cluster of techniques created by David Freeman; these techniques seek to evoke in gamers a breadth and depth of rich emotions to keep them engaged in playing a game.

enumeration: A group of names that refers to values. These names can be used in your scripts. You can also omit values to have the group automatically assign successive values starting from zero.

F

feng shui: The theory that people's moods and reactions can be orchestrated by the placement of objects in a room or, in the case of game design, placed on the computer screen.

fetch quest: A common type of quest whereby the player must find and return with a particular item in her possession.

file transfer protocol (FTP): A set of instructions that allows you to upload and download files to and from a web server.

flowchart: A schematic representation of an algorithm or other step-by-step process, showing each step as a box or symbol and connecting them with arrows to show their progression.

Foley sounds: Sounds that are not natural but are custom recorded to emphasize sounds as they should be heard in context.

function: The most common statement within an object-oriented programming language and a part of sequential logic.

G

game: Any activity conducted in a pretend reality that has a core component of play.

game design document: A written document that tells the team all the details of the game, including which levels and characters will be in the game and how the player controls will work.

game developer: A person who, frequently with the help of others, designs video games using specialized computer software.

game loop: A cycle of repetitive steps the player takes to win at any given game challenge.

game pace (or flow): The speed at which a player makes interactive actions and is guided through the game.

game proposal: A written document intended to knock the socks off of potential publishers and investors, and which puts a game in its very best light.

game prototype: A raw, unfinished game demo often used for business pitches.

game school: A place of higher education that offers degree or certificate programs in game development and/or design.

game testing: Often done iteratively to ensure there are no glaring mistakes; this means that testing is done every step along the way, and after a mistake is fixed, the game is tested again to make sure the fix didn't break something else.

Game view: A view rendered from your game cameras in Unity and a direct representation of your final, rendered game, as shown in Figure G.4. It is most often used for play-testing your game. *See also* Scene view.

Figure G.4
A Game view of a soldier game with the statistics information toggled on.

game world: A complete background setting for a game.

GameObject: Every object in your game is technically a GameObject, a container for information, and the information you apply to a GameObject (components) defines what the GameObject can and cannot do in-game.

gameplay: The way a game is played, especially in the way player interaction, meaningful direction, and an engaging narrative come together to entertain the player.

gimmick: A clear and representational image of an idea; in level design, gimmicks are archetypal level types that are immediately memorable for players because of their familiar themes. For example, a sewer level, mine-cart ride, or lava field are all in-game gimmicks.

global variable: A variable that is accessible from all functions. There are no true global variables in Unity's languages, but you can simulate them by having a script on an object that has easily accessible member variables.

gold master: The final edition of a game with all the bugs removed.

graphical user interface (GUI): The look of the shell extension of a game, including the windows, interactive menus, and heads-up display.

green light: When you hear this, it means that a game development group has completed the pre-production phase, the required tools and finances to begin proper game creation have been acquired, and the team is now geared up to start development in earnest.

H-J

Hierarchy tab: A Unity editor panel that contains every GameObject in the current scene. Some of these are direct instances of asset files like 3D models, and others are instances of prefabs. You can select and group together (parent) objects in the Hierarchy tab.

high-concept statement: A two-to-three sentence description of a game, akin to film/TV blurbs.

Huizinga's Magic Circle: A concept stating that artificial effects appear to have importance and are bound by a set of made-up rules while inside their circle of use.

human-machine interfacing (HMI): The way in which a person, or user, interacts with a machine or special device, such as a computer.

immersion: A key element of a game's popularity that creates addictive gameplay by submerging players in the entertainment form; with immersion, you get so engrossed in a game that you forget it's a game.

inheritance: In Unity, all classes have a base class that gives them some properties and methods. For example, your scripts are derived from base class `MonoBehavior` and inherit methods like `GetComponent`, events like `Update`, and properties like `enabled` from it.

Inspector tab: A Unity editor panel used to view and edit properties of many different types, including the components of selected GameObjects.

instantiation: One difficult subject in networking games online is ownership of an object. Who controls what object? Network instantiation determines the logic for you.

Internet: A global network of networks.

iOS: The operating system developed by Apple for its mobile technology, including the iPad, iPod Touch, and iPhone.

JavaScript: A prototype-based C-style scripting language that is dynamic and supports object-oriented programming styles.

L

levels: Basic units, like chapters in a book, used for subdividing and organizing progress through a game.

lights: How you illuminate your scenes in Unity. While meshes and textures define the shape and look of a scene, a light defines the color and mood of your 3D environment. You'll likely work with lots of different sized and colored lights in each scene. Placing them and making them work together requires practice, but the results can be amazing.

local area network (LAN): A local infrastructure system of multiple computers connected over a single network; are often used to support multiplayer gaming.

lock mechanism: A structure that prevents the player's access to some area or reward in a game until the moment when the player beats the challenge and unlocks the next area or recovers the reward.

ludology: The academic study of games for the features that are distinctly related to play, including rules and simulation.

M

massively multiplayer online game (MMO): Any game played over a network or the Internet that can be played by many gamers simultaneously.

massively multiplayer online role-playing game (MMORPG): A genre role-playing game played over a network or the Internet that can be played by many gamers simultaneously. *See also* multi-user dungeon (MUD) and role-playing games (RPGs).

Master Server: Similar to a game lobby where servers can advertise their presence to clients; the Master Server is also a solution to enabling communication from behind a firewall or home network. When needed to, it makes it possible to use a technique called NAT punch-through to make sure your players can always connect with each other.

materials: Define which textures to use for rendering, which colors to use when rendering, and other assets, such as a cubemap, required by the shader for rendering.

member variable: A variable that is attached to an object of a class. In JavaScript, these are variables declared outside of functions.

meshes: 3D assets consisting of triangles with textures applied over them. Meshes in Unity are rendered with renderer components. Meshes make up a large part of your 3D worlds. You don't build meshes in Unity, however, but in a 3D art application, such as Maya, Cinema 4D, 3D Studio Max, Modo, Lightwave, or Blender. Unity prefers FBX files but can also read DAE, 3DS, DXF, and OBJ file types.

method: A function attached to an object of a class. This function has access to any of the other methods and member variables of the class. All of your JavaScript functions are considered methods as you can't create standalone functions in Unity.

milestone: A realistic step of production that can be accomplished on a game production timeline.

MonoBehavior: The master class that all (normal) Unity scripts are derived from. It gives you easy access to common components on the same GameObject as the script. It also provides a set of events automatically called within your script.

monomyth: Also known as the "hero's journey," this is a pattern of legendary steps that follow one another in a chain of events common among most myths, fairy tales, and stories.

motion cycle: A looping animation of a character or other object going frame-by-frame through its motions.

moveset: A list of animations documenting a character's movements for a game, often described in the character section of a game design document.

multi-user dungeon (MUD): One of the first types of online multiplayer role-playing games, MUDs are often text-based games. Popular examples include *Age of Chaos* and *Dark Prophecy*. *See also* massively multiplayer online role-playing game (MMORPG).

N-O

NetworkView: A Unity component you use to share data across a network. They are extremely important to the correct functioning of online games.

non-player characters (NPCs): Characters not controlled by the player but by the computer artificial intelligence. Figure G.5 shows some NPCs.

Figure G.5
NPCs you might see in a fantasy role-playing game (RPG).

object: An object does not necessarily have to be a GameObject; rather, it is a particular instance of item from your Project tab and may include static meshes, classes, scripts, and materials.

Objective-C: A simple object-oriented programming language used primarily on Apple's Mac OS X and iOS operating systems.

online communities: Websites designed to foster communication and social networking; they've been compared to bulletin boards, social clubs, and schoolyard.

orthographic view: A 3D term meaning that you can see only two of three dimensions at one time. *See also* perspective view.

P

parallax scrolling: A method in 2D side-scrolling games whereby dissimilar planes of graphics scroll by at unlike rates of speed depending on their perceived relation to the viewer, used to create the illusion of depth. *See also* side-scrolling.

particles: 2D images rendered in 3D space (see Figure G.6). They are primarily used for effects such as smoke, fire, water droplets, snow, or falling leaves. A particle system is made up of three separate components: a particle emitter, a particle animator, and a particle renderer. You use a particle emitter and renderer together to create static particles and the particle animator to move those particles in different directions and change their colors.

Figure G.6
This particle
system
simulates fire.

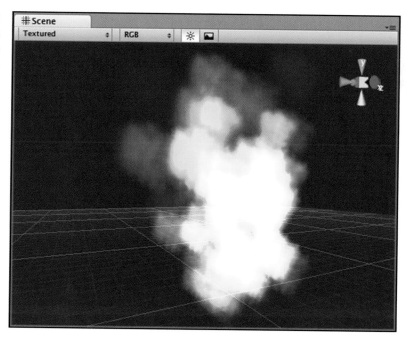

perspective view: A 3D term meaning that you can see more than two dimensions at the same time. *See also* orthographic view.

physics: Unity has NVIDIA PhysX physics engine built-in. This allows for unique emergent behavior that is actually pretty cool. To put an object under physics control so it acts just like a "real" object would, you just add a Rigidbody component to it. When you do this, the object will be affected by gravity and will collide with other objects in your scene.

pick-your-path game book: A book in which the narrative is not linear but branching, and the reader must make decisions that carry the story forward to multiple possible endings.

pixel: A tiny square of color, one of many that make up a bitmap, that has a dot of red, green, and blue information in it that sets the color tone for that square. *See also* bitmap.

play: Any grouping of recreational human activities, often centered on having fun.

player interaction: A complex human-computer interface where the player gives her input or feedback to the game engine and the engine responds proportionally; this interaction can reside on mouse and keyboard or on a handheld game controller, but it comes in the form of key or button combinations and directs the course of action in game.

plot: The sequence of events that take place over time, from beginning to end.

polygon: A closed plane figure bounded by three or more straight edges.

portfolio: A list, often visual in nature, of what a designer has accomplished in his or her career thus far.

post-production phase (of game development): During this development phase, testing, quality assurance, and bug-fixing are initiated, followed by a public relations campaign to get a game noticed by its target audience. *See also* production phase, pre-production phase.

prefab: A type of asset within Unity that is a reusable GameObject stored in your Project tab. Prefabs can be inserted into any number of scenes, multiple times per scene. When you add a prefab to a scene, you are creating an instance of it. All prefab instances are linked to the original prefab and are essentially clones of it, so if you edit your prefab, you will simultaneously update all existing instances in your scenes.

pre-production phase (of game development): The phase that takes place before designers ever get their tools out and get started. *See also* post-production phase, production phase.

private: Member variables or functions that are accessible only from the class they belong to are considered private. In Unity's JavaScript, you use the private keyword to stop member variables from appearing in the Inspector tab, as well as to prevent other scripts from tampering with these values. *See also* public.

production phase (of game development): During this phase of development, the artists design the assets, characters, and environments on their computers, the writers set out dialogue and scripted events, the programmers code the controls and character behaviors, and the leaders make sure no one walks off the job. *See also* post-production phase, pre-production phase.

Project tab: A Unity editor panel used to store all assets making up your current game project, including scenes, 3D models, textures, audio files, and prefabs. If you right-click on any asset in the Project tab, you can choose Reveal in Finder (or Reveal in Explorer for Windows users) to actually see the asset file in your file system.

property: Behaves similar to a member variable but might also have a function attached to it to handle the data in a particular way. JavaScript doesn't use properties, but the Unity API does; anything, such as `enabled`, which lets you get or set a value, is a property.

protagonist: Another word for the central character or hero of a story. *See also* antagonist.

public: These are member variables or functions that are accessible to any class. In C# and Boo, you have to explicitly code a variable as public to make member variables appear in the Inspector tab. In JavaScript, all member variables are made public automatically. *See also* private.

Q-R

quality assurance (QA): Apart from game testing and beta testing, testing must be done to look at the game as a whole and check it against the initial concept for consistency.

quests: A special set of challenges that takes place in both stories and games, thus linking narrative and play.

ramping: A game gets increasingly harder the longer someone plays it.

randomization: A method by which a computerized system can change the way in which a game is played.

rapid iterative prototyping: A production method where designers test ideas daily, see what's working and what's not, and abandon hurdles that are too difficult to get over.

reactive environments: The game world responds to the player in logical and meaningful ways that help immerse the player in that game world.

remote procedure call (RPC): A method of calling a function on a remote machine. This may be a client calling a function on the server or the server calling a function on all or specific clients.

replayability: The "sweet spot" for game designers, where the player doesn't play the game only once through but wants to play the game repeatedly, either motivated by the need to excel or by the sheer excitement that comes from experiencing a compelling narrative.

Rigidbody: Program controls that simulate physical objects they are attached to in Unity. You use Rigidbody controls for things the player can push around, such as crates and barrels. You can also use Rigidbody scripts to bring vehicles to life. *See also* Character Controller.

rogue-like game: Any game in which the world is not persistent but changes every time the game is played.

role: The part a player plays in a game, especially a role-playing game, often reflected as an avatar.

role-playing games (RPGs): Games in which the main goal is for the players to gain enough experience or treasure for completing missions and beating monsters to make their near-infinitely customizable characters stronger. *See also* massively multiplayer online role-playing game (MMORPG).

runtime class: A class that's relevant to the game rather than the editor and usually runs during the gameplay.

S

scene: In Unity a complete 3D environment by itself. You can add more than one scene to a game and create pass-through connections for players between them, and then the scene becomes synonymous with a game level. You place and move objects in your scene through Unity's Scene view.

Scene Gizmo: The gray, red, green, and blue compass in the upper-right corner of the Scene view that is used to display the scene camera's current orientation and allows you to quickly modify the view angle. See Figure G.7.

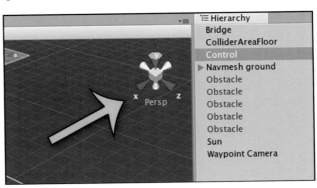

Figure G.7
The Scene Gizmo helps you steer your view of the Scene view.

Scene view: Your interactive sandbox in Unity. You use the Scene view to select and position environments, the player, the camera, enemies, lights, and all other GameObjects as they will appear in your game. Maneuvering and manipulating objects within the Scene view is one of the most important functions in the Unity editor. *See also* Game view.

scrum: A relatively new project management process that helps keep game teams organized and progressing towards product completion in a timely manner. Using this iterative, incremental process, developers check their progress at fairly regular intervals and have a playable work-in-progress early on.

search engine: A program that searches the web for specific keywords and returns a list of documents in which those keywords are found.

shader: All rendering done within Unity is done with shaders, which are small scripts that let you configure how the graphics hardware is set up for rendering objects. Unity ships with more than sixty built-in shaders, but you can extend this by making more yourself.

shadows: All types of lights used in Unity support shadows. Using shadows can be as simple as choosing Hard Shadows or Soft Shadows on a light object. Unity Pro makes it possible to use real-time shadows on any light object. Curiously enough, though, the best shadows are non-real-time ones. Computing shadows offline always results in better quality and performance than displaying them in real time.

shooters: Games in which the characters are equipped with firearms and focus on fast-paced movement, shooting targets, and blowing up nearly everything in sight.

side-scrolling: A visual technique in games where the player's character starts on the left side of the screen (usually) and the player navigates the character to the right side of the screen; the invisible camera that the game is viewed from is locked onto the player character, following its movements. *See also* parallax scrolling.

sound effects (SFX): Short recorded sounds that are interjected relative to visual effects to enhance the whole experience and give aural clues to what's happening onscreen.

spawning: Making an object appear in-game at a specific or random location, often referring to the dynamic generation of enemies or pick-up items.

sprint: A short iteration in project development using the scrum method.

sprite: A 2D rectangular bitmap image that makes up most of the visual elements in a 2D game. *See also* animated sprite.

state synchronization: A method of regularly updating a specific set of data across two or more game instances running on a network.

static sprite: A single sprite image that consists of a non-animating character, object, or element.

strategy games: Mental-challenge-based games, where the players build an empire, fortress, realm, world, or other construct, manage the resources therein, and prepare against inevitable problems like decay, hardship, economic depravity, revolution, or foreign invaders. See Figure G.8.

Figure G.8
The Settlers is a strategy game for the iPad.

T

tabletop role-playing game: Any role-playing game that is played with pencils, paper, and dice and/or around a table with multiple players at once.

target market: A specific group of people to sell to.

textures: Bring your meshes, particles, and interfaces to life; they are 2D image or movie files that you lay over or wrap around various objects in Unity. As they are so important, textures have a lot of various properties. You can put any image file inside your Unity project that you like, regardless of file extension. If it meets the size requirements, it will get imported and optimized for game use. This extends to multi-layer Photoshop or TIFF files, too; they are flattened on import, reducing their file size.

tile-based map: Any regularly spaced grid that reuses the same set of tiles.

tiles: Flat 2D images, which can be static or animated, that are repeated over and over in the background to make up the terrain or surface area of the game world.

touchscreen: An electronic visual display that detects the presence and location of a touch within the display area. This generally refers to touching the device's display surface with a finger or hand.

triple-A (AAA) title: A game that sells big, in other words has a high cost to make and a higher return-on-investment; refers to an individual title's success or anticipated success if it is still in development.

V-X

variable: Any observable attribute in a programming language that changes its values when ordered to.

vertex: A point in Cartesian space made up of three coordinates (X, Y, and Z) and often the point at which the sides of an angle intersect.

voiceovers (VOs): Sounds done by artists recorded reading dialogue and narration scripts in a recording studio for purposes of providing spoken dialogue and narration in games.

web browser: A software program that is used to locate and display web pages.

web pages: Specially formatted documents created using languages such as Hypertext Markup Language (HTML) and Extensible Hypertext Markup Language (XHTML).

web server: A computer that is hooked up to the Internet 24/7 that might have one or more websites stored on it at any given time.

work breakdown: A project management plan that breaks down the overall project into tasks and sub-tasks, assigns team members to those tasks, and estimates the time it will take to get those tasks done.

World Wide Web (WWW or the Web): A subset of the Internet that supports web pages.

Xcode: A suite of tools developed by Apple specifically for developing software for the Mac OS X and iOS operating systems.

Index

YOUR ULTIMATE RESOURCE

Beginning Java SE 6
Game Programming, Third Edition
1-4354-5808-7 • $34.99

Game Development with Unity
1-4354-5658-0 • $39.99

Visual Basic Game Programming
for Teens, Third Edition
1-4354-5810-9 • $34.99

PSP Game Creation for Teens
1-4354-5784-6 • $34.99

Beginning C++ Through
Game Programming, Third Edition
1-4354-5742-0 • $34.99

Multi-Threaded
Game Engine Design
1-4354-5417-0 • $59.99

Torque for Teens, Second Edition
1-4354-5642-4 • $34.99

iPhone 3D Game Programming
All in One
1-4354-5478-2 • $39.99

Introduction to Game AI
1-59863-998-6 • $39.99

C# Game Programming:
For Serious Game Creation
1-4354-5556-8 • $49.99

XNA Game Studio 4.0
for Xbox 360 Developers
1-58450-537-0 • $49.99

Game Programming Gems 8
1-58450-702-0 • $69.99

Available from Amazon, Barnes & Noble, and other retailers nationwide and online.
Visit us online at courseptr.com or call 1.800.354.9706.

COURSE TECHNOLOGY
CENGAGE Learning
Professional • Technical • Reference

courseptr.com